Excel Charts For Dummies®

Cheat Sheet

D1536555

Selecting the Correct Chart Type

To Do This	Use This Type of Chart
Compare items from more than one series, and/or more than eight categories	Bar or Column
Compare items from a single series with eight or fewer categories	Doughnut or Pie
Show change over time or over categories	Area or Line
Show a stock's open, high, low, and close	Stock
Show relationships between sets of data	Bubble, Radar, Scatter, or Surface

Troubleshooting Charts

Problem	Solution
A series is hidden behind another series.	Reorder the series.
The lines are all scrunched up together.	Change the value-axis scale to a narrower range.
One or more lines are pressed up against the top or bottom of the plot area.	Change the value-axis scale to a wider range, or plot the problem series on the secondary axis.
The lines are too light and/or they all look alike.	Use the Format Data Series dialog box to change the lines. Make some thicker, use data markers, and change colors.
The category labels are all squished together.	Change the category-axis scale settings so fewer category labels are shown.
The background is dark, making it hard to see the series.	Change the Area setting of the chart area or plot area to None.
The series are plotted incorrectly or are not visible.	On the Data Range tab in the Source Data dialog box, change the Series In setting from Rows to Columns or vice versa.

For Dummies: Bestselling Book Series for Beginners

Category-Axis Scale Settings (Non-Time-Scale)

Setting	What It Does
Value (Y) Axis Crosses at Category Number	Positions the value axis somewhere along the category axis. Usually, this value is 1, which puts the value axis on the left side of the chart. Setting the number to the number of categories moves the value axis to the right side of the chart. Any number in between positions the value axis in the middle area of the chart.
Number of Categories Between Tick-Mark Labels	Determines how category labels are displayed. A setting of 1 forces all category labels to display. This may not be desirable. Increasing the number reduces the clutter.
Number of Categories Between Tick Marks	Determines how many small tick marks are displayed along the axis. A setting of 1 places a tick mark for each category. Increasing the number reduces the number of displayed tick marks.
Value (Y) Axis Crosses Between Categories	Determines whether to plot at the category points or between them. If unchecked, data is plotted directly above the category positions. If checked, data is plotted offset to the category positions.
Categories in Reverse Order	Reverses how categories are presented (for example, December through January instead of January through December). Saves you the trouble of having to alter the sort of the source data.
Value (Y) Axis Crosses at Maximum Category	Positions the value axis to cross the category axis at the last category. For a horizontal category axis, this places the value axis at the right side of the chart. Works the same way as setting the Value (Y) Axis Crosses at Category Number to the total number of categories.

Value-Axis Scale Settings

Setting	What It Does
Minimum	Sets the bottom value of the value axis.
Maximum	Sets the top value of the value axis.
Major Unit	Sets how the full range of the value axis is delineated. Provides the setting for the gridlines. This setting cannot exceed the maximum value.
Minor Unit	Sets where tick marks will appear along the axis. For example, a setting of 20 on a value range of 0 to 110 would produce 5 tick marks. This setting cannot exceed the major unit.
Category (X) Axis Crosses At	Determines where the category axis is positioned along the value axis. Allows placing the category axis anywhere from the bottom to the top by using numbers that fall within the value range.
Logarithmic Scale	Alters the range of the value axis to follow a logarithmic scale. This is useful for data that covers a wide range of values.
Values in Reverse Order	Reverses how the value axis range is displayed. For example changes a range of 0 to 100 to a range of 100 to 0.
Category (X) Axis Crosses at Maximum Value	Positions the category axis to cross the value axis at the maximum value of the value axis. For a vertical value axis, moves the category axis to the top of the chart. Works the same as setting the Category (X) Axis Crosses At to the maximum setting of the value axis.

Excel™ Charts

FOR

DUMMIES®

Excel™ Charts

FOR
DUMMIES®

by Ken Bluttman

WILEY

Wiley Publishing, Inc.

Excel™ Charts For Dummies®

Published by
Wiley Publishing, Inc.
111 River Street
Hoboken, NJ 07030-5774

Copyright © 2005 by Wiley Publishing, Inc., Indianapolis, Indiana

Published by Wiley Publishing, Inc., Indianapolis, Indiana

Published simultaneously in Canada

For general information on our other products and services, please contact our Customer Care Department within the U.S. at 800-762-2974, outside the U.S. at 317-572-3993, or fax 317-572-4002.

For technical support, please visit www.wiley.com/techsupport.

Wiley also publishes its books in a variety of electronic formats. Some content that appears in print may not be available in electronic books.

Library of Congress Control Number: 2005923418

ISBN-13: 978-0-7645-8473-2

ISBN-10: 0-7645-8473-1

Manufactured in the United States of America

10 9 8 7 6 5 4 3 2 1

1O/RW/QV/QV/IN

WILEY

About the Author

Ken Bluttman has been working as a software developer for over 15 years. He works with many technologies, including Office/VBA, Visual Basic .NET, SQL Server, as well as ASP.NET and other Web goodies. He is the author of *Excel Formulas and Functions For Dummies, Access Hacks,* and *Developing Microsoft Office Solutions.* Ken lives in New York with his wife, son, dog, and assorted amphibians and crustaceans.

Dedication

To my two artists. You bring light and color into our home.

Author's Acknowledgments

Bringing a book from concept to reality is a team effort. I want to thank Elizabeth Kuball for her outstanding project management and editorial work. Thanks to Tom Heine and the wonderful Wiley staff for all the behind-the-scenes activities. And thanks to Doug Klippert for his technical prowess.

Publisher's Acknowledgments

We're proud of this book; please send us your comments through our online registration form located at www.dummies.com/register/.

Some of the people who helped bring this book to market include the following:

Acquisitions, Editorial, and Media Development

Project Editor: Elizabeth Kuball

Acquisitions Editor: Tom Heine

Technical Editor: Doug Klippert

Editorial Manager: Robyn Siesky

Media Development Supervisor: Richard Graves

Editorial Assistant: Adrienne Porter

Cartoons: Rich Tennant, www.the5thwave.com

Composition Services

Project Coordinator: Nancee Reeves

Layout and Graphics: Lauren Goddard, Stephanie D. Jumper, Barry Offringa, Lynsey Osborn, Melanee Prendergast, Julie Trippetti

Proofreaders: Leeann Harney, Jessica Kramer, Dwight Ramsey; Charles Spencer, TECHBOOKS Production Services

Indexer: TECHBOOKS Productions Services

Publishing and Editorial for Technology Publishing

Richard Swadley, Vice President and Executive Group Publisher

Barry Pruett, Vice President and Publisher, Visual/Web Graphics

Andy Cummings, Vice President and Publisher, Technology Dummies

Mary Bednarek, Executive Acquisitions Director, Technology Dummies

Mary C. Corder, Editorial Director, Technology Dummies

Publishing for Consumer Dummies

Diane Graves Steele, Vice President and Publisher

Joyce Pepple, Acquisitions Director

Composition Services

Gerry Fahey, Vice President of Production Services

Debbie Stailey, Director of Composition Services

Contents at a Glance

Table of Contents

Introduction

· ·

Charts are everywhere! In newspapers and magazines, on TV, on roadside billboards, and on your utility bill. Some are gorgeous, and some are dull but functional. Some provide you with useful information, and some pull the wool over your eyes.

Charts have a purpose or two — to tell you something useful, and to tell it to you in a way faster than words would. When you're creating a chart, you hope that someone looking at it won't have to take long to figure it out! Let that be a guiding principle in chart design: If it takes too long for someone to figure out what he's looking at, you need to rethink and redesign that chart.

About This Book

This book takes you through the chart-making power of Excel. Charts are an essential part of Excel but perhaps not understood to the degree that number crunching and math are. Often, when someone needs to make a chart, she just opts for a catch-all Line chart or perhaps a Column or Bar chart. Make it a 3-D Column or Bar, and who can complain when they see how beautiful it is? But the fact is that artsy, beautiful charts are not always the best way to present the facts about the data.

This book give you lots of useful information about creating charts, so that you're a wiser chart designer. I guide you through some key issues, such as how to know which chart type to use, how to format all the parts of a chart, and even how to deliver the chart via Word, PowerPoint, or a Web page.

Along the way, I give you step-by-step instructions to create and edit charts. I explain in detail how the Chart Wizard works, what a series is, how the axes work, and much more. And the great thing: how visual this all is! I show you lots of charts to view, including 16 full-color charts in the center of the book! (Can you tell I'm excited about that?)

Foolish Assumptions

In this book, I assume you already know how to use Excel. I hope I'm right on that score, but if not, check out *Excel 2003 For Dummies* by Greg Harvey (published by Wiley).

Even though I assume you have a basic understanding of Excel, it's okay if you're new to making charts — that's what this book is for.

How to Use This Book

This book is divided into five parts, and you may find yourself reading one or two of the parts more than you read the others. That's fine! You don't have to read the book straight through.

Each chapter stands on its own merit. Occasionally, I refer you to another chapter or two, but for the most part, you'll be able to pinpoint just the chart knowledge you need at the moment, without having to read any of the other chapters.

How This Book Is Organized

This book is organized in five parts. I cover the basics at the start, and each successive part addresses a key facet of chart creation and use. Here is what you can find in each part.

Part 1: Getting Started with Excel Charts

Part I introduces you to charts. If you've never worked with charts, or you've only had the occasional need to make one, Part I is a great place to uncover the basics. Charts have distinct components, and knowing about them goes a long way toward making great charts. Not all charts are the same, nor are they meant to be used in the same situations.

Chapter 1 is the basic get-to-know-what-charts-are chapter. You get a brief heads-up about chart types. Chapter 2 goes into more detail and covers a lot of territory including all the parts of a chart, chart types and subtypes, series data, and where to place charts in the workbook. Chapter 3 is an important chapter, because it explains how to use the Chart Wizard, the Excel utility you use to create charts. Knowing the ins and outs of how the Chart Wizard works will make your chart creation chores much easier.

Part II: Exploring Chart Types

Part II dives into the chart types. There are reasons why one chart type is more appropriate than another, and this part of the book tells you why. (**Hint:** It all has to do with the data and understanding which chart type is best for telling the facts about the data.)

Chapter 4 discusses chart types that support comparative data. For example, a Column chart is ideal to see how one entity compares with another. Chapter 5 shows how to use charts to display changing values over time. The classic chart in this arena is a Line chart that shows how a stock or other investment fares over time.

Chapter 6 shows you how to use charts that are a little less common and a little more complex. These are the XY (Scatter), Radar, Bubble, and Surface charts that look so cool but are confusing to figure out. This chapter gives examples of how and why to use each of these interesting chart types.

And Chapter 7 shows you how to work with custom chart types.

Part III: Formatting Charts

Charts are visual, so formatting them is a key element to good presentation. Part III is devoted exclusively to formatting techniques and issues. There are eight chapters in this part and that nugget on its own should speak to how valuable formatting is!

Chapter 8 discusses chart placement. There are advantages and disadvantages to placing charts on worksheets or dedicated chart sheets. This chapter tells you all about it.

Chapter 9 tells you about formatting the chart area and the plot area. Knowing how to insert gradients, textures, patterns, and pictures into these areas opens the door to making very exciting-looking charts. In this chapter, you also find out how to use gridlines.

Chapter 10 explains the details of formatting axes' lines and using tick marks and tick-mark labels.

Chapters 11 and 12 are vital to understanding how to use the scale settings for the axes. Knowing how to control the settings and the methodology for selecting settings is key to creating presentable charts.

Chapter 13 is devoted to the formatting of the data series. You can do quite a bit to format data points as a group or to format individual data points. You also find out here about drop lines, up-down bars, overlaps, gap widths, and even how to isolate a slice of a Pie chart.

Chapter 14 tells you all about working with 3-D charts. There are settings used in 3-D charts that aren't relevant to flat charts. Knowing how to adjust perspective, elevation, and rotation lets you make the best of presenting data in 3-D.

Chapter 15 shows you how to insert and use custom graphics and shapes in your charts. This opens the door to making distinctive charts.

Part IV: Advanced Chart Techniques

Part IV covers advanced topics, including trendlines, pivot charts, and posting charts on Web pages. Mastering the material in this part will really provide you with a well-rounded knowledge of chart smarts.

Chapter 16 shows you how to apply trendlines to your charts. Chapter 17 discusses combination charts — vital for displaying mixed data on the same chart. Chapter 18 shows you how to save chart layouts for future use. This is a great thing to know — if you find yourself always formatting charts in a similar way, you can just save a reusable chart layout with the incorporated formatting.

Chapter 19 tells you how to create pivot tables and pivot charts. Knowing how to use the PivotTable and PivotChart Wizard is a main detail of this chapter. Chapter 20 shows you how to have your chart appear on a Web page and even be interactive!

Part V: The Part Of Tens

No Dummies book is complete without a Part of Tens. In this part, I include two chapters. Chapter 21 is an exposé of bad charts, with guidelines to their improvement. This chapter points out incorrect charting issues you'll want to avoid. Chapter 22 showcases a handful of unique, cool-looking charts. This chapter can serve as an inspiration for your charting endeavors.

Icons Used in This Book

Icons are little pictures in the margins, designed to draw your attention to particular kinds of information. Here's what they mean:

Text marked with a Tip icon gives you a extra-helpful information on the subject at hand, including suggestions on how to do things better or faster.

I use the Remember icon when I'm presenting some basic concept that you'll want to keep tucked away somewhere in your brain.

As the bomb implies, the Warning icon is serious stuff. These icons tell you to be careful, usually because you can accidentally erase your data or some such horrible thing.

Once in a while, I get carried away and tell you some tidbit that is interesting but not essential to making charts. You can read them or ignore them as you see fit.

Where to Go from Here

Make charts! Experiment! The best way to become a charting master, or at least be comfortable with it, is to make charts. Start with some data. You can make some up or find some sitting around or even find some on the Internet. Data is everywhere. You can write down the temperature for five days in a row and then plot the data.

If you want to work your way from the ground up and build a good chart foundation, start with Part I. If you're familiar with making charts, but you want to find out how the different chart types are used, Part II is the place for you.

Look for the chapters that will fill in the gaps of your chart knowledge. You can bounce around from chapter to chapter — you won't get lost, I promise!

Part I
Getting Started with Excel Charts

The 5th Wave — By Rich Tennant

"MY GIRLFRIEND RAN A SPREADSHEET OF MY LIFE, AND GENERATED THIS CHART. MY BEST HOPE IS THAT SHE'LL CHANGE HER MAJOR FROM 'COMPUTER SCIENCES' TO 'REHABILITATIVE SERVICES.'"

In this part . . .

Are you new to charts? Or have you dabbled a bit and want to find out more? In Part I, I take you through chart boot camp, or if you prefer, Excel Charts 101. This is where I explain all the facets of charts.

Do you know your category axis from your value axis? (I hope I'm not asking anything personal!) By the time you finish reading the first part of the book, you'll be talking the chart talk and walking the chart walk. Not only will you discover all the necessary components and chart types, but you'll also be on a first-name basis with a great wizard. Yes, it's the great Chart Wizard and, boy oh boy, are you going to be glad to make that acquaintance.

Chapter 1

Harnessing the Power
of Excel Charts

*Y*ou live in a sea of information. Lucky for you, you can boil down information into bits and pieces that you can make use of. Using charts to convey information is one way to do that.

Excel, as you already know, is fantastic at handling data, crunching numbers, and making snazzy reports. Throw charts into the mix and you really have all bases covered.

Excel can handle all your charting needs, from the simple line to 3-D surface maps and everything in between. This book guides you through all you need to know — from deciding which type of chart to use, to making the chart, to formatting the chart to look as good as you need it to be.

First things first, though! Diving right in is a good way to get started, so here you get your first chart out. Don't worry — I go easy on you for your first chart. You'll just use some basic data, shown in Figure 1-1.

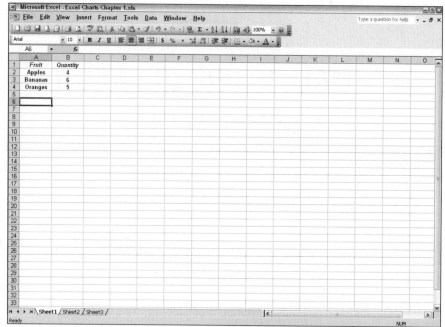

Figure 1-1:
Preparing
basic data
to plot.

Creating Charts with Excel

A chart is a visual representation of data. Before you can make a chart, you need some data on which to base it. The data shown in Figure 1-1 is ideal for a simple chart. It has all the necessary elements of the data:

- ✔ **Categories:** The names of the fruits (Apples, Bananas, Oranges) are the categories, and for each category there is an associated value, which is plotted on the chart.

- ✔ **Values:** The actual numbers associated with each category (each fruit).

- ✔ **Series name:** In this example, the series name is Quantity.

Charts can have more than one series.

Here's how to create the chart:

1. **On a worksheet, enter the information, as shown in Figure 1-1.**

2. **Select the data by clicking the mouse in the first cell and dragging the mouse over the data while keeping the mouse button down.**

   Figure 1-2 shows how the data should look when it's selected.

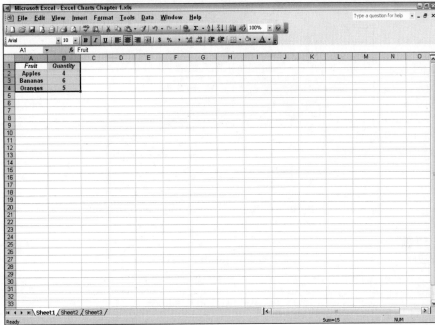

Figure 1-2:
Selected
data.

3. Choose Insert ➪ Chart.

The Chart Wizard, shown in Figure 1-3, appears.

Figure 1-3:
Using
the Chart
Wizard to
make a
chart.

4. Click Finish.

You'll end up with a chart on your worksheet. Figure 1-4 shows how mine came out.

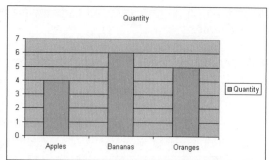

Figure 1-4:
Viewing the
completed
chart.

Congratulations! You made a chart! Here's a review of a couple points about all the excitement that just transpired:

- ✔ Data existed on which to create the chart.
- ✔ The Chart Wizard made the chart for you.
- ✔ The chart is a column chart, one of many types.
- ✔ The chart has categories and values.

After selecting the data, you can bypass the Chart Wizard and just press F11 to create the *default chart* (a certain chart type and formatting that Excel uses when no other selections are made).

In this book, I show you much more about the elements of a chart, how to use the Chart Wizard, and the different chart types (and much more of course!). Chapter 2 explains the parts of a chart. You find out about data series, axes, the legend, chart subtypes, and so forth. Chapter 3 explains the full nuts and bolts of using the Chart Wizard. In the example chart you just finished, I had you just accept all the defaults, thereby skipping most of what the Chart Wizard has to offer. Chapter 3 is where you discover more about using all of the Chart Wizard's magic powers.

Excel offers several chart types, and each type is used for a specific purpose. In Chapters 4 through 7, I show you these in detail with plenty of examples for you to try out.

Looking At the Different Types of Charts

Excel provides a good number of chart types: Column, Bar, Line, Pie, XY (Scatter), Area, Doughnut, Radar, Surface, Bubble, and Stock. Excel has even more chart types, but the others are just variations of these main types. Many of these chart types can be two-dimensional (with a flat appearance); others are three-dimensional. Not all chart types can be formatted as 3-D.

Figure 1-5 shows a few of the chart types. These four charts are of the same data, used in the earlier example.

Changing a chart from one type to another is easy! Here's how to change the chart from the earlier example:

1. **Click once on the chart to select it.**

   You'll notice that Chart is now an option on the worksheet menu bar (it replaces the Data menu item as long as a chart is selected).

2. **Choose Chart ⇨ Chart Type.**

   The Chart Type dialog box, shown in Figure 1-6, appears.

   The Standard Types tab should be on top; if it isn't, click on it to bring it to the top.

3. **In the Chart Type list, select another chart type.**

   I suggest selecting Bar, Line, or Pie.

   You can select a new chart type and then click on the Press and Hold to View Sample button to see how the chart looks without closing the dialog box.

4. **After you've selected a new chart type, click OK.**

   Figure 1-7 shows my chart, which I changed to a Bar type.

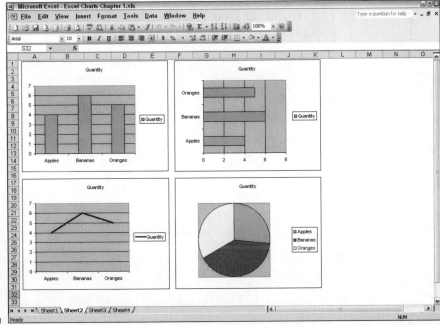

Figure 1-5: Top-left: Column chart; top-right: Bar chart; bottom-left: Line chart; bottom-right: Pie chart.

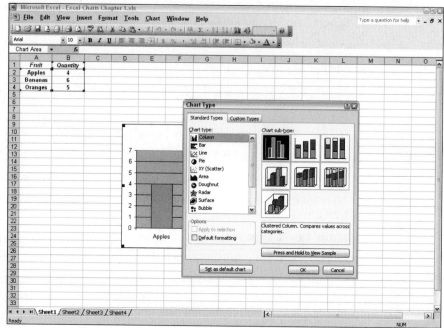

Figure 1-6:
The Chart
Type dialog
box.

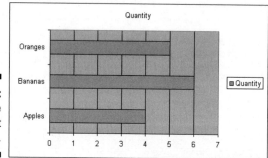

Figure 1-7:
Viewing the
new chart
type.

Some chart types require two or more data series. I tell you more about these in Part II of this book.

You can also select a chart subtype. Here's what to do:

1. **Click once on the chart to select it.**

2. **Choose Chart ⇨ Chart Type.**

   The Chart Type dialog box appears.

   The Standard Types tab should be on top; if it isn't, click on it to bring it to the top.

3. **The chart type is already selected on the left. On the right, select a different chart subtype.**

   You may have one or more 3-D chart subtypes to choose from. Go for it!

4. **Click OK.**

   The dialog box closes and the chart updates to the new subtype.

Making Your Chart Look Good

You may have noticed that the charts generated by the Chart Wizard, as they are, are not all that good looking. They may be the wrong size, the background may be a dull color, the font size may be too small, and so on.

The good news: You can change all of that, and this book shows you how. For example, Chapter 9 tells you how to format the chart area and the plot area. These two areas compose most of the chart's space, so knowing how to spiff them up is a good thing. Chapter 10 talks about font formatting, among other things. Chapters 11 and 12 tell you how to format the axes, a key thing to know!

Other chapters tell you about formatting the data series, formatting the 3-D views, and using graphics. My point: Getting up to speed on how to format charts will serve you well. How about a quick shot at it now? Here's how to format your charts a bit:

1. **Double-click directly in the middle of your chart, in an area that seems empty — in other words, not on a line, bar, column, and so on.**

   The Format Plot Area dialog box, shown in Figure 1-8, appears.

   In my charts the *plot area* (the area behind where the data is being plotted) has been coming out dark gray. I'm going to remove the color, and you can, too.

2. **In the Format Plot Area dialog box, in the Area section on the right, select None.**

3. **Click OK to close the dialog box and see the change on the chart.**

   You can also click anywhere on the worksheet to deselect the chart.

   Figure 1-9 shows how my chart now looks.

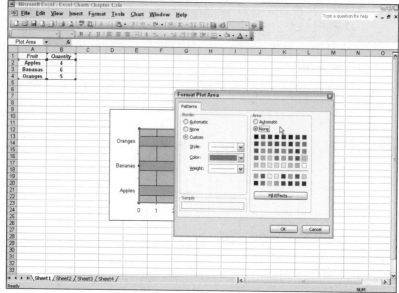

Figure 1-8:
Preparing to
format the
plot area.

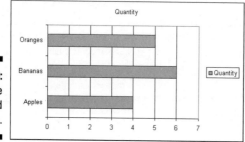

Figure 1-9:
The
improved
formatting.

I also see a need to make my chart bigger. You may see the need to do the same. This is easy enough. Here's what you do:

1. **Click on the chart once to select it.**

2. **Move the mouse over one of the handles (the little black boxes) around the border of the chart.**

3. **Click and hold down the mouse button.**

4. **With the mouse button down, move the mouse out from the center of the chart.**

    As you move the mouse, an outline of the chart border is visible. Figure 1-10 shows how it looks.

5. **Release the mouse button when the desired size is arrived at.**

    Figure 1-11 shows how my chart now looks.

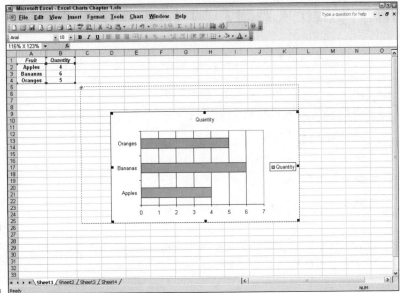

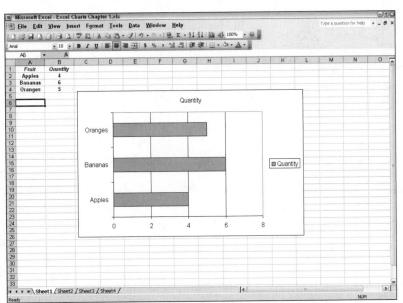

Note: This is just the tip of the iceberg. Many formatting attributes are out there for you to find out about and conquer. If you work through some of the other chapters in this book, you'll be a pro in no time!

Taking Your Chart to the Next Level

You can use charts and make them work best for your data in many ways. In this book, I show you interesting items such as:

- Working with time-scale data
- Creating combination charts
- Working with 3-D
- Creating your own custom chart formats
- Creating pivot tables and pivot charts
- Placing your charts on Web pages

As you can see, there are many interesting facets to charts to find out about. I'm excited for you — working with charts is one of the more fun things you can do with Excel. (Yes, I am a chart geek.)

Chapter 2

Understanding How Charts Are Constructed

*A*ll charts share a number of common components. Even though a Pie chart, for example, looks significantly different from a Line chart, they both have a plot area, are dependent on underlying data, and benefit from descriptive labeling.

Some charts are simple and some are fancy. Formatting options play a key role, as does the inclusion of clip art, photographs, or other graphics. Graphics are not always necessary; in fact, some people believe that graphics distort the presentation of the data and its value. Keep in mind that as much as charts are meant to point out particulars about the underlying data, they can also be used to *hide* particulars about the underlying data.

This reminds me of when I have a chat with my Aunt Gertrude. Every time I ask a question, she answers with a question of her own! Is she giving me answers or hiding them?

An Overview of Charts

Charts, simply put, are visual representations of data. The old saying "A picture is worth a thousand words" applies perfectly to charts. All charts are dependent on underlying data. To be precise (and I like to be precise even though it drives my wife batty sometimes), you *can* create a chart without data by using some fancy computer art program, but all that creates is a picture. A real chart sits on top of data. I just hope the data isn't getting squished.

Figure 2-1 shows — what else? — a chart. The chart title tells you what you're looking at, and you can easily see the direction of the data being presented. That is, you can easily see the ups and downs of the underlying data simply by viewing the ups and downs of the series line in the middle of the chart.

The chart in Figure 2-1 shows the closing value of the Dow Jones Industrial Average (DJIA) for each trading day in October 2004. The title at the top of the chart tells you that data for the October 2004 DJIA is being displayed, and the legend (on the right) tells you the data comprises the closing values.

The horizontal axis (or x-axis) along the bottom displays the start date, a midpoint date, and the end date of the data's range of dates; this is the *category axis.* The vertical axis (or y-axis) along the left side displays a range of values within which data falls; this is the *value axis.*

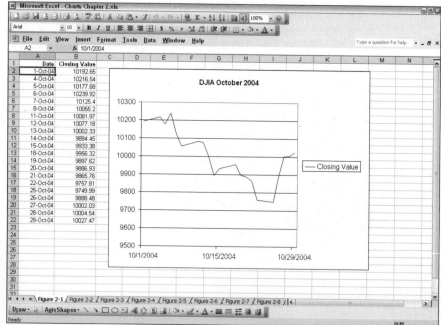

Figure 2-1:
Seeing what
a chart is
made of.

The chart in Figure 2-1, therefore, clearly states what it is presenting, and the data itself is well presented. Note how this chart immediately conveys information. Within a blink of an eye, you can easily see that the highest value occurred near the beginning of the period, and that the value went downhill from there. Only toward the end of the period did the value rebound a bit, but it didn't gain back enough to match the value at the beginning of the period.

Using titles, legends, and other labeling makes it easy to understand what a chart is presenting.

Charts are visual displays of information. The chart in Figure 2-1 is no exception. Its data, the closing prices of the DJIA, is freely available public information. (I especially like the free part!) Figure 2-2 shows a worksheet with this data.

By the way, a great place to find data like this is Yahoo! Finance. It has oodles of historical stock prices available for free download. Visit `http://finance.yahoo.com`.

Not all charts are built the same way. A Pie chart is a good contrast to the Line chart in Figure 2-1. Whereas a Line chart displays changing values (such as differing prices over a period of time), a Pie chart displays the breakdown of components that make up a whole. A Pie chart has no category axis or value axis.

Figure 2-2:
Looking at the underlying data.

Date	Closing Value
1-Oct-04	10192.65
4-Oct-04	10216.54
5-Oct-04	10177.68
6-Oct-04	10239.92
7-Oct-04	10125.4
8-Oct-04	10055.2
11-Oct-04	10081.97
12-Oct-04	10077.18
13-Oct-04	10002.33
14-Oct-04	9894.45
15-Oct-04	9933.38
18-Oct-04	9956.32
19-Oct-04	9897.62
20-Oct-04	9886.93
21-Oct-04	9865.76
22-Oct-04	9757.81
25-Oct-04	9749.99
26-Oct-04	9888.48
27-Oct-04	10002.03
28-Oct-04	10004.54
29-Oct-04	10027.47

Figure 2-3 shows a Pie chart that displays the revenue streams for a hypothetical bicycle store. Each slice of the pie relates to one of the income streams. Taken together, the different revenue streams make up the whole pie.

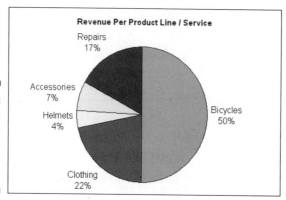

Figure 2-3:
Using a Pie chart to see the breakdown of the components.

Throughout this book, I show you how to create and enhance charts, but I bet you're just itching to make a chart! So, here's how to create a Pie chart:

1. **In one column of a worksheet, type in a few labels.**

   These could be names, items, or anything that identifies data. Only enter a few. Anything more than eight or so makes for an unintelligible pie chart.

2. **In the next column to the right, in the adjacent cells, enter some numbers.**

3. **Select the labels and the data.**

4. **Click the Chart Wizard button on the Standard toolbar (as shown in Figure 2-4) or choose Insert ⇨ Chart.**

   The Chart Wizard appears.

5. **Select Pie as the chart type, as shown in Figure 2-5.**

6. **Click Finish.**

   I fill you in on the Chart Wizard options in Chapter 3. For now, clicking Finish tells the Chart Wizard to use default settings.

All charts depend on underlying data.

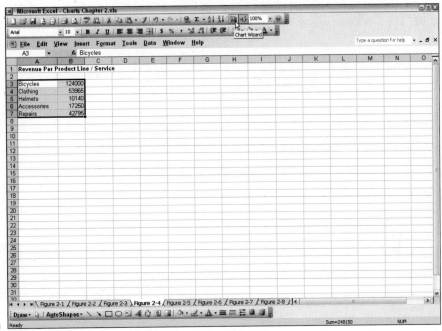

Figure 2-4:
Starting
up Chart
Wizard.

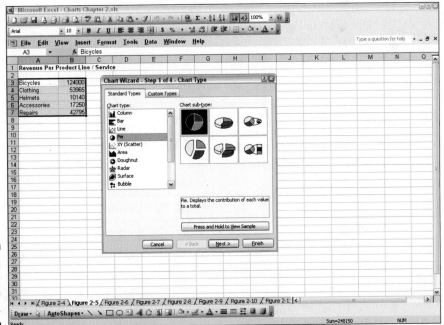

Figure 2-5:
Selecting
the Pie
chart type.

Reviewing Basic Chart Components

All charts share some common components. Other components may or may not be present, depending on the type of chart, and a number of optional components are available.

At the very least, a chart plots a *series,* which is a collection of related data values. But just seeing a plotted series by itself is not an efficient method to present the data. Figure 2-6 is a case in point.

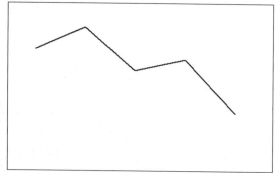

Figure 2-6:
A too-basic
chart.

The chart in Figure 2-6 is useless. You can easily see that whatever is plotted started at a given value and then ended lower. Is this good or bad? If the plot is consumer confidence, or attendance for the local square dance, this is bad. If the plot is the rate of inflation, or the price of admission to the local disco-theque, this is good.

Believe it or not, labels are optional — but clearly their value is paramount. The chart in Figure 2-1 is good because the intent of the chart is clear. Figure 2-7 shows the chart from Figure 2-1. Table 2-1 identifies and explains the components of the chart in the figure.

Table 2-1	The Components of Figure 2-7	
Item Number	*What It Is*	*Comments*
1	Title	Optional. Identifies the chart.
2	Legend	Optional. Identifies the series. The series is the data being displayed. There can be more than one data series and, therefore, more than one series identifier in the legend.

Item Number	What It Is	Comments
3	Value axis	Required for chart types that use it. Often referred to as the y-axis. In an XY (Scatter) chart, there are two values axes.
4	Value axis tick-mark labels	Optional. Identify the values being plotted. *Tick marks* are incremental divisions, similar to the lines on a ruler.
5	Category axis	Required for chart types that use it. Often referred to as the x-axis.
6	Category axis tick-mark labels	Optional. Identify the categories of the plotted data.
7	Plot area	Required. A chart could not be plotted without a plot area.
8	Data series	Not strictly required, but without at least one data series, you would have nothing to plot. Without at least one series, the plot area appears empty.

All in all, not many of the components of a chart are required. Yet the optional elements are often what clarifies a chart's intent. The labeling elements in particular — the title, legend, and tick-mark labels — are key to creating a chart that makes sense.

Charts can be as stark or busy as necessity calls for. However, letting an abundance of supporting elements be more noticeable than the data itself isn't a good idea. The KISS principle ("Keep it simple, stupid") applies to charts.

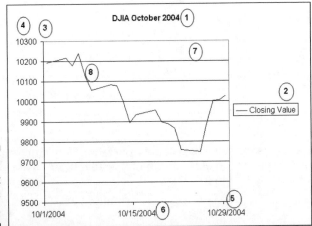

Figure 2-7: Seeing what a chart is made of.

Using Charts to Display Prominent Information about Your Data

The purpose of a chart is to make the facts about the underlying data easy to understand. A successful chart conveys a point or two about data that would generally require a more detailed perusal of the data itself to conclude the same result.

Maybe you're the type of person who likes to look at numbers. There's nothing wrong with that! But a lot of folks out there will take a picture over numbers any day of the week.

Here is a small data sample that contains the cost components that go into a few products:

Component	Product A	Product B	Product C
Labor	22	24	48
Parts	17	27	16
Fees	30	38	25

Quick! Which product has labor as at least half the total cost? Have to look at all the numbers first to figure this out? You need a chart! Figure 2-8 displays this data in a stacked Column chart — perfect for contrasting the components of a whole and comparing one whole to another.

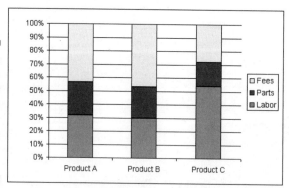

Figure 2-8: Using a stacked Column chart to compare item components.

Product C has at least half its costs come from labor. How much exactly? I don't know. But a quick scan of the Product C is all it takes to note, visually, that the labor portion dominates.

A stacked Bar or Column chart displays components as a percentage of a total percentage of 100 percent — regardless of whether the actual data sums up to 100.

Understanding Series Data

Data is fed into charts as series. A series is a set of related individual data points that together become a plot of data in a chart. Most chart types can display multiple series. This is a key value of charts — it becomes easy to see how different sets of data compare, relate, or correspond to each other.

Back to the DJIA example (maybe I was a stockbroker in another life). Wouldn't it be great to compare the DJIA of October 2004 with another stock index from the same period? How about the NASDAQ? Can this be done?

Certainly! First, you need the extra data. The NASDAQ data becomes a second series of data on the chart, while the DJIA maintains its place as the first series.

Figure 2-9 shows the DJIA and NASDAQ both plotted on the same chart. You can easily see how these two series run similar to each other.

Figure 2-9: Plotting two series on the same chart.

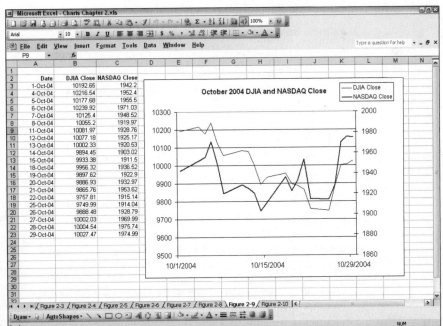

For the most part, the DJIA and NASDAQ correlate quite closely. Over the period of October 2004, they moved together in direction up and down, except for a short period of October 19 through 21. During that time, the DJIA went down while the NASDAQ went up.

To be precise this chart is a *combination chart.* Combination charts are useful when the multiple series of data to be plotted together don't share a similar range of values. Case in point, the DJIA hovers around 10,000 and the NASDAQ stays around the 1,930 mark. These series could not possibly share a common value axis. The high values of the DJIA would force the small values of the NASDAQ to appear as a flat line near the bottom of the chart.

A combination chart is used to display multiple series that do not share a close range of values.

It's high time I get you, dear reader, to try your hand at working with series data. Here's how to make a chart that has two series of data:

1. **In one column of a worksheet, type in a few categories.**

   These could be names, items, or anything that identifies data. In my example, I use the first six months of the year.

2. **In the next column to the right, in the adjacent cells, enter some numbers that span a reasonable range of values.**

   In my example, I use random numbers between 20 and 28.

3. **Enter a header in the cell at the top of the values.**

   In my example, I enter 2004.

4. **In yet another column to the right, in the adjacent cells, enter some other numbers that span a reasonable range of values.**

   Keep these values similar to the ones created in Step 2. By doing this, the two series will be able to share a common value axis. In my example, I use random numbers between 28 and 36.

5. **Enter a header in the cell at the top of the values.**

   In my example, I enter 2005.

   Figure 2-10 shows how my example is shaping up. I've created three columns of data. The first column contains labels. The second and third columns contain values.

6. **Select the categories and data, including the headers.**

   It may seem odd, but the top-left cell in the selection is empty. That's okay.

7. **Click the Chart Wizard button on the Standard toolbar or choose Insert ➪ Chart.**

   The Chart Wizard appears.

8. **Select Line as the chart type, and then select the first chart subtype (see Figure 2-11).**

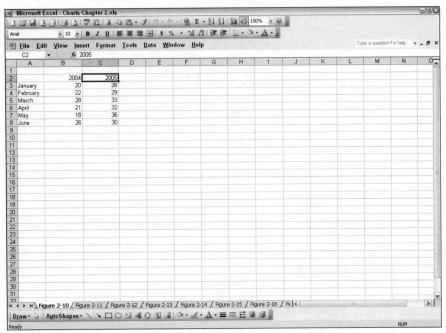

Figure 2-10:
Preparing
data.

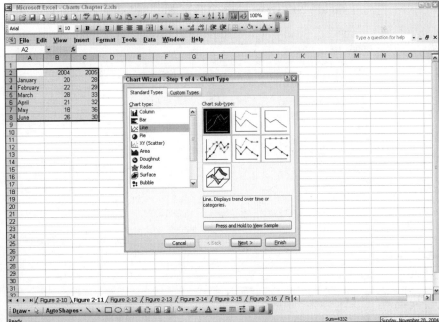

Figure 2-11:
Selecting
the chart
type and
chart
subtype.

9. **Click Finish.**

I cover the Chart Wizard options in Chapter 3. For now, clicking Finish tells the Chart Wizard to use the default settings.

You now have a Line chart that displays two data series. Yours should look something like mine (refer to Figure 2-9). The formatting is probably different: Your plot area may be a different color; the size of your chart may be different; and the series lines themselves may be different. Charts often need a bit of formatting to be pretty. The Chart Wizard delivers the chart — it's up to you to enhance its appeal. I show you how to do this in Part III.

Why stop here? How about adding a third series to the chart? You can continue to add data to a chart without using the Chart Wizard. The old drag-and-drop method works fine here.

10. **Enter another series of data on the worksheet.**

The values should again be within a similar range as the other two series.

11. **Enter a header label in the cell above the new data.**

12. **Select the series, including the header.**

13. **Move the mouse pointer to the border of the selected data.**

14. **When the mouse pointer changes shape to four arrows, click and keep the mouse button pressed.**

Figure 2-12 shows how this looks.

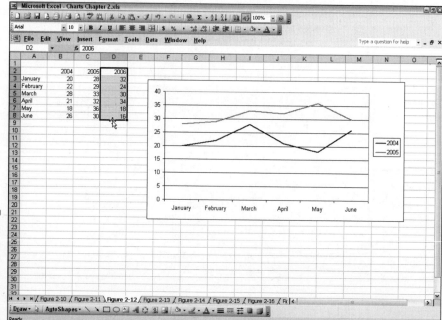

Figure 2-12:
Getting
ready to
drag the
data to the
chart.

15. **Drag the selected data over the chart and let go.**

    That's it! Figure 2-13 shows my example with the third series in place. Excel has given your new data series a color that differs from the other two.

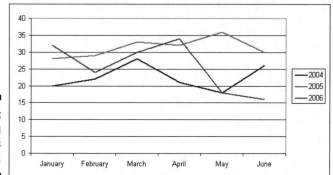

Figure 2-13: Displaying three series on a chart.

These colors, weights, and styles of the lines can be formatted. Chapter 13 delves into the details of doing this.

Series data is displayed differently in various chart types. Just for a quick look-see, do the following to change the chart type:

1. **Select the chart by clicking on it once.**

   The Menu Bar now has a Chart menu item.

2. **Choose Chart ➪ Chart Type.**

   The Chart Type dialog box appears.

3. **Select the area chart type.**

4. **Select the fourth chart subtype, named "Area with a 3-D visual effect."**

   Figure 2-14 shows how these selections are made in the Chart Type dialog box.

5. **Click OK to complete the operation.**

   The Line chart has now been changed to an Area chart. The chart still displays the three data series. Figure 2-15 shows how my example looks.

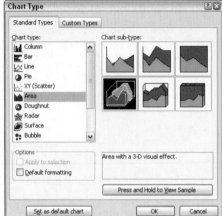

Figure 2-14: Changing the chart type.

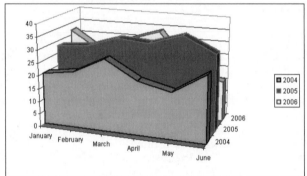

Figure 2-15: Same data, different chart.

Introducing the Standard Chart Types

Excel provides several chart types to use for displaying data. You can select a chart type when using the Chart Wizard to create a chart, or when the Chart Type dialog box is displayed while editing an existing chart.

The standard chart types are summarized in Table 2-1.

Table 2-1	Standard Chart Types
Chart Types	**Comment**
Bar, Column, Cone, Cylinder, Pyramid	Use to compare items. The main difference between a Column and Bar chart is the orientation. A Column chart displays data points vertically and a Bar chart

Chart Types	Comment
	displays data points horizontally. Either way, the variance among data points is easy to see. Cylinder, Cone, and Pyramid chart types are just stylized Column and Bar charts. When using Cylinder, Cone, or Pyramid charts, you have the choice to orient them as columns or bars. In a Column chart, values are shown on the vertical (y) axis. In a Bar chart, values are shown on the horizontal (x) axis.
Area, Line, Stock, Surface	Use to show change over time or category. These chart types display values in a series' data at different points of measurement. The points of measurement are most often time-based (for example, displaying the value of some entity at different points in time). The category axis comprises the points of measurement. Although the categories *are* most often time-based, they don't have to be. For example. you can measure the value of an entity at different locations.
Doughnut, Pie	Use to analyze components of an entity. These chart types make it easy to see how big or small each component is. These charts can display only a single data series.
Bubble, Radar, XY (Scatter)	Use to display relationships,dependencies, and corre lation among sets of data. These chart types are helpful to show how one set of data affects, or is related to, another.

Different chart types are used to display different facts about data. There is an art to selecting the right type of chart. How many series are in the data? Does one series correlate to another? (For example, does a drop in temperature cause more fractured ankles?) Do you need to emphasize the dominant factor of a sum of items?

An incorrect chart type can produce a great-looking chart and yet still not display the correct information.

Refer to Figure 2-14 to see where you select the chart type. For each chart type, there are chart subtype options, explained in the following section.

Looking At Chart Subtypes

Each chart type has a number of chart subtypes to select from. These subtypes give enhancement options on how the chart should be displayed and, possibly, how the data is interpreted.

Figure 2-16 shows the Chart Wizard with the Area chart type selected. The chart subtypes are displayed to the right. A description in the lower right explains how the selected subtype works.

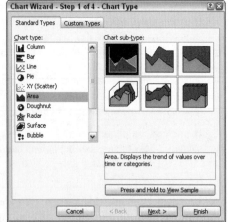

Figure 2-16:
Selecting
a chart
subtype.

Understanding Custom Chart Types

Excel provides a good assortment of chart types, but if you're fussy, there are several custom chart types to choose from as well. In either the Chart Wizard or the Chart Type dialog box, you'll see a Custom Types tab, which allows you to display the available custom chart types.

Figure 2-17 shows the Chart Type dialog box, with the Custom Types tab selected. In this tab are several custom types.

Unlike the standard chart types, the custom chart types do not have subtypes to select from. However any custom chart can be further formatted.

Custom chart types are not really unique. They're just stylized versions of standard chart types.

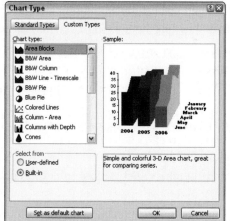

Figure 2-17:
Selecting
a custom
chart type.

Here's how to create a custom chart:

1. **Enter some labels in a column of a worksheet and enter some values in the next column to the right, in the adjacent cells.**

   The first cell in each list should be a heading. Figure 2-18 shows my example.

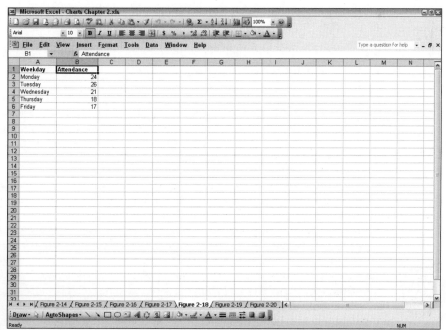

Figure 2-18:
Preparing
some data.

2. **Select the labels and data, including the headers.**

3. **Click the Chart Wizard button on the Standard Toolbar or choose Insert ⇨ Chart.**

   The Chart Wizard appears.

4. **In Step 1 of the Chart Wizard, click the Custom Types tab and click on the various chart types.**

   As you click on each, you can see a preview of how your data is charted. Some previews won't seem correct, because the data in the example won't make sense for the chart type.

5. **Click Finish to finish creating the chart, or just click Cancel to stop making the chart.**

In the Chart Type dialog box, shown in Figure 2-17, you have options for selecting a chart type from user-defined or built-in types. The example in this section had you preview the built-in custom types. User-defined custom chart types are something you create and then save. (I explain all this to you in Chapter 18.)

Deciding Whether to Use an Embedded Chart or a Chart Sheet

Charts can be used two ways:

- ✔ Embedded on a worksheet
- ✔ As a separate chart sheet

Embedded charts on worksheets can be moved, resized, and easily integrated with text on the worksheet. Plus, multiple charts can be embedded on a worksheet, which makes for numerous possibilities of how to present data.

Embedded charts are really *chart objects*.

Figure 2-19 shows a group of embedded charts on a worksheet. Although they may appear too small to make out the numbers or categories, this type of "thumbnail" approach is great for displaying comparisons across charts. Without reading the actual values in any particular chart, you can easily see which months had fairly uniform data — such as March or April — and which months had wider variation — such as May or June.

The other option of chart placement is to use a dedicated *chart sheet*. This is a special type of sheet. You cannot enter any data on it. In fact, the underlying data must be on a worksheet. Only one chart is displayed. The advantage here is a clean, full-size chart, for which you do not have to consider its place on a worksheet or its size. Figure 2-20 shows a dedicated chart sheet.

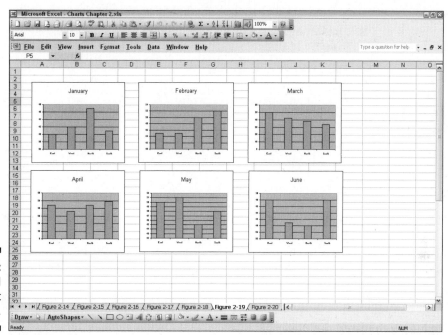

Figure 2-19:
Embedded
worksheet
charts.

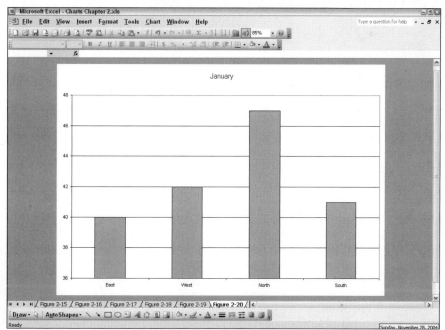

Figure 2-20:
Displaying a
single chart
on a chart
sheet.

The decision whether to use embedded charts or a chart sheet is subjective. Often the choice rests on whether the chart should physically sit near its data or with any other supporting information. In this case, an embedded chart on a worksheet is required. I cover working with the chart's location in Chapter 8.

You can print an embedded chart by itself, without the underlying worksheet, by selecting the chart before printing.

Chapter 3

Making Great Charts with the Chart Wizard

*I*magine a mighty wizard, one that takes care of all your charting needs. If only there were such a great and powerful wizard. Well, actually there is! The Chart Wizard is a huge help when creating Excel charts.

You provide the data and the Chart Wizard can do the rest. You can make decisions along the way about certain aspects of the chart, or you can just let the Chart Wizard create a chart abracadabra, zippo presto. Let the magic fly.

Besides you can always change it later.

Starting Up the Chart Wizard

You can start up the Chart Wizard in one of two ways: Choose Insert ⇨ Chart, or click the Chart Wizard button on the Standard toolbar.

Figure 3-1 shows how to start the Chart Wizard using the button on the Standard toolbar. Just a single click and you're on your way!

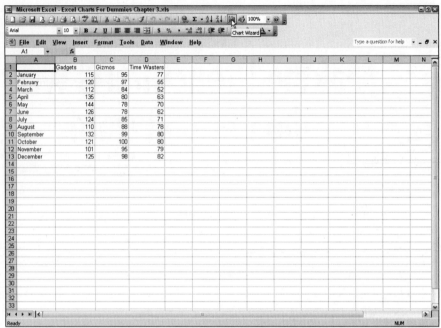

Figure 3-1:
Starting up
the Chart
Wizard.

The Chart Wizard walks you through four steps. Each step helps fill in the facts about a certain aspect of the chart being created.

Chart Wizard Step	What You Do
Step 1	Select the chart type and subtype.
Step 2	Define the data.
Step 3	Select chart options.
Step 4	Decide where the chart is to be placed.

Each of these steps has several settings to work with. The myriad of choices may seem overwhelming at first. Fret not! I explain each of the steps in this chapter, with all the choices noted. Soon you'll be making charts like a pro.

At any point while using the Chart Wizard, you can press the Finish button. The Chart Wizard will use default settings to complete the chart. If you want, you can change these settings after the chart is created.

Selecting Source Data

One key point to consider before starting up the Chart Wizard is whether to select the data first, or to select the data during Step 2. This is not a make-or-break kind of decision. You can select the data at either point and the Chart Wizard will accommodate you.

In Figure 3-1, the Chart Wizard was about to be launched without the data being selected. Figure 3-2 shows the alternative — the data *is* selected first. Isn't that nice to have a choice?

Deciding whether to select the data first isn't a big deal. The only real ramification is that if you do *not* select data first, start the Chart Wizard, and just click the Finish button to use all the default settings, you end up with an empty chart, shown in Figure 3-3.

All is not lost. If this happens just delete the empty chart object and start over. To delete a chart object:

1. **Click on the chart once to select it.**

2. **Press Delete on the keyboard.**

You have a choice whether or not to select the data before starting up the Chart Wizard.

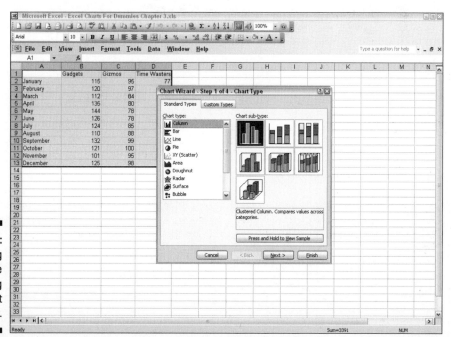

Figure 3-2:
Selecting
data before
starting
the Chart
Wizard.

So before I show you the Chart Wizard proper, make sure you have some data in place. To make this a snap, I guide you through setting up the sample data I use. You can re-create mine or enter your own similar data. Here's what to do:

1. **On an empty worksheet, enter January in cell A2.**

2. **Enter the remaining months, February through December, under-neath, in cells A3:A13.**

   You can enter them manually, or you can use the fill handle to have them entered for you. To do this make sure cell A2 is the active cell, and then move the mouse pointer to the little square in the lower-right corner of the cell. The mouse pointer changes shape to a thin black cross. Click and hold the mouse button down and drag down over cells A3:A13. Release the mouse button when you've dragged down to cell A13. The cells will be auto-filled with the remaining months. Figure 3-4 shows this operation in action.

3. **In cells B1, C1, and D1, enter headers.**

   These become the names of the data series. They can be anything. I used Gadgets, Gizmos, and Time Wasters.

4. **Finally, enter numeric values in columns B, C, and D, for each month.**

   Refer to Figure 3-1 to see how the data should look.

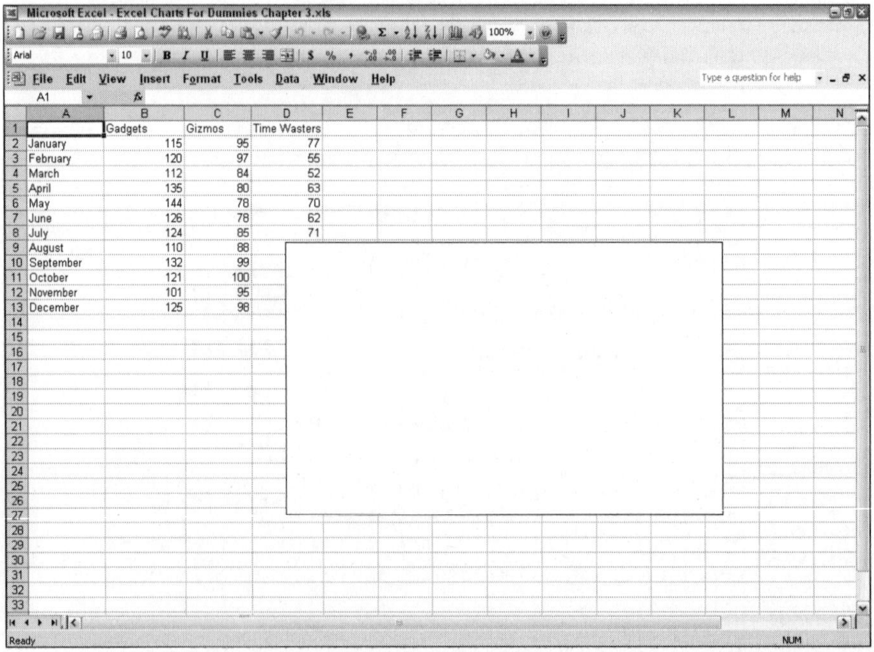

Figure 3-3: Creating an empty chart, by accident.

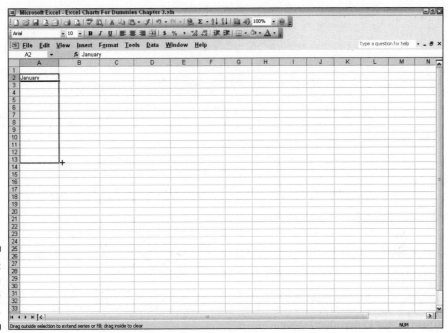

Figure 3-4:
Filling in the
months the
easy way.

As I said earlier, you have a choice whether to select the data before running the Chart Wizard. I discuss both approaches in the "Establishing the Source Data with the Chart Wizard Step 2" section, later in this chapter.

Selecting a Chart Type with the Chart Wizard Step 1

Step 1 of the Chart Wizard is where you choose the type of chart to create. You have several chart types to select from, and then there are subtypes to boot! Luckily, though, Excel does not hold you to your decision. You can always change the chart type after the fact.

One important note at this point: This section explains how to select standard chart types. Refer to Figure 3-2 and you can see there are two tabs: Standard Types and Custom Types. This chapter is focused on standard chart types. I cover custom chart types in Chapter 7.

And now to the nitty-gritty of making charts!

I've decided to select the data first and then start up the Chart Wizard. Here's how you can do this:

1. **Select the data, including the column with labels and the row with headers.**

2. **Choose Insert ➪ Chart, or click the Chart Wizard button on the Standard toolbar.**

   The Chart Wizard starts.

The first thing Chart Wizard will walk you through is choosing a chart type. This could be a Bar, Column, Pie, Line, or any other type of chart listed in the first step.

Determining which chart type to use

Selecting the correct chart type is key to making a good chart. The data typically drives this decision. It's easy to think how nice a 3-D Pie chart or an Area chart, or a cute little chart with pyramids might look, but, unfortunately, that is not how you go about selecting the chart type.

The data should drive the chart selection. You don't want to select a chart type first, and then try to get the data to fit.

Looking at my example data (refer to Figure 3-1) a couple of key facts are evident:

✔ **The data is time-based.** This is clearly the case, because the first column contains a series of months.

✔ **There is more than one series of data.** Not all chart types can display multiple series of data.

✔ **The three column of data (columns B:D) run within a similar range.** This means that all the data can be plotted using one value axis.

Chapter 2 includes a guide to selecting chart types. Time-based data such as the data in this example is plotted on a Line, Area, Surface, or Stock chart. Taking this a step further, a Surface chart is not appropriate here; a Surface chart delineates colors in a chart by the value axis major unit (explained in Chapter 6), instead of applying color to each series. A Stock chart won't cut it with this particular data either; a Stock chart takes three series of data, but then displays them specifically in a combined way to show high, low, and closing values of a stock or similar investment vehicle.

That leaves two chart types that make sense for the example data: a Line chart or an Area chart.

Figure 3-5 shows the first step of the Chart Wizard, which is where you select the chart type. You select the chart type from the Chart Type list on the left. If you haven't yet figured out what type of chart to use, you can get a preview of what your data will look like with the selected chart type.

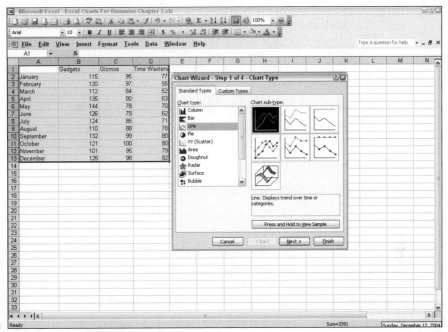

Figure 3-5:
Selecting a
chart type.

This preview feature is great — it saves a lot of time. To make use of this
feature, click the Press and Hold to View Sample button in the lower right.
Presto! You get a preview of the chart, as shown in Figure 3-6.

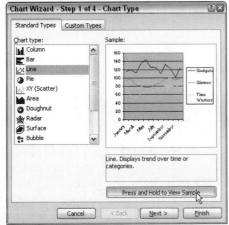

Figure 3-6:
Previewing
the chart.

You can only preview charts in the Chart Wizard if you selected the data
before starting up the Chart Wizard.

You can put the preview feature to good use! The following steps let you see what your data looks like as a Pie chart. Note that previewing only works if the data was already selected. Otherwise, how would Chart Wizard know what to show you? Just because it's a wizard doesn't mean it's a mind reader!

1. **In the Chart Type list, select Pie.**

2. **Click the Press and Hold to View Sample button.**

   Figure 3-7 shows what the steps look like with my data.

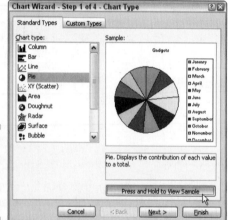

Figure 3-7:
Previewing
the data
displayed as
a Pie chart.

Did you notice anything unusual? A Pie chart appeared in the preview — nothing funny about that. But the Pie chart displays just one series. Case in point about selecting the correct chart type. A Pie chart can only display one data series.

By using the preview feature in the Chart Wizard, you can quickly see which chart types make sense for your data. The Chart Wizard won't decide for you, but it does give you a method to make a quick decision.

Choosing a chart subtype

After you've selected the correct chart type, you select a chart subtype. Decisions, decisions! This can get overwhelming. Take a deep breath — in this section, I give you some tips.

First, consider your data. What do you need to represent? Here are a few points to consider:

✔ **Is there more than one series of data?** When there is just one data series, the subtype decision is easier. For several chart types, the related subtypes are useful in presenting ways to work with multiseries data. If there is just one series, using any subtype that "stacks" the data has no effect.

✔ **Do the multiple data series work together to provide a summed value?** For example, in a time-based set of data, is there any need for a running total? If you have data points say for the 12 months of the year, do you need to see how the data points are contributing to a grand total? If so, a "stacked" subtype is useful.

✔ **Should each series be represented independently?** If so, stacking is not an option.

This is not an exhaustive list of considerations when selecting chart subtypes. In fact the decision on selecting the correct formatting may play a bigger role — to 3-D or not to 3-D, that is the question.

Let the data drive the decision on charts and chart subtypes. Consider what you need to point out about the data, and then locate an appropriate subtype to use.

Often, the chart subtypes are not all that unique. For example, the Line chart type has seven subtypes, as shown in Figure 3-8. But really there are just three subtypes for the Line chart type. Seven are available because some variations on formatting are offered. To be specific, one subtype plots the data series as independent lines; one subtype plots the lines in a stacked method (you can find out what this means in Chapter 4); and one subtype plots the lines as percentages of a stacked whole.

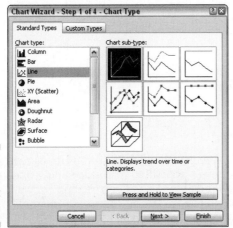

Figure 3-8: Reviewing chart subtypes.

Whew! Putting aside what some of that means, the point is that the subtypes present three different ways to process the *data*. Each of the three subtypes in the top row of subtypes leads to a way to process the data. Each subtype in a *column* of available subtypes offers a variation of how to format the chart.

Try this yourself. Here's a way to see how the Line chart subtypes are organized. You'll preview all seven subtypes and will come to see that there are really only three subtypes with formatting options:

1. **Make sure you've selected the data and you've started up the Chart Wizard.**

2. **Select the Line chart type**

3. **Click on the first chart subtype and click the Press and Hold to View Sample button to see a preview of the chart.**

   Make note of the shape of the lines and the range of values that are listed along the vertical axis (that's the value axis) on the left.

4. **Click on the chart subtype *below* the first one, and click the Press and Hold to View Sample button to see a preview of the chart.**

   You'll see that the shape of the lines and the values along the vertical axis have not changed! All that has changed is that there are now data point markers. This is a change in format. The data is still displayed the same way with regard to the values represented by each individual series line.

5. **Click on the last chart subtype (the bottom one in the first column of subtypes), and click the Press and Hold to View Sample button to see a preview of the chart.**

   This subtype presents a 3-D Line chart. However, this is still just a formatting change. The line shapes and range of values on the value axis have not changed.

   The three Line chart subtypes in the first column of subtypes, therefore, are just variations of one chart subtype. Doesn't that make it easier to work with the chart subtypes?

6. **Click on the second chart subtype (the second one in the first row of subtypes), and click the Press and Hold to View Sample button to see a preview of the chart.**

   This one is different! This is a stacked data chart. The cumulative values from preceding series are added to create each succeeding line. Immediately, you should be able to see that the range of values along the vertical axis has changed. Figure 3-9 shows how my example preview looks.

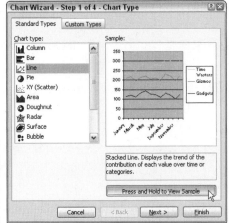

Figure 3-9:
Previewing
a Stacked
Line chart.

7. **Click on the subtype below the second subtype, and click the Press and Hold to View Sample button to see a preview of the chart.**

   As you probably expect by now, this preview processes the data in the same manner as the chart subtype above it. The only difference is that data markers have been added — a formatting change.

8. **Click on the third chart subtype (the third one in the first row of sub-types), and click the Press and Hold to View Sample button to see a preview of the chart.**

   Once again, the data is presented in a different way. This subtype displays how each data series contributes as a percentage, as the values are stacked. This is like the stacked subtype from Step 6, but instead of showing the summed values, it shows how the values are contributing as a percentage. Therefore, the vertical value axis stops at 100 percent. Can't get any higher than that! Also, the last data series becomes a flat line at 100 percent, because its contribution, by design, brings the summed contributions to the 100 percent mark.

9. **Finally, click on the subtype *below* the third chart subtype, and click the Press and Hold to View Sample button to see a preview of the chart.**

   I bet you're just itching to tell me that this is just a change in format. Correct! The data is processed in the same manner as the subtype above it, just with the addition of data markers.

For the most part, the chart subtypes work this way. For example, when working with Bar charts, you have three subtypes, and each has a variation of formatting. Figure 3-10 shows the Bar chart subtypes. The subtypes going across are Clustered Bar, Stacked Bar, and 100% Stacked Bar. The second row offers formatting variations of these three subtypes.

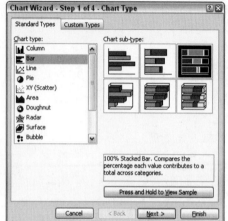

Figure 3-10:
Looking at
Bar chart
subtypes.

Establishing the Source Data with the Chart Wizard Step 2

The second step in the Chart Wizard is where you define the data you'll use. Not only do you define the range of the data, but you can also work with the individual data series. Bear in mind that a chart may present more than one series of data, so being able to work on them individually is a great thing!

Wait! How to do you get to Step 2? By clicking the Next button, of course! If you have the Chart Wizard running, and you're on Step 1, click Next. If the Chart Wizard is not running, refer to the "Selecting a Chart Type with Chart Wizard Step 1" section, earlier in this chapter.

A wizard usually has a set of buttons: Back, Next, Cancel, and Finish. The Next button takes you through each successive step of the Chart Wizard.

Figure 3-11 shows the Chart Wizard Step 2 screen. There are two tabs at the top:

- **Data Range:** Used for selecting and displaying the range of the full set of data, inclusive of all data series. Also, lets you tell the Chart Wizard which way the data is situated — in rows or columns.

- **Series:** Lets you work with each individual data series, with regard to range and where the name is found. You can even add and delete individual series. This is great because if you forgot to select some data beforehand, you can add it now — and vice versa (if you selected too much data, you can delete some).

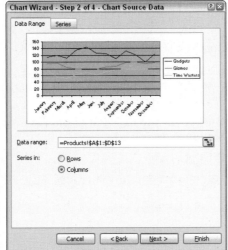

Figure 3-11:
Checking
out the tabs
in Step 2.

Selecting the data range and orientation

When you started up the Chart Wizard, you may or may not have first selected
the data. If you did, the Chart Wizard displays the range of data in the Step 2
screen (refer to Figure 3-11). If you didn't select the data first, Step 2 looks
empty, as shown in Figure 3-12.

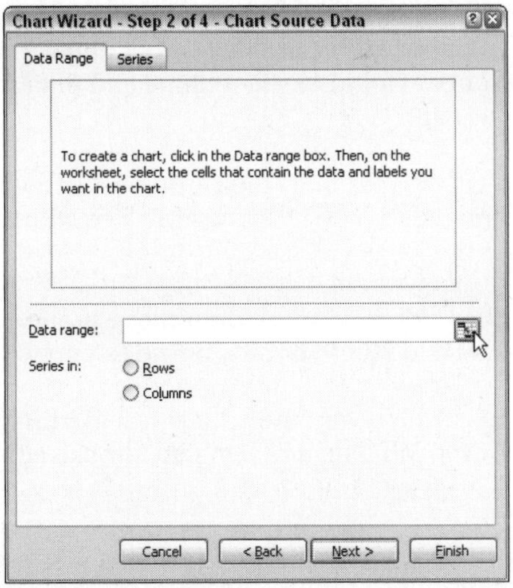

Figure 3-12:
Step 2, with
no data.

If you didn't select the data before starting the Chart Wizard, now is the time to select the data. Here's what you do:

1. **Click the control that lets you select data.**

   In Figure 3-12, the mouse pointer is on top of it. As soon as you click on it, the Chart Wizard shrinks in size to just display the Data Range entry box. Figure 3-13 shows what this looks like.

2. **Position the mouse pointer over the first cell of the data range, and then click and hold the mouse button.**

3. **Drag the mouse over the data range.**

   The Data Range entry box fills in with the data range. Figure 3-14 shows how this now looks.

4. **Press Enter.**

   The Chart Wizard is back to its original size, as shown back in Figure 3-11. A preview of the chart is visible in the Step 2 screen.

An alternative method to select worksheet data while the Chart Wizard is running is to first click in the entry box. Then you can use the mouse to click and drag over the worksheet to select the data. Or you can even just enter in the range of the data!

On the Data Range tab, the Data Range box displays the worksheet and range of the selected data:

```
=Products!$A$1:$D$13
```

In detail, this comprises an equal sign (=), the worksheet name (Products, in my example), and the data range. The worksheet name and data range are separated by an exclamation point.

If your worksheet name has any spaces in it, the worksheet name will be enclosed in single quote marks. Also note how the absolute address indicator ($) is included.

You can, of course, type in the reference to the data range in the Data Range entry box. This strategy works in a pinch, but it's prone to entry errors.

Another important setting tells which way the data is oriented. The actual setting in Step 2 has the Series In labeling and lets you choose either Rows or Columns.

The Chart Wizard sets the setting for you based on its best analysis of the selected data. But even so, that doesn't mean the Chart Wizard is always right! A wizard may be wise, but it can still make a mistake.

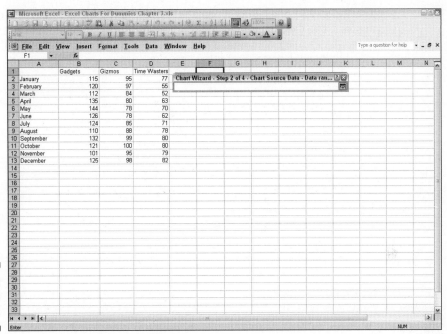

Figure 3-13:
Preparing to
select data.

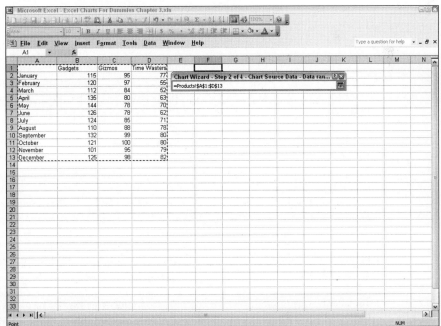

Figure 3-14:
The data
range is
selected.

In my example, the Chart Wizard set the Series In setting to Columns (refer to Figure 3-11). This choice was the correct one. In my data, there are more rows than columns: My data has 12 categories (1 for each month) and just 3 columns (1 for each product).

However, this can be changed by selecting Rows instead. Figure 3-15 shows how the data is presented (as a preview) when Rows is selected for the Series In setting.

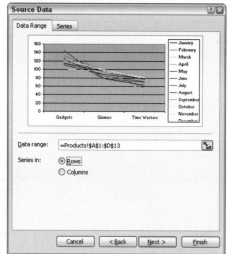

Figure 3-15:
Selecting Rows for the Series In setting.

Given a choice, a chart looks and reads better when there are fewer data series being plotted. The intention with the data in this example is to show how the 3 products fared in each of the 12 months. With the Rows setting, the chart displays how the 12 months fared in each of the 3 products! Yes, that sounds strange, and I'm not even sure it makes sense.

The chart displayed in the preview in Figure 3-15 doesn't do a good job of presenting the data. Technically, the lines do correctly plot the values found at the intersections of month and product, but overall the chart incorrectly describes the data — plus, it's just plain unreadable! With 12 series lines all crunched together, you can't easily follow any individual series.

Figure 3-16 displays two completed charts based on the example data. The one on the left locates the data in columns; the one on the right locates data in rows. Amazingly, as I was writing these very words, my 7-year-old son came over and gave me his unsolicited opinion that the chart on the right looks strange. My praise to the second-grade curriculum, which already covers how to make charts!

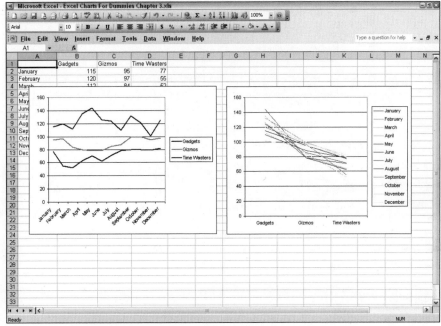

Figure 3-16:
Comparing
the right and
wrong way
to present
data in a
chart.

In Figure 3-16, the chart on the left clearly shows how each product fared per month. The lines are distinctive and the shape of each is easy to discern. The chart on the left has 12 categories along the horizontal axis and plots just 3 products. The chart on the right reverses this orientation and produces a confusing mess of series lines.

Plotting more categories and fewer series is best.

Working with individual data series

Clicking the Series tab in the Chart Wizard Step 2 provides the way to work with each individual series. Even though the range of the full set of data is entered in the Data Range entry box, within the Data Range tab, you can adjust the data range of individual series, where the names for the series are found, and where category labels are found.

Figure 3-17 shows what's found on the Series tab. The series are listed in the Series list on the left. By the way, the names found in this list are a reflection of how the Series In setting was applied on the Data Range tab. In other words, the Series names listed in the Series list must coordinate with the setting that says where the series are found.

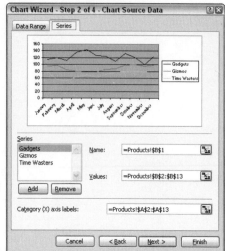

Figure 3-17:
Viewing the
series.

As each series is selected in the Series list, the Name and Values entry boxes display a cell or range:

- ✔ **Name:** On a chart, each series usually has a name to identify the data. Although not required, including a name is a really good idea — otherwise, you won't know what you're looking at! The reference for each series name is to a single cell.

- ✔ **Values:** The range of the individual data series. The fact that you can alter the range individually by series opens up possibilities. For example, you can plot one series full of data of January through December, and for a second series, just plot January through June.

Also note the Category (X) axis labels shows the range where the category labels are found.

Adding and removing series is as easy as a click of a button. A great way to test this is to remove a series and then add it back. Here's how:

1. Select a series in the Series list.

2. Click Remove.

Now that was easy! And consider how useful this is. If you needed to remove a series from your chart and this feature weren't available, you'd have to start all over! Go, Wizard, go!

Figure 3-18 shows how my example looked when I removed a series. The series (Time Wasters) is no longer in the Series list, and the preview shows just the two remaining series.

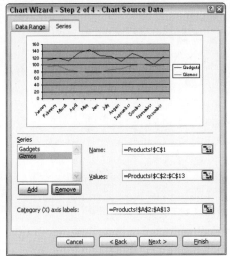

Figure 3-18:
Removing
a series.

Now you can get that series back:

3. Click the Add button.

A new generically named series, such as Series3, is added to the Series list. Note that the Name and Values entry boxes need to be populated with the correct references. The generic series name will update to the correct name as its reference is added.

4. Click in the Name entry box.

5. On the worksheet, click on the cell that contains the name of the series.

This is a single cell, not a range. In my example, the name Time Wasters is in cell D1, and that's where I click. By clicking the cell, the Name entry box automatically fills with the reference.

6. Click in the Values entry box, and delete anything that's in the box.

7. On the worksheet, click on the first cell of data for the series being added.

In my example, this is cell D2, the cell just under the name.

8. Keep the mouse button pressed, drag over the rest of the data for the series, and let go of the mouse button.

Figure 3-19 shows how my worksheet now looks. Time Wasters is back.

You can use the Add button to add as many additional series as you need. For each one, you'll need to identify the reference to the name and the data.

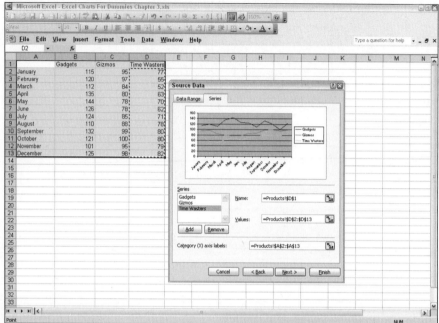

Figure 3-19:
Defining the
series name
and data
range.

The Category (X) Axis Labels entry box works the same way as the Name and Value entry boxes. A reference is established to the category labels. In my example, the names of the months are the categories. The Chart Wizard correctly identified them, and the reference to them is in the entry box.

Rounding Out a Chart's Appearance with the Chart Wizard Step 3

The third step in the Chart Wizard is where you work with several chart options. These include using titles, using a legend, and using labels for the data series. Although none of these is strictly required, their inclusion makes a big difference. Without some type of identifying information, a chart has no meaning. Other options include how to apply gridlines. *Gridlines* are lines that can appear running up and down and/or left and right through the plot area. A last option is whether to attach a table of the data to the chart.

All settings that can be entered or set in the Chart Wizard Step 3 are optional. You can always change the settings after the chart is created.

To get to Step 3 of the Chart Wizard, click the Next button on the Step 2 screen. Figure 3-20 shows how the Chart Wizard Step 3 appears.

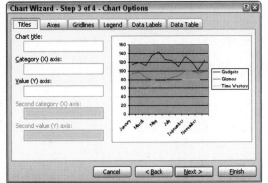

Figure 3-20:
The Chart
Wizard
Step 3.

A number of tabs are along the top. The chart type drives which of these tabs is present, so you may not see them all. Here is a summary of the tabs and what they are used for.

Tab	What It's Used For
Titles	Enter a title for the chart. Enter a title for any or all available axes. The chart type drives which axes are available.
Axes	Choose which axes to display. This does not affect the data. It does affect identifying the data.
Gridlines	Inserts lines horizontally and/or vertically through the plot area.
Legend	Identifies the series by associating the name with the formatting settings for the series.
Data Labels	Gives the option to place labels at the actual data points. Could be useful, but could also create an overly busy-looking chart.
Data Table	Append the data as a table to the chart. Has some merit for small sets of data.

The following sections show all the wonderful things you can do in Step 3 of the Chart Wizard.

Using titles

If the Titles tab is not on top, click the Titles tab.

In this tab, you enter titles for the chart and for the axes. Just which axes are available to receive titles depends on the chart type.

Giving a chart a title is always a good idea. A title lets viewers know what they're looking at. Unless some of the recipients of your charts are mind readers, how else will they know what the chart conveys?

Figure 3-21 shows where I've filled in a chart title and a title for the value axis.

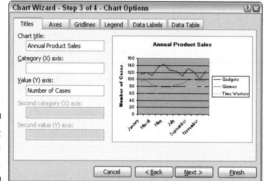

Figure 3-21:
Adding titles.

In particular, I've added a chart title, "Annual Product Sales," and a value axis title, "Number of Cases." This immediately provides important information about my data. Even though each product clearly has a value for each given month, there was no indication of what the value was. It could have been a sales figure, a count of defective units, a price, a cost, and so on. Now it's clear that it's a sales figure.

And that's not all! In fact, it isn't an actual sales figure per unit. The title of the value axis states that it's the number of cases. Therefore, each value displayed in the chart is a number of cases sold. Whew! I feel much better knowing that!

I intentionally left the category axis title blank. In my example, the categories are the names of the months. What title could possibly go here that explains the categories any better than the category names themselves? In other words, I could use a title like "Months," but you already know what they are. Adding a redundant title only adds clutter to the chart.

Even though titles help describe what a chart conveys, avoid using titles that don't add any value to understanding the chart.

Selecting axes

If the Axes tab is not on top, click on the Axes tab.

In this tab, you choose whether to display the axes. The available settings differ depending on the chart type. Not all chart types use the same axes.

Figure 3-22 shows the Axes tab. Because my example is of a Line chart type, the options are presented to display both the category and value axes.

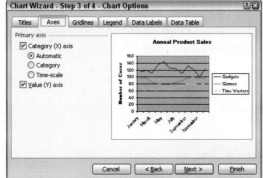

Figure 3-22:
Selecting axes attributes.

Figure 3-22 shows both the Category (X) Axis and the Value (Y) Axis as being selected for display. Further, there are choices on what the category axis should display:

- ✔ **Automatic:** The Chart Wizard decides what is best.
- ✔ **Category:** The categories are used as is, from the referenced range of category names. In my example, these are the names of the months.
- ✔ **Time-scale:** When time-based categories are used, additional settings become available to control the scaling attributes of the category axis. I explain these settings in Chapter 11.

By the way, selecting Automatic or Category as the suboption in my example produces the same result. When you choose Automatic, the Chart Wizard selects Category as the best choice.

There are many more settings to be applied to the axes. The Chart Wizard lets you get the basic task of displaying them accomplished. After the chart is created, further settings can be applied. I discuss these additional settings in Chapters 10, 11, and 12.

Choosing gridline types

If the Gridlines tab is not on top, click on the Gridlines tab.

Have you ever used a ruler or other straightedge to follow columnar information along a page? This is the idea behind gridlines. The purpose is to make it easy to follow data points in the plot area across or down to the axes to see the actual category or value.

Axes have major and minor demarcations. For example the value axis may cover a range of 0 to 100. The major demarcation might be 20 and the minor demarcation might be 5. These actual numeric settings are not available to set in the Chart Wizard. You can alter these settings after the chart is created. I discuss these settings in Chapters 9, 11, and 12.

For now, the Chart Wizard at least lets you choose whether to display major and minor gridlines, shown in Figure 3-23.

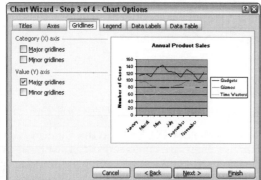

Figure 3-23:
Choosing whether to display gridlines.

Deciding to use a legend and where to place it

If the Legend tab is not on top, click on the Legend tab.

The legend is a visual key to identifying the data series. The legend is optional. Avoid using a legend altogether when there is just a single data series. If the chart and axes titles are correctly worded, you can skip the legend because it becomes redundant. Also, the legend takes up room. If it isn't needed, skipping its inclusion makes for a cleaner chart and a larger plot area.

When there is more than one series, you'll find a legend necessary. The Chart Wizard automatically assigns a different color to each series line. These colors, along with the names of the series, are what is displayed in the legend.

Figure 3-24 shows the Legends tab in the Chart Wizard Step 3. The tab includes the choice of whether to display the legend and where to place it.

After the chart is created, you can resize the legend and move it around. Balancing the room needed for the plot area with the room needed for the legend is a challenge sometimes.

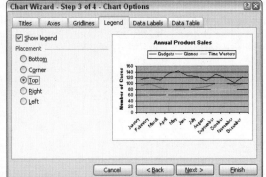

Figure 3-24:
Displaying
and placing
the chart
legend.

Working with data labels

If the Data Labels tab is not on top, click the Data Labels tab.

Data labels are informative descriptors that are situated with the individual data points. In this way, the value, series name, or other attribute of the data point is right next to it. The theory is that this makes understanding the data clear. In practice, though, data labels can lead to very busy charts. Somebody call the clutter busters!

Seriously, if there are many data points, using data labels leads to, well, many data labels. Because labels take up room, a chart with many data labels can look like a mess. Figure 3-25 shows just such an overly busy chart.

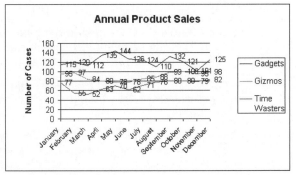

Figure 3-25:
Creating
clutter with
data labels.

On the other hand, data labels are great when applied with an eye to creating a well-balanced chart. The chart type also makes a difference when using data labels. Line type charts such as that in Figure 3-25 are usually not great candidates for data labels, simply because there are usually many data points.

On the other hand, a Pie chart often benefits from some data labeling. Figure 3-26 shows a Pie chart in which each part's contribution is expressed as a percentage of the whole. The data labels are not obscuring the data, and they provide instant useful information.

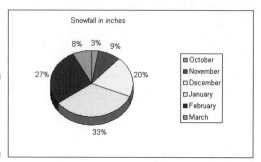

Figure 3-26:
Applying
useful data
labels.

A few types of data labels can be used in charts. The availability of each is dependent on the chart type. Here are the types.

Data Label Type	What It Does
Series Name	Displays the series name with its individual data points. Duplicates the purpose of the legend. Often unnecessary and creates clutter. Appears useful with stacked Area charts, but trial and error is the best way to tell.
Category Name	Displays the categories with the individual data points. Often unnecessary and creates clutter. Trial and error is the best way to tell.
Value	Plots data point values next to the data points themselves. This can be helpful when it doesn't create clutter. Trial and error is the best way to tell.
Percentage	Applies to Pie charts and Doughnut charts. Displays the percentage of the whole that a data point contributes.
Bubble Size	Applies only to Bubble charts. Displays the size of the bubble, derived from the third data series.

Figure 3-27 shows the Chart Wizard Step 3 with the Data Labels tab on top. The result of clicking on and off the various data label types shows up in the preview box.

Additionally, there is a selection of the separator. The separator is used only when more than one type of data label is selected. For example, if choosing to display the category names and values, you then can choose how the two types are separated at each data point. The choices are: space, comma, semi-colon, period, and new line.

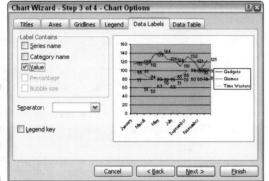

Figure 3-27: Previewing the application of data labels.

There also is a check box to display the legend key, but doing so is really unnecessary. It displays a marker that is the same color as the series line, next to data points along the series line. What's the point of that? This is like telling you that a blue line is really blue, by putting a swatch of blue next to it.

Deciding to show the data table

If the Data Table tab is not on top, click the Data Table tab. The data table literally is the data that makes up the chart. Even though the data is on a worksheet, you can select to have the data itself appear in the chart. When selected, it will appear in a table format underneath the horizontal axis.

Figure 3-28 shows the Data Table tab. When the Show Data Table check box is checked, there is an additional choice to show legend keys.

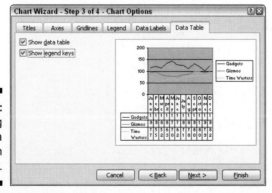

Figure 3-28: Including the data table with the chart.

The data table is anchored to the categories along the horizontal axis. Therefore, the orientation of the data in the data table may differ from the way the data appears in the worksheet. To the left of the data table are the series names. The Show Legend Keys option places a color marker next to the series names.

Including the data table makes sense only if there is a small amount of data. If there is too much data, it won't all be displayed, or it'll be so compacted together as to become difficult to read. When there is just a small amount of data, the data table may do a better job of showing the individual data values compared to the option to display value data labels. It's all a matter of trial and error — and personal preference. When a chart is on a separate chart sheet, the data table may display enough data, because there is more room on the sheet.

You can do further formatting of the data table, including formatting the lines in the table and the font attributes, after the chart is completed.

Choosing Where the Chart Will Go with the Chart Wizard Step 4

The fourth step in the Chart Wizard is a quickie. You just tell the Chart Wizard where to put the chart. You may have felt that it took a while to set all the data references and options in the previous Chart Wizard steps. Now you just want to get the chart displayed already! Luckily, you have just two options:

✔ On a new chart sheet

✔ As an object on an existing worksheet

Figure 3-29 shows the Chart Wizard Step 4 screen. You select one type of placement or the other.

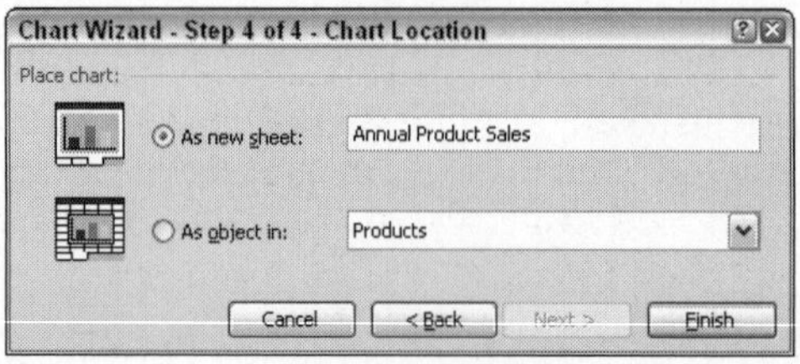

Figure 3-29:
Deciding
where to put
the chart.

Chart Wizard - Step 4 of 4 - Chart Location

Place chart:

○ As new sheet: Annual Product Sales

○ As object in: Products

Cancel   < Back   Next >   Finish

Selecting to have the chart appear on a separate chart sheet

The first choice is to have the chart appear on its own chart sheet. Chart Wizard prompts you to enter a name for the chart sheet. In my example, I've entered Annual Product Sales for the sheet name.

Figure 3-30 shows the chart as placed on a separate chart sheet.

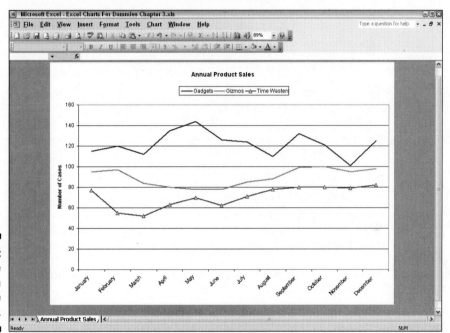

Figure 3-30: Placing the chart on a separate chart sheet.

Putting a chart on a worksheet

By default a chart is placed as an object on a worksheet. This approach has some advantages. First, you can resize and move the chart object around the worksheet, which gives you full control of where to place the chart *and* how big it should be. For example, you may opt to place the chart near its source data and then resize it such that when you print, the data and the chart fit nicely together on a single sheet of paper.

Figure 3-31 shows how a chart's size and placement is advantageous. If a client or a manager asks to see the chart and the data, no sweat!

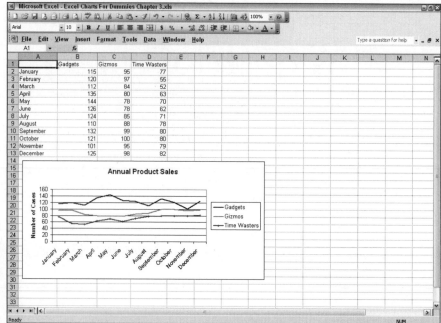

Figure 3-31:
Placing a
chart as an
object on a
worksheet.

In the Chart Wizard Step 4, when selecting to place the chart as on object on a worksheet, the drop-down list to the right of where the worksheet name goes gives you the list of all the worksheets in your workbook. You can place the chart on any worksheet, regardless of which worksheet holds the data.

The data that a chart is based on and the chart itself do not have to be on the same worksheet.

Part II
Exploring Chart Types

The 5th Wave — By Rich Tennant

"WELL, SHOOT! THIS EGGPLANT CHART IS JUST AS CONFUSING AS THE BUTTERNUT SQUASH CHART AND THE GOURD CHART. CAN'T YOU JUST MAKE A PIE CHART LIKE EVERYONE ELSE?"

In this part . . .

Part II is the real roll-up-your-sleeves-and-get-to-work part of the book. Here I break out the charts by type and divide it into four chapters to aid in your chart crash course. I have a lot to cover, but it's all fun. Just to whet your appetite, I show you pies, doughnuts, pyramids, and cylinders. Of course, you'll also hear about the standard Line, Column, and Bar charts, and also about the more obscure types, such as Surface and Radar charts. Chapters 4, 5, and 6 cover the standard chart types. The last chapter in this part, Chapter 7, takes you on a tour of a group of specialty charts that you can use in a number of imaginative ways.

Chapter 4

Creating Charts That Compare Items

*W*hich city has a larger population? Who sold more? What percentage of the team's output did Ken contribute?

These types of questions infer that items are to be compared to each other, or against the total. Consider comparing the population count of a few cities. Whatever the population is for any city, it has no relation to another city's population count. Another example is comparing grades on a test. Whether Sally gets an A or a B is independent of whatever grade Susan or Sarah gets. But you may need to compare the results nonetheless.

The charts I show you in this chapter are used to compare these types of items. I also show you how items are compared to the sum or whole of the items. In this way, too, each item is independent of the others, but instead of looking at an item-to-item comparison, you can see an item-to-total comparison.

Working with Comparison-Based Data

A common requirement is to compare performance, counts, or another measurable attribute. This is achieved by comparing values of some measurable item for each category. The worksheet in Figure 4-1 shows a perfect example of this. The data in Figure 4-1 compares vacation packages sold (the measurable item) for each office (the category).

Each of the five offices (identified by the city) sold a given number of A and B vacation packages. Looking at the column for Vacation Package A, you can see that the highest number sold goes to the Winnipeg office. On the other hand, Toronto sold the most B packages.

This type of data is not meant to uncover any relationships between the offices. That Toronto sold more of package B is a fact, but its value of 86 B packages sold would not change if, say, the Montreal B package figure were changed.

I'm starting to think that one of the vacation packages will be a nice treat for next year's summer vacation!

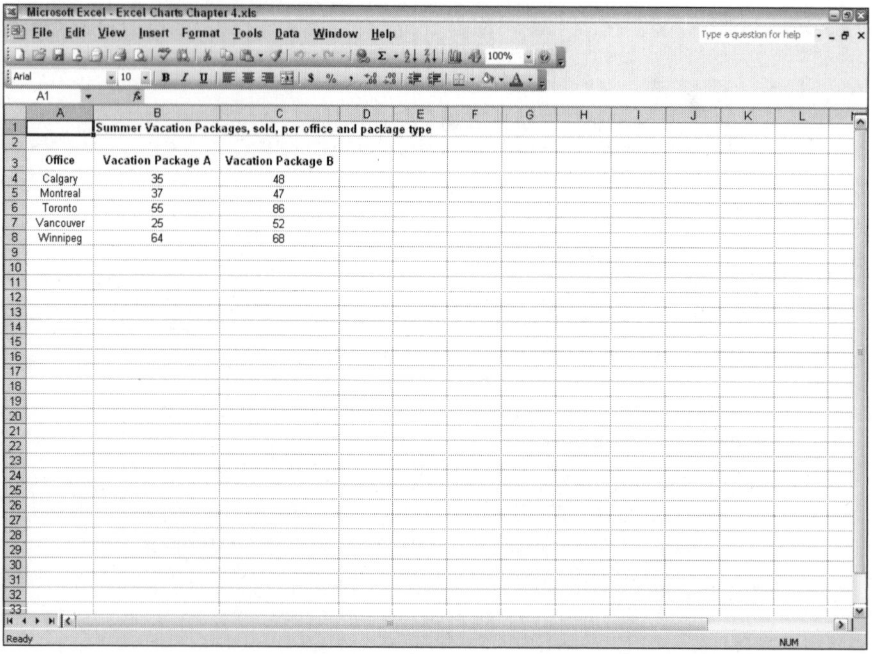

Figure 4-1:
Comparing
values.

Throughout this chapter, I show you how to plot this data in the guise of different chart types. If you want, you can use my data or create your own. Here's what you need to do:

1. **On a blank worksheet, enter three headers in three columns, across a row.**

   In my example, I entered Office, Vacation Package A, and Vacation Package B.

2. **Underneath the first header, enter five category values.**

   These are not the actual measurements. In my example, I used the names of five Canadian cities.

3. **Enter numeric values under the second header.**

   The values should be somewhat close to each other. This will help the chart present reasonably well. In other words, the range of the value axis will not become so wide that the data ends up looking flat.

4. **Enter numeric values under the third header.**

   These values should not, as a group, vary greatly from the values under the second header. This, too, helps keep the reasonable range in the value axis.

The value axis has to accommodate the range of the values. When there is a great difference between the lowest and highest values, seeing how the data is plotted can be difficult.

Bear in mind that the data you just created contains two data series. For some charts, both will be used, and for others just the first will be used.

Putting Items Side-by-Side with Column and Bar Charts

Column and Bar charts are effectively the same. The difference is that Column charts display vertical columns and Bar charts display horizontal bars. On a Column chart, the values are on the vertical (y) axis. On a Bar chart, the values are on the horizontal (x) axis. They each process data the same way. Column and Bar charts are great to compare items side-by-side. Also, they handle multiple data series — a key point when considering which chart type to use.

Making a Column chart

The first task is to plot the data:

1. **Select the data, including both series and headers (all three columns).**

2. **Click the Chart Wizard button on the Standard toolbar or choose Insert ⇨ Chart.**

   The Chart Wizard opens with the Column chart type selected by default. It doesn't get any easier than that!

   Figure 4-2 shows the Chart Wizard with the Column chart type selected, and the first subtype. This is what you want.

Figure 4-2:
Selecting a
Column
chart.

3. **Click the Next button twice.**

   The Chart Wizard should now be on Step 3.

4. **Click the Titles tab.**

5. **Enter an appropriate title for the chart.**

   In my example, I entered Summer Vacation Packages Sold. Yes, the title is optional, but it's my duty to show you proper chart etiquette.

6. **Click Finish.**

Figure 4-3 shows how the chart turned out. The categories (the cities) are correctly placed under the category axis. The legend clues you in to which column represents which data series. This is made possible by the fact that each data series has its own color.

There always must be a way to differentiate multiple series. This is accomplished by applying formatting attributes — color, patterns, line styles, markers, and so on. Each series is somehow uniquely formatted.

Figure 4-3:
Reviewing
the number
of sold
vacation
packages.

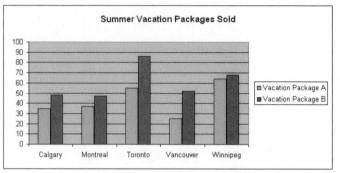

The chart in Figure 4-3 shows how the individual data points, from the two data series, are anchored to their respective categories. The two data series are differentiated by color. This chart makes it easy to see a few key points about the data:

✔ Winnipeg sold the most of Vacation Package A, and Toronto sold the most of Vacation Package B.

✔ Overall, Calgary and Montreal performed very similarly.

✔ Winnipeg sold almost an even amount of A and B packages.

In other words, the Column chart in Figure 4-3 makes it easy to compare values, whether comparing multiple series per category, or comparing across categories. For example, you can easily see that Toronto outperformed all other cities with regard to Vacation Package B.

Changing the chart type to a Bar chart

The next task is to display the data in a different format. A Bar chart presents data in the same way as a Column chart, but it does so horizontally instead of vertically. Here's what you do to change the chart type:

1. **Click once on the chart to select it, if it is not already selected.**

   The menu bar now displays the Chart menu item where the Data menu item usually is found. Figure 4-4 shows the Chart menu with its various submenus.

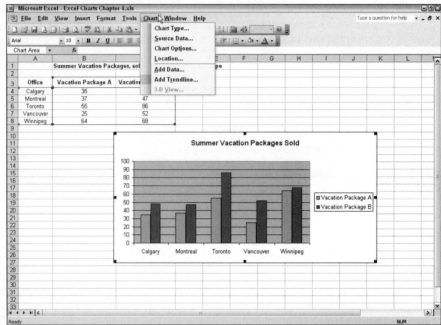

Figure 4-4:
Accessing
the Chart
menu item.

2. **Choose Chart ⇨ Chart Type.**

   The Chart Type dialog box opens (see Figure 4-5).

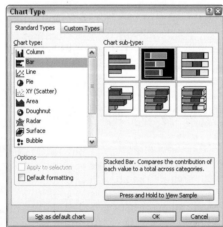

Figure 4-5:
Changing
the chart
type.

3. **Select the Bar chart type, and the first subtype (Clustered Bar).**

4. **Click OK.**

Presto! The Column chart is now a Clustered Bar chart. Figure 4-6 shows the result of all this effort (hardly an effort at all!). The values of the two vacation packages are still anchored to their respective categories, now along the vertical axis.

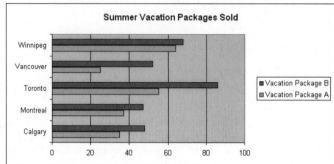

Figure 4-6: Displaying the data in a Bar chart.

A Bar chart typically has the categories on the vertical axis and the values on the horizontal axis.

Seeing How Data Stacks Up with Stacked Column and Bar Charts

Another way to display comparative data is in a stacked fashion. This means that, for each category, all values of the multiple series are stacked on top of each other. The idea that the stacking is on top implies here a Column chart. A Bar chart would stack horizontally to the right.

Changing the chart subtype

Here's how to change the chart to a Stacked Bar:

1. **Click on the chart once to select it.**

2. **Choose Chart ⇨ Chart Type.**

   The Chart Type dialog box appears.

3. **Select the second chart subtype (Stacked Bar), that is the second one in the first row of chart subtypes.**

4. **Click OK.**

Figure 4-7 shows how my example looks.

Figure 4-7:
Changing
the chart
subtype to
display
stacked
data.

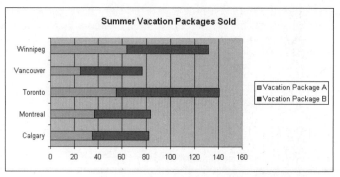

The stacked chart in Figure 4-7 uses the same data, but for each category all the series are added successively to the right (because this is a Bar chart). There are only two series, so each category displays a bar with two colors.

Stacking shows a successive, or running, total of the values found in the data series, per category. The advantage to this is the immediate recognition of which category has the overall highest achievement. Looking back at the chart in Figure 4-6, it could be difficult to see which office sold the most over-all vacation packages — Winnipeg or Toronto. The stacked view shown in Figure 4-7 removes any doubt. For a grand total of vacation packages sold, Toronto is in first place. The Toronto stacked line is the longest.

Note, too, that the value of ranges of the value scale (along the bottom) have increased. By necessity, the range has increased to accommodate the new summed (er, stacked) total values.

Displaying a Stacked Column chart

Now it's time to look at a Stacked Column chart, and then a 100% Stacked Column chart. First, though, follow these steps to change the chart into a stacked column:

1. **Click on the chart once to select it.**

2. **Choose Chart ⇨ Chart Type.**

    The Chart Type dialog box appears.

3. **Select the Column chart type, and the second chart subtype (that is, the second one in the first row of chart subtypes — Stacked Column).**

4. **Click OK.**

    Your chart should now look something like the one in Figure 4-8.

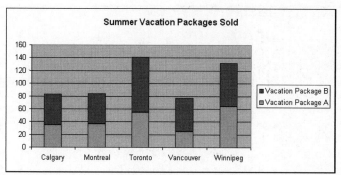

Figure 4-8:
Looking at a
Stacked
Column
chart.

The Column chart in Figure 4-8 is identical to the Bar chart in Figure 4-7, except for the direction. Stacking data horizontally or vertically is a matter of preference. Both chart types serve well to present the data. For example, in either the Column or the Bar chart, Toronto stands out.

Displaying a 100% Stacked Column chart

The cumulative stacked values are interesting to see, in that you receive visual feedback of how each series value contributes to a full sum, for each individual category. In other words, in Figure 4-8, you can easily see that for Vancouver, Package B clearly was sold more than Package A.

Sometimes you need to compare items not by an actual amount, but rather by a percentage. Why? Imagine this — a contest is on to see which office sold the highest percentage of Package B vacations, compared to the total for the office. Comparing results by an actual amount often isn't sensible. For example, Toronto may easily outsell Vancouver by virtue of more salespeople. However, getting any size office to sell more of a given item, as a percentage of its overall sales, is equally challenging to all offices.

Let's see how the offices are doing with vacation package sales as percentages:

1. **Click on the chart once to select it.**

2. **Choose Chart ⇨ Chart Type.**

   The Chart Type dialog box appears.

3. **Select the third chart subtype (that is, the third one in the first row of chart subtypes — 100% Stacked Column).**

4. **Click OK.**

   A 100% Stacked Column (or Bar) levels the playing field, at least in looking at results. Figure 4-9 shows how my example stacks up.

Funny contest tricks

I once worked in the sales department of a major book publisher. A group of us salespeople each handled similarly sized sales territories. I was fairly consistent in being the best performer. Then, one day, management came out with a contest named "Who's the Best." The winner would be determined by who increased his own sales by the greatest percentage over a three-month period. The odds were for me to fail, because I was already at full capacity. The odds for the winner were on the worst performer in our group. All that person would have to do is just start working a bit harder. Increasing — even doubling — sales if you have hardly any sales in the first place should be easy. To make a long story short, the worst performer and I both worked very hard. I won the contest, and the worst performer came in second. Is there a lesson somewhere in here about how hard work only benefits those who already work hard?

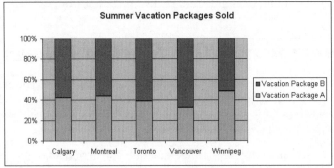

Figure 4-9:
Viewing
data as
percentage
s of a whole.

In a 100% stacked chart the value axis displays a range of percentages from 0 to 100 percent. All stacked categories reach from bottom to top (or left to right in a 100% Stacked Bar chart). And sure enough, an interesting fact is uncovered: As a percentage of its own overall sales, Vancouver did the best with Vacation Package B. The charts in Figure 4-8 and Figure 4-9 plot the same data; and as you can see, the 100% stacked chart can make it easier to discern results.

Getting Jazzy with Cylinder, Cone, and Pyramid Charts

Cylinder, Cone, and Pyramid charts are fancy versions of Column and Bar charts. I ask you, why use a plain old column when a cool-looking cone is yours for the taking?

Figure 4-10 shows the Chart Type dialog box. In the left in the list of chart types — the Cylinder, Cone, and Pyramid are found near the bottom of the list.

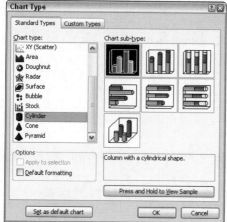

Figure 4-10:
Seeking out
the Cylinder,
Cone, and
Pyramid
chart types.

The Cylinder, Cone, and Pyramid are all identical in practice and use. Only their actual appearance differentiates them. The subtypes for the Cylinder, Cone, and Pyramid are also identical. An interesting twist, though, in the subtypes is that they give you the choice of applying the Cylinder, Cone, or Pyramid as a Column or Bar chart. That is, you can go for the horizontal or vertical look. (Just what *is* this year's style anyway?)

The chart subtypes provide the variety of standard, stacked, and 100% stacked choices, as I show you earlier with Column and Bar charts.

The Cylinder, Cone, and Pyramid charts are all 3-D charts.

If you still have the 100% Stacked Column chart on your worksheet, here is what you do to change it to one of these fancy charts:

1. **Click on the chart once to select it.**

2. **Choose Chart ⇨ Chart Type.**

   The Chart Type dialog box appears.

3. **Scroll down in the Chart list if you need to, and then select the Cylinder, Cone, or Pyramid chart type.**

4. **Click OK.**

   Figure 4-11 shows the data displayed as a Pyramid chart, in splendid 3-D.

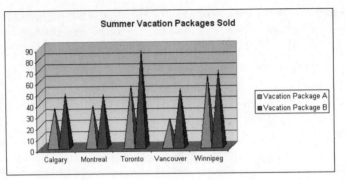

Figure 4-11:
Using a 3-D
Cone chart
to display
the data.

Changing the Data Orientation to Make a Series-Segregated Side-by-Side Comparison

I just couldn't leave this one out. By changing the direction in which the data is interpreted, you can create a chart that compares data values of categories but with each series plotted separately. You'll have an easier time understanding this by first looking at Figure 4-12, which shows just such a chart, and then reading my explanation of it.

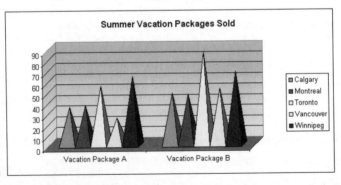

Figure 4-12:
Comparing
data
values as
independent
series.

To be clear, this is a trick of perception. So far, you've seen comparisons of offices in cities. The cities were the categories. In the chart in Figure 4-12, the series and categories have been swapped. Now, the two vacation packages are the categories, and the cities have become the series. Yet, you still could use this chart to *think of* the vacation packages as the series. It's all in the mind.

It seems I've broken my own rule about having more categories and fewer series (I mention this in Chapter 3), but what the heck! This twist of chart items makes it easy to distinguish, individually, how the two vacation packages fared among the offices.

Here's how to change the data orientation:

1. **Click on the chart once to select it.**

2. **Choose Chart ⇨ Source Data.**

   The Source Data dialog box appears.

3. **Select Rows for the Series In setting.**

   Figure 4-13 shows where this change is made.

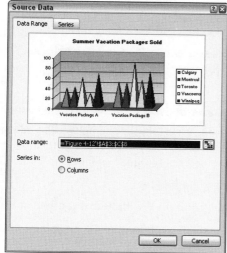

Figure 4-13:
Changing the way the chart displays data.

4. **Click OK.**

Comparing Slices of Data with Pie Charts

Pie charts are used to compare components of a whole. Considered in percentages, the components together add up to 100 percent. The cool thing about a Pie chart is that, visually, a circular shape is whole. Slicing up a circle allows the instant perception of gauging how a slice of the circle compares to the whole.

Too many data points makes for an unusable Pie chart. No exact number makes or breaks this decision, but you could use the number 8 as a guide to when a pie chart is no longer the best choice.

Using a single series to make a Pie chart

Pie charts display just a single series. To work with a Pie chart, the vacation package data has been altered. Vacation packages A and B have been added together. In this way, there is just one series to plot. Figure 4-14 shows the data and the Chart Wizard on its way to creating a pie.

Here's how to create a Pie chart:

1. **On a blank worksheet, enter two headers in two columns, across a row.**

   In my example, I entered Office and Vacation Packages Sold.

2. **Underneath the first header, enter five category values.**

   These are not the actual measurements. In my example, I used the names of five Canadian cities.

3. **Enter numeric values under the second header.**

   A large discrepancy in values will cause the smallest or smaller values to show as very thin slices of the pie — not necessarily a bad thing, just don't be surprised if they're hard to find.

4. **Select the data, including the headers.**

5. **Click the Chart Wizard button on the Standard toolbar or choose Insert ➪ Chart.**

   The Chart Wizard opens.

6. **In Chart Wizard Step 1, select Pie as the chart type.**

7. **Select the second chart subtype (the second along the first row of subtypes — Pie with a 3-D visual effect).**

8. **Click Finish.**

   You now have a Pie chart. The cities are listed in the legend, and the color of each identifies which pie slice belongs to which city. Figure 4-15 shows how mine looks.

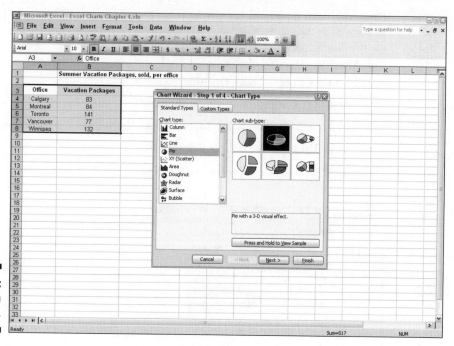

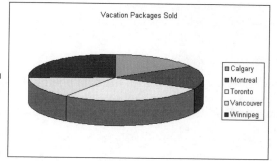

Figure 4-15:
Displaying
components
of a whole.

Using labels to point out the exact values

Unlike some other chart types, you can't display a value axis on a Pie chart. Therefore, there are no immediate clues to the actual values of the slices, bearing in mind that each slice represents a data point in the series.

Often, leaving out labels on a Pie chart is fine. A Pie chart is meant to show the contribution of each data point to the total. By using a complete circle as the total, you can easily grasp a data point's contribution by the size of its slice. They may be all you need — a general idea of the data point's contribution.

However, sometimes you'll need to know the exact values. The way to do this is by adding data labels:

1. **Click on the chart once to select it.**

2. **Choose Chart ➪ Chart Options.**

   The Chart Options dialog box appears.

3. **Click the Data Labels tab to bring it to the top (if it isn't already).**

4. **Check Value in the Labels Contain box.**

   Figure 4-16 shows what this looks like.

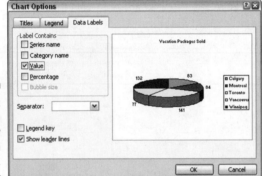

Figure 4-16: Selecting to display values on the chart.

5. **Click OK.**

   Figure 4-17 shows the Pie chart now with the data point values situated next to the slices. If your chart looks slightly different, perhaps flatter, it's because I adjusted the angle of the 3-D view. I show you how to do this in Chapter 14.

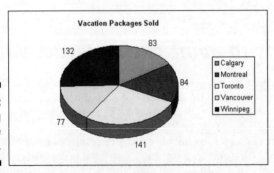

Figure 4-17: Displaying values in the Pie chart.

Comparing Bites of Data with Doughnut Charts

Doughnut charts are a variation of Pie charts. Of course, if you want to be philosophical, you could say Pie charts are then a variation of Doughnut charts, but I get to call the shots here.

Seriously, Doughnut charts use a circular shape to represent the whole (100%), and the doughnut becomes sliced into relative pieces that represent the data points. In this respect, Doughnut charts are the same as Pie charts. You can use them for the same reason (showing how components compare to the whole).

Doughnut charts have an additional feature that is both their saving grace and their downfall. Unlike Pie charts, Doughnut charts can display multiple series. You would think that would be a good thing, until you make such a chart.

Displaying multiple series in a Doughnut chart

Figure 4-18 shows a Doughnut chart that displays the two series vacation packages used throughout this chapter. The legend has the names of the cities — nothing new there. But upon looking at the chart, how easy is it to tell anything about comparisons among the two series, or city to city?

Figure 4-18:
Using a
Doughnut
chart to
present a
confused
multiple-
series view.

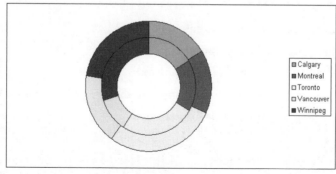

A little farther down in this section, I show you how to make sense of the confusion. But first it's time to make the chart — you can alter it later. If you still have the data used throughout the chapter, skip the first four steps.

1. **On a blank worksheet, enter three headers in three columns, across a row.**

   In my example, I entered Office, Vacation Package A, and Vacation Package B.

2. **Underneath the first header, enter five category values.**

   These are not the actual measurements. In my example, I used the names of five Canadian cities.

3. **Enter numeric values under the second header.**

   The values should be somewhat close to each other.

4. **Enter numeric values under the third header.**

   Also here, the values should not vary greatly.

5. **Select the data, including the headers.**

6. **Click the Chart Wizard button on the Standard toolbar or choose Insert ⇨ Chart.**

   The Chart Wizard opens.

7. **Select the Doughnut chart type, and the first subtype (Doughnut).**

8. **Click Finish.**

You should now have a Doughnut chart that resembles the one in Figure 4-18. Putting aside the fact that you didn't enter a chart title, would you agree that telling much of anything is difficult? In fact, you can't tell which circle represents which series! Is the outer circle Vacation Package A or Vacation Package B? You can only tell by looking at the source data and trying to figure it out.

Even so, the chart can be improved:

1. **Click on the chart once to select it.**

2. **Choose Chart ⇨ Chart Options.**

   The Chart Options dialog box appears.

3. **Click the Data Labels tab to bring it to the top (if it isn't already).**

4. **Check Value in the Labels Contain box.**

5. **Click OK.**

   That's a little better (see Figure 4-19). The data points are now identified with their value. Still, no way to identify which circle belongs to which series. You can insert text to clarify the data — I show you the technique in Chapter 15. You can also select to display the series name along with the values. This will make for a messy chart, though.

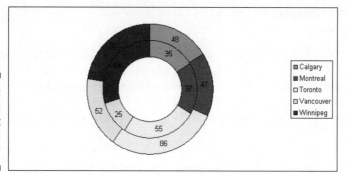

Figure 4-19:
A little
clearer, but
is it good
enough?

Displaying a single series in a Doughnut chart

Perhaps a Doughnut chart is best used to display a single series. This is a subjective decision. Here's a quick way to remove a series and be left with just one series:

1. **Click on the chart once to select it.**

2. **Choose Chart ⇨ Source Data.**

   The Source Data dialog box appears.

3. **Click the Series tab to bring it to the top (if it isn't already).**

4. **Click one of the series in the Series list.**

   Figure 4-20 shows how my example looks.

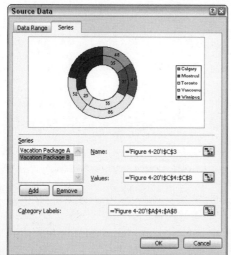

Figure 4-20:
Removing
a series.

5. Click Remove.

6. Click OK.

Figure 4-21 shows the results of my efforts (clicking buttons is hard work!). With just a single series, trying to compare delineations along one circle with those along another is no longer necessary. Guess what — removing the second series took care of another problem. Like magic, a chart title has appeared identifying the series. It doesn't get any better than that!

Figure 4-21:
Putting a
Doughnut
chart to
good use.

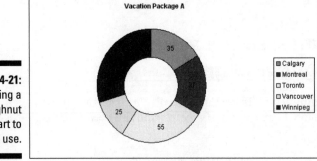

Chapter 5

Creating Charts That Show Change

*N*umerous charts are used to show how an item changes in value over time. The quintessential example is a Stock chart. How is your investment doing? This question involves time, for only the change over time answers the question.

In chart talk, the concept is to analyze the change of an entity over a set of categories, and most often the categories are intervals of time. This can be seconds, hours, days, months, centuries, or anything in between. It's not that the categories have to be fixed to a rigid sense of typical time intervals, such as hours or days. What matters is that the categories make sense of the data. Categories could be in milliseconds, four-day intervals, double decades, and so on. If you're measuring the change of something every 20 years — say the lobster population off the coast of Maine — then double-decade categories are just what you need.

Although most often the change is over time, it doesn't have to be. The categories can be anything. What matters is seeing how the measurable entity has changed over the categories, whatever the categories are (for example, measuring how a fund-raising trip is doing as it travels from city to city). Figure 5-1 shows just such an example.

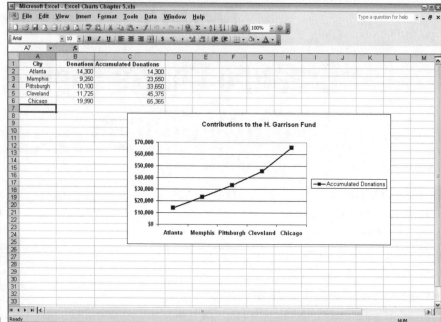

Figure 5-1:
Displaying
change over
a non-time-
based
category.

In the chart in Figure 5-1, the categories are cities and the values are dollars. Time is not a factor in this chart. There is an important point here: Looking at the data and what has been plotted, note that a column of accumulated donations has been calculated. This is the data that is plotted, not the column of raw donations per city. This chart is measuring the growth of the proceeds across the cities, but not the funds received per city.

Just to make this point clear, Figure 5-2 displays the cities with the amounts received per city. The problem with the chart in Figure 5-2 is that it looks like it's attempting to show how the fund fared as each successive city is considered. This is not the case — the donations received in each city are independent facts. This is the wrong chart type to plot the donations per city. Better would be a Bar or Column chart — to compare the data values *per* category.

Using the wrong chart type isn't always evident. A chart can *appear* correct yet still misrepresent the data.

Someone could look at the chart in Figure 5-2 and conclude that Memphis is tied in to a retraction of the fund. That's just wrong!

Okay, enough chart theory. In this chapter, I focus on change over time, because that's predominantly the use of charts that show change.

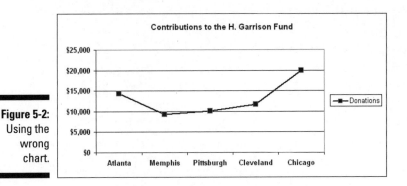

Figure 5-2:
Using the
wrong
chart.

Working with Data That Contains Change over Time

Ups and downs are a fact of life, and a fact about the life of a data series. If all the measurements along a series of data were the same, the plot would be of a flat line — not too exciting! Putting together the points of a data series, across (time) categories makes it possible to see performance over time.

One expectation is that plotting change over time will reveal a pattern of performance, and often, you hope, serve as a guide to what can be expected in the future. That is, you hope there is some useful trend to uncover. Seemingly random data produces a seesaw squiggly kind of chart — no pattern in that! On the other hand, meaningful data produces a meaningful chart, which is exactly what you're going for.

Looking at a plot of time-based performance

Figure 5-3 shows a plot of the closing price for IBM stock, for the year 2003. (I bet there are some financial analysts who would know it's IBM just by looking at the line. The rest of us need the chart title!)

Like all good charts, the one in Figure 5-3 immediately conveys useful information. The value of IBM stock was higher at the end of 2003 than it was at the start. The value bounced around in the $75 to $90 range for most of the year and then "broke out" in mid-September to reach new highs. For the rest of the year the stock yo-yoed around $90. (That Stock Analysis 101 course I took way back when is finally paying off!)

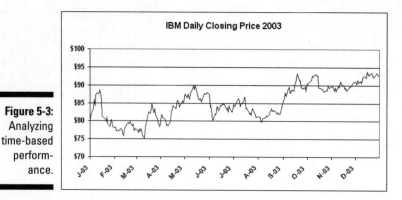

Note, too, a few other attributes about the chart in Figure 5-3. The values on the vertical (value) axis have been formatted to dollars. The categories along the horizontal axis are the 12 months of the year, even though there are over 252 data points. This means there are 252 categories. But listing each individually would be unreadable. Finally, there is no legend. Its inclusion would leave less room for the chart itself. More importantly, though, the legend would serve no purpose. The single data series is the daily close price. You already know this from the chart title.

Looking at the data

When time-based data is plotted, the time delineations themselves become the categories. Figure 5-4 shows the source data of the chart in Figure 5-3. These are the daily close figures for IBM stock through the year 2003.

The data in Figure 5-4 covers 252 rows. I've added a small summary section that points out the lowest and highest values, along with their dates. You can see that the chart in Figure 5-3 accurately shows these to be the low and high points on the plotted line.

When dates are the categories, the category axis uses a time-scale approach to displaying categories. A time-scale category axis accommodates nuances of daily data. See Chapter 11 for more information.

To get cracking on making some charts, you need some data. I created a reasonable set of time-based data (see Figure 5-5). There are 12 months — the categories — and there are three series. You'll be plotting multiple data series.

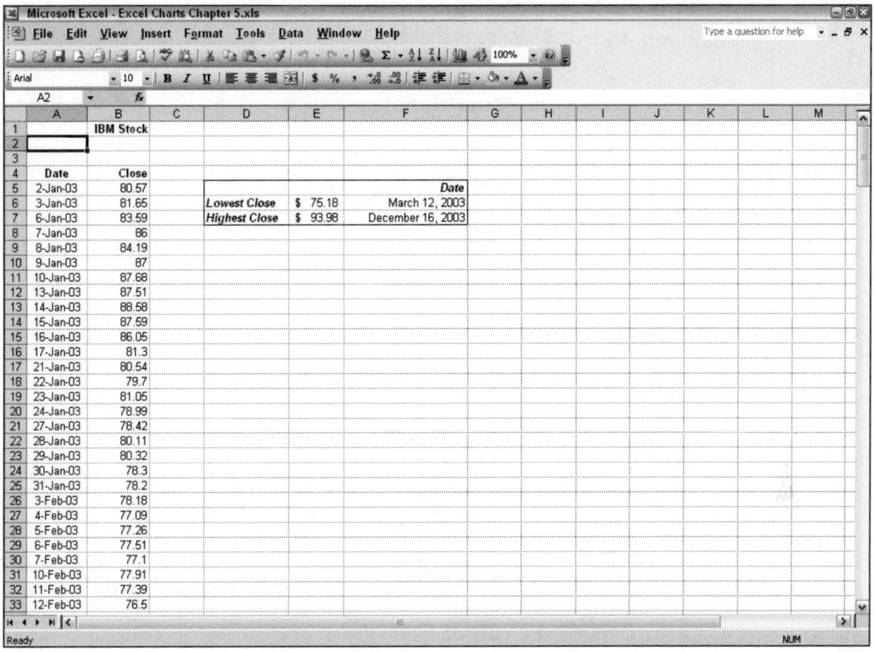

Figure 5-4: Reviewing the data behind the chart.

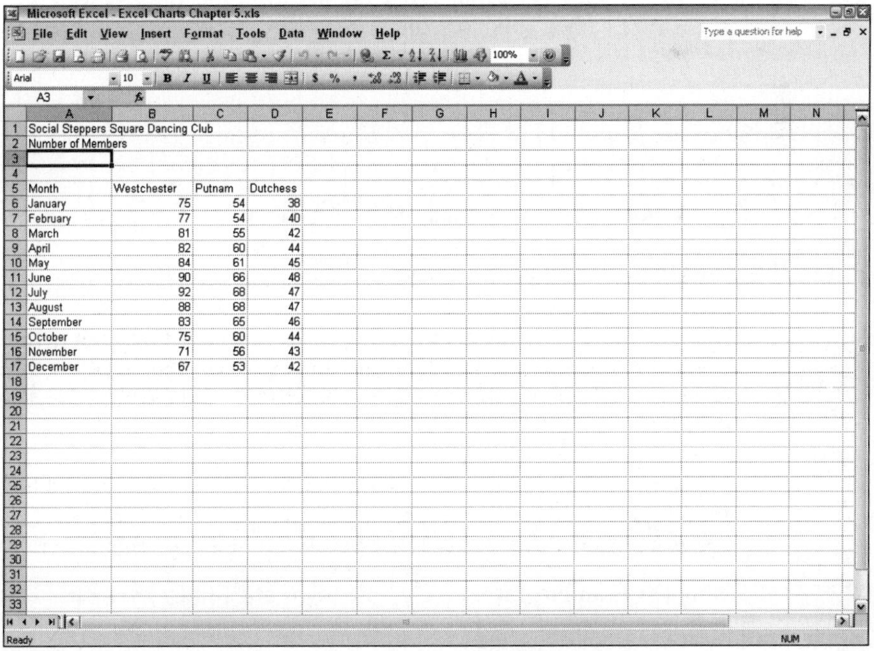

Figure 5-5: Creating time-based data.

Here's how to create data for making the charts in this chapter. You can use mine exactly, or create some that pertain to you:

1. **On a blank worksheet, enter four headers in four columns, across a single row.**

   In my example, I entered Month, followed by Westchester, Putnam, and Dutchess (counties near where I live).

2. **Underneath the first header, enter the names of the 12 months.**

   These are the categories.

3. **Enter numeric values under the second header.**

   The values should be somewhat close to each other, to help the chart present reasonably well. In other words, the range of the value axis will not become so wide that the data ends up looking flat.

4. **Enter numeric values under the third header.**

   The values should be somewhat close to each other. Also, these values should not, as a group, vary greatly from the values under the second header. This, too, helps keep the reasonable range in the value axis.

5. **Enter numeric values under the fourth header.**

   The values should be somewhat close to each other. Also these values should not, as a group, vary greatly from the values under the second or third header. This, too, helps keep the reasonable range in the value axis.

Time to plot!

Laying Out the Sequence of Data Points with Line Charts

Because lines are continuous, using them makes it easy to see the flow of the data points across the categories. A single series can be plotted, as can multiple series. When multiple series are plotted, you have the option of stacking the data.

Charting a single time-based series

Using the example data, here's how to create a line chart with a single series:

1. **Select the categories (months) in the first column and the first data series (in the second column), including the headers.**

For now leave out the other series. Figure 5-6 shows just which section of the data to select.

2. **Click the Chart Wizard button on the Standard toolbar or choose Insert ➪ Chart.**

   The Chart Wizard opens.

3. **Select the Line chart type, and select the first subtype (Line).**

4. **Click Finish.**

   Figure 5-7 shows how my chart turned out. A few formatting changes will help the appearance.

The Chart Wizard is great at making charts, but it can be mediocre at formatting them.

If your chart came out like the one in Figure 5-7, take note that the values axis (the vertical one) is covering a range of 0 to 100. Starting the range at 0 is not necessarily a bad thing. The side effect, though, is that the data becomes a little squished. The lowest value in the data in the first series is 67. Most of the plot area, therefore, is not used.

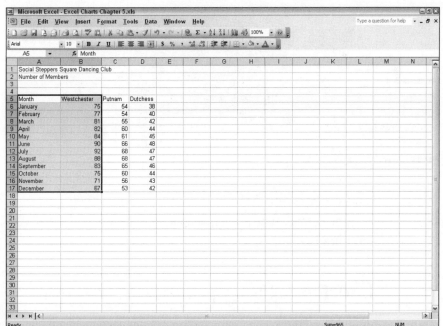

Figure 5-6:
Selecting a
portion of
the data.

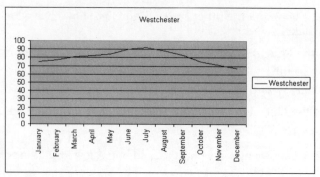

Figure 5-7: Plotting a single time-based series.

In my example, the plot area is gray, which obscures the line a bit. Here's how to change the value range and the plot area color. These procedures are discussed fully in Chapters 9 and 12.

1. **Right-click directly on the value axis.**

   Figure 5-8 shows where and how this is done.

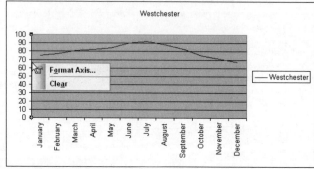

Figure 5-8: Preparing to change axis attributes.

2. **Choose Format Axis.**

   The Format Axis dialog box appears.

3. **Click the Scale tab.**

   Figure 5-9 shows what this tab looks like.

   There are a number of scale settings. For now, though, there is just one to change — Minimum. The Minimum and Maximum values define the range the axis displays.

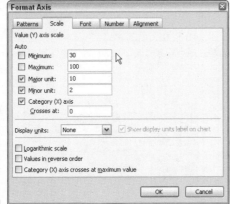

Figure 5-9:
Reviewing
the axis
scale
settings.

4. If you've used my data, change Minimum to 30.

If you've used other data, change the minimum to a value that is less than the value of the lowest data point *among all three series.* I chose 30 because it's a little lower than 38, which is the lowest value found among all three series. The other two series will be added to the chart in the next section. You may end up leaving the Minimum at 0.

Figure 5-10 shows the change in the axis range. The shape of the line has changed — it isn't as flat.

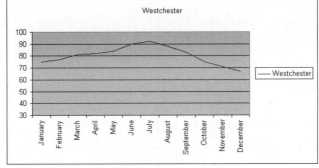

Figure 5-10:
Bringing the
series line
to life.

5. Right-click directly on the plot area, but not on the series line or on a gridline.

Figure 5-11 shows where and how this is done.

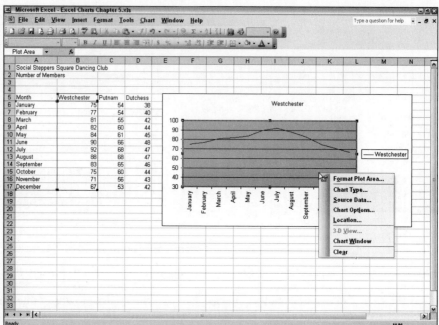

Figure 5-11:
Selecting
the plot
area.

6. Choose Format Plot Area.

The Format Plot Area dialog box, shown in Figure 5-12, appears.

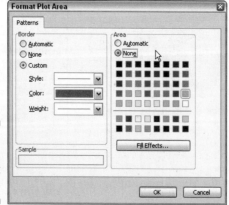

Figure 5-12:
Formatting
the plot
area.

7. In the Area box on the right, select None.

8. Click OK.

Figure 5-13 shows the result of these steps. The series line is easier to follow (it isn't as flat), and it's easier to see (it stands out better without a dark background).

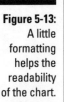

Figure 5-13:
A little formatting helps the readability of the chart.

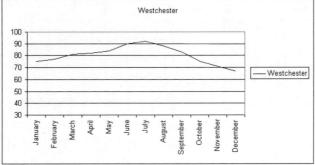

You can apply other formatting changes; experience will become your guide.

Plotting multiple-series time-based data

A common use of charts that show change over categories is to compare multiple series among the common categories. This makes seeing where a data series acted in a similar or dissimilar way, in relation to the other series, easier.

Some charts, such as Bar charts, compare items at individual categories, and other charts, such as Line charts, compare movement among categories.

The task at hand is to add the other data series to the chart:

1. Select the other two series, including the headers.

2. Move the mouse pointer over the border of the selected data area.

The mouse pointer changes to a small black cross. Figure 5-14 shows what this should look like.

3. Click and hold down the mouse button, and then drag the data over the chart.

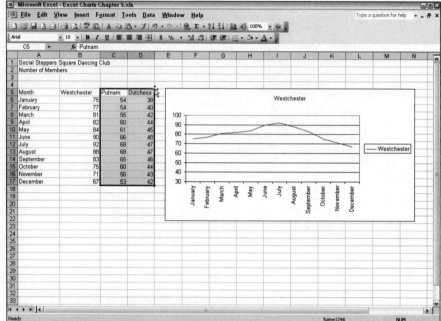

Figure 5-14:
Getting
ready to
drag more
data to the
chart.

4. Release the mouse button.

In Figure 5-15, the chart now displays all three data series. The value range, set at 30 to 100 in my example, does the data justice. The range helps accommodate all three series with regard to not having them appear too flat.

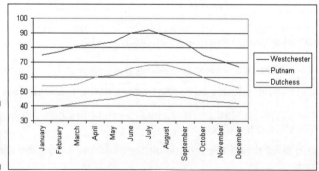

Figure 5-15:
Displaying
three series.

In my example, the three series follow a similar pattern. During the summer months, membership goes up in all counties. During the winter, membership dips in all counties.

Stacking multiple series in a Line chart

Stacking lets you see a combined result. In my example, I've plotted how each of the three counties fared on membership, but I haven't considered how combined membership is making out over the course of the year.

An easy way to see this is to stack the data, by changing the chart subtype:

1. **Click on the chart once to select it, if it isn't already selected.**

2. **Choose Chart ⇨ Chart Type.**

   The Chart Type dialog box appears.

3. **Select the second chart subtype — that is, the second one in the first row of chart subtypes (Stacked Line).**

4. **Click OK.**

If you don't see any change — in particular, if there is still only one series presented — use these optional steps:

1. **Right-click directly on the value (vertical) axis.**

2. **Choose Format Axis.**

   The Format Axis dialog box appears.

3. **In the Format Axis dialog box, make sure the Minimum and Maximum check boxes are checked.**

   Note that the Minimum and Maximum values have changed to accommodate the wider range needed to display stacked results. Leave the new values as they are.

4. **Click OK.**

   Figure 5-16 shows how the stacked data appears. There are three lines as before, but each successive line, from bottom to top, is the sum of the lines below it. In other words, the middle line is a plot of data that is the sum of the first two series. The top line is a plot of the sum of all three series. You can see this is so: Take any given month, add the three values together, and see that the top line matches the total, at the position of the month you added together.

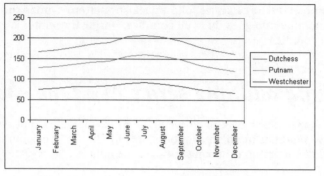

Figure 5-16:
Using
stacked
data to
see how all
the data
adds up.

Look carefully at the charts in Figures 5-15 and 5-16. At first glance, they seem nearly alike. But the range on the vertical axis gives it away: The former is a standard plot; the latter is a stacked plot.

There are other subtypes to apply to Line charts. The 100% Stacked data plots against a value axis in the range of 0 to 100 percent. The other subtypes are variations on the Standard, Stacked, and 100% Stacked subtypes.

Giving Perspective to Data with Area Charts

Area charts have the same functionality and purpose as Line charts. Values are plotted with regard to looking at results across categories. The difference is in the effect. Area charts fill the plot area from the plotted points downward. In other words, imagine a Line chart (better yet, just look at Figure 5-16), in which someone took a crayon and filled in the area from a line down to the category axis.

If you have the data created earlier in the chapter, great! If not, follow the instructions in the "Looking at the data" section, earlier in this chapter.

Here are the steps to create an Area chart:

1. **Select the data, including the categories, all three series, and the headers.**

2. **Click the Chart Wizard button on the Standard toolbar or choose Insert ➪ Chart.**

   The Chart Wizard opens.

3. **Select the Area chart type, and select the first subtype (Area).**

4. **Click Finish.**

Figure 5-17 shows how my chart came out. The three series are present. An interesting twist with my data is that none of the series crosses another series. The effect of this is that each series is fully visible.

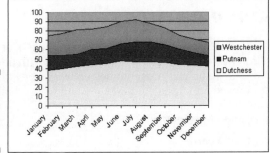

Figure 5-17:
Displaying data as areas.

Watching out for hidden data

In Area charts, you can easily have hidden data points. The areas are solid and not transparent. Therefore, if and when a data point (or more than one point) from one series crosses the range of another series, something gets covered up.

To show a quick example of this, in my data I've changed the Westchester June figure from 92 to 42. Figure 5-18 shows the effect of the plot.

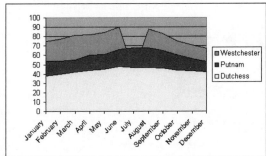

Figure 5-18:
A data point is hidden.

As is evident, the order in which the series appear, with regard to depth (front to back), makes a difference. Luckily, there is a way to adjust the order of the series; a detailed example appears in Chapter 6.

The order of the series can make a big difference in how an Area chart displays. Applying 3-D attributes can be a workaround to reordering the series.

Stacking data in an Area chart

Area chart subtypes include the typical three: Standard, Stacked, and 100% Stacked. This is no different than what a Line chart has, but with an Area chart, at least the 100% Stacked chart presents better. Here's how to change the chart to the 100% Stacked subtype:

1. **Click on the chart once to select it.**

2. **Choose Chart ⇨ Chart Type.**

   The Chart Type dialog box appears.

3. **Select the third chart subtype (that is, the third one in the first row of chart subtypes — 100% Stacked Area).**

4. **Click OK.**

   Figure 5-19 shows how mine turned out. With all 100% Stacked charts, the upper series is flat along the top of the chart. At least with an Area chart, you can get a sense of it being there. In a Line chart, you can easily miss seeing the top line in a 100% Stacked chart, because the line sits adjacent to the top of the plot area.

Figure 5-19:
See how
data stacks
up in
percent-
ages.

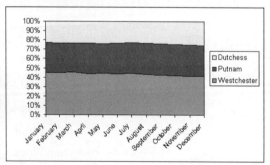

Tracking Price Fluctuations with Stock Charts

One of the more common uses of a chart is to plot the performance of an investment over time. Back in Figure 5-3 is a plot of IBM stock, based on the daily closing price. A Line chart is perfectly fine for tracking a stock and one of its price attributes.

However, there are several attributes of stock price and activity. The number of things that can be tracked, analyzed, sliced and diced, and generally held to scrutiny is overwhelming. For our purposes though, only five need be considered (phew, isn't *that* a relief). These are:

✔ **Open:** The opening price of the stock or investment, at the start of the timeframe being measured, usually daily.

✔ **High:** The high price of the stock or investment, within the timeframe being measured, usually daily.

✔ **Low:** The low price of the stock or investment, within the timeframe being measured, usually daily.

✔ **Close:** The closing price of the stock or investment, at the end of the timeframe being measured, usually daily.

✔ **Volume:** Typically, the number of shares being traded, within the timeframe being measured, usually daily.

Excel provides a special Stock chart type for plotting these specific data points. Each of the Stock chart subtypes requires a certain configuration of these data points.

Figure 5-20 shows the Stock chart type with its available subtypes.

The four chart subtypes are:

Subtype	*Requirement*
High-Low-Close	Time-based categories and three data series
Open-High-Low-Close	Time-based categories and four data series
Volume-High-Low-Close	Time-based categories and four data series
Volume-Open-High-Low-Close	Time-based categories and five data series

Although Stock charts are meant to display investment-based results, you can use them with other types of data, as long as the number of required series is present.

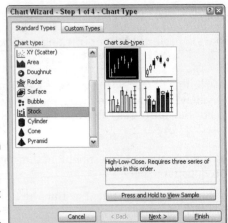

Figure 5-20:
Reviewing
Stock chart
subtypes.

Finding and plotting financial data

Rather than give you steps on entering data, here are a couple of sources to find stock data for publicly held companies:

- ✔ **Yahoo! Finance** (`http://finance.yahoo.com`)**:** The Yahoo! Finance site contains a vast store of financial data. Generally, to find and download data, you look up a specific stock, fund, or index; find the link to the historical prices; select the range of dates; and find the link to download the data (you may have to scroll to the bottom of the page to find this link).

- ✔ **MSN** (`http://moneycentral.msn.com/home.asp`)**:** MSN contains a wealth of business news and data. Generally, to find historical pricing, look up a specific stock, fund, or index; follow the link to the charts; enter a range of dates; click the Show Table button; and click the Download File button.

Instructions on how to download data from these Web sites can become outdated as Web sites are updated. You may need to do some sniffing around to figure out how to do it.

Figure 5-21 shows a download of Microsoft (MSFT) stock historical prices. All the necessary fields are present: Open, High, Low, Close, and Volume.

	A	B	C	D	E	F	G	H	I	J	K	L	M	N	O
1	Date	Open	High	Low	Close	Volume	Adj. Close*		Microsoft (MSFT)						
2	2-Jan-04	27.58	27.77	27.33	27.45	44487700	24.56								
3	5-Jan-04	27.73	28.18	27.72	28.14	67333696	25.17								
4	6-Jan-04	28.19	28.28	28.07	28.24	46950800	25.26								
5	7-Jan-04	28.17	28.31	28.01	28.21	54298200	25.24								
6	8-Jan-04	28.39	28.48	28	28.16	58610800	25.19								
7	9-Jan-04	28.03	28.06	27.59	27.66	67079900	24.74								
8	12-Jan-04	27.67	27.73	27.35	27.57	55845200	24.66								
9	13-Jan-04	27.55	27.64	27.26	27.43	51555900	24.54								
10	14-Jan-04	27.52	27.73	27.47	27.7	43907000	24.78								
11	15-Jan-04	27.55	27.72	27.42	27.54	58604100	24.64								
12	16-Jan-04	27.71	27.88	27.53	27.81	63983400	24.88								
13	20-Jan-04	27.98	28.2	27.93	28.1	63068500	25.14								
14	21-Jan-04	28.13	28.3	27.85	28.3	53570600	25.32								
15	22-Jan-04	28.36	28.44	27.94	28.01	78425200	25.06								
16	23-Jan-04	28.28	28.76	28.22	28.48	127259104	25.48								
17	26-Jan-04	28.49	28.83	28.32	28.8	58299600	25.76								
18	27-Jan-04	28.64	28.72	28.22	28.25	63196200	25.27								
19	28-Jan-04	28.3	28.44	27.47	27.71	71336000	24.79								
20	29-Jan-04	27.81	27.95	27.57	27.91	63748400	24.97								
21	30-Jan-04	27.84	27.9	27.55	27.65	40528700	24.74								
22	2-Feb-04	27.61	27.8	27.24	27.4	62891800	24.51								
23	3-Feb-04	27.4	27.55	27.18	27.29	47993800	24.41								
24	4-Feb-04	27.22	27.43	27.01	27.01	60648000	24.16								
25	5-Feb-04	27.06	27.17	26.83	26.96	55527500	24.12								
26	6-Feb-04	27.03	27.19	26.93	27.08	47209600	24.23								
27	9-Feb-04	27.19	27.23	26.85	26.9	48108500	24.06								
28	10-Feb-04	26.87	27.15	26.82	27.02	37790600	24.17								
29	11-Feb-04	26.97	27.23	26.85	27.15	51515300	24.29								
30	12-Feb-04	27.09	27.15	26.93	26.95	44537000	24.11								
31	13-Feb-04	26.98	27.06	26.5	26.59	67541104	23.79								
32	17-Feb-04	26.72	27.1	26.59	26.99	43477000	24.15								
33	18-Feb-04	26.9	27.11	26.74	26.77	50334700	23.95								

Figure 5-21:
Looking at
downloaded
financial
data.

Not all financial data is what it appears to be. Note in Figure 5-21 that the Close and Adjusted Close columns contain different numbers. This can be because of stock splits and other financial particulars.

Here's how to make a basic High-Low-Close stock chart:

1. **Select the Date, High, Low, and Close columns in your data.**

   The columns in the downloaded stock data may not be in the order you need them. In other words the Date, High, Low, and Close columns may not be all next to each other. To select noncontiguous data, press the Ctrl key while selecting with the mouse.

2. **Click the Chart Wizard button on the Standard toolbar or choose Insert ⇨ Chart.**

   The Chart Wizard opens.

3. **Select the Stock chart type, and select the first subtype (High-Low_ Close).**

4. **Click the Next button twice.**

5. **In the third step of the Chart Wizard, enter a chart title.**

   This should be the name or symbol of the stock, and the period covered in the chart.

6. **Click Finish.**

Figure 5-22 shows how my chart came out. I used the data for Microsoft stock (ticker symbol: MSFT) for January 2, 2004, through January 8, 2004.

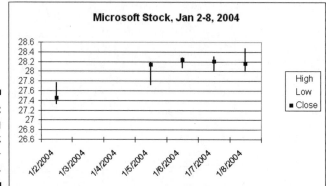

Figure 5-22:
Tracking
stock
perform-
ance.

Stock charts differ from other charts in that the lines that appear are the result of the three series being plotted — high, low, and close in this case. The size of each plotted line is based on the high and low values for the category. For example, January 2 shows a high of 27.77 and a low of 27.33. These figures define the top and bottom of the line based on the values in the value axis. The close figure is presented as the marker in the middle of each line.

Plotting volume with price data

Volume can be plotted on the same chart with the price data. In the data itself, the volume data must follow directly after the categories (the dates), and before the price data. Here are the steps to plot volume and price together:

1. **Rearrange the data so the columns are in the order of Date, Volume, High, Low, Close (or Date, Volume, Open, High, Low, Close).**

2. **Select the data, including the headers.**

3. **Click the Chart Wizard button on the Standard toolbar or choose Insert ➪ Chart.**

   The Chart Wizard opens.

4. **Select the Stock chart type, and select the third subtype (Volume-High-Low-Close) if you did *not* include the open data or the fourth subtype (Volume-Open-High-Low-Close) if you *did* include the open data.**

5. Click the Next button twice.

6. In the third step of the Chart Wizard, enter a chart title.

This should be the name or symbol of the stock, and the period covered in the chart.

7. Click Finish.

Figure 5-23 shows how my chart came out. Because volume falls in a much higher range than the price data, the chart has been formatted as a Combination chart.

Combination charts make it possible to display two different ranges of data in the same chart. A Combination chart has two value axes, one on each side. Each value axis has a different range, and each series is plotted against one value axis or the other. I cover Combination charts in Chapter 17.

Figure 5-23:
Displaying
volume and
price data
on the same
chart.

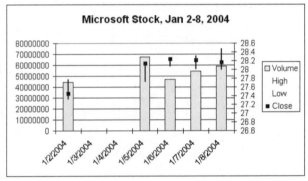

Analyzing stocks and the charts that present the data can be fascinating (well, at least for nerdy types like myself). For example, the chart in Figure 5-23 shows that, on January 5, the volume was highest and the stock closed near the high point of the day. You can tell this because the close marker is at the top of the high-low line. If only I had known this was going to happen the day *before* it actually did!

Chapter 6

Creating Charts That Display Data Relationships

*Y*ou get hammered with advice all the time: Eat fewer calories and you'll lose weight; get a college education and you'll earn more money; brush your teeth and you'll get fewer cavities.

This is great advice! And the reason these facts are known to be true is that the actions and the results are measurable. This is the type of data that has cause and effect. For example, four years of education results in increased average earnings of $20,000. Cause and effect. Or, the world of charts, before and after. No matter what you call it, the point is that there is a relation — one set of data is affected by the other.

This chapter shows how data like this is plotted. But there is an extra bonus to this — you find out how to make some really cool-looking charts! These are not the type of charts you see every day (unless you go out of your way to find some). Knowing how to use these charts will increase your value as a grand chart maker.

Working with Data That Is Related to Other Data

Figure 6-1 shows a worksheet with three columns of data. The first two columns are raw data, and the third measures the relationship of the first two columns. In particular, column A shows the number of survey letters peri-odically sent out. Column B shows the number of responses. The values in column D are calculated to show the response rate.

The values in columns A and B have a relationship. I don't mean they're going out on dates or anything like that. What's apparent is that, when 100 letters were sent out, 12 responses were returned. The number of responses is a function of the number of letters sent. Column A or B considered on its own does not provide any useful information; it's the two together that tells the story.

The response rates in column D are the type of numbers that make business managers jump for joy — or hide under their desks. It all depends on the interpretation. One person's great result is another person's failure. Direct-marketing efforts — where ads are sent out in the mail — are aimed at large groups of people in the hopes of getting a small percentage to respond. Achieving even a 1 to 2 percent response rate is considered successful in some situations.

Looking at the data in Figure 6-1, you can see that, as more letters are sent, the number of responses also rises. This trend continues until 220 letters are sent and then the number of responses starts to stall. Now look at the response rate in column D. The response rate begins to slide downhill starting when just 140 letters are sent.

Number of Letter Sent	Number of Responses	Response Rate
100	12	12%
120	15	13%
140	17	12%
160	18	11%
180	18	10%
200	19	10%
220	20	9%
240	20	8%
260	22	8%
280	22	8%
300	24	8%

Figure 6-1: Reviewing the num-ber of responses.

If this were your direct-mail campaign, you would review these results and make some decisions about future mailings.

Let's look at some more related data. Figure 6-2 shows the number of rainy days for each month of the year, and the number of customers that came in the store.

A quick perusal of this data brings to light that the number of rainy days has little to do with the number of customers. For example, January had 17 rainy days and 74 customers. March had 24 days of rain and 79 customers. You could conclude, then, that more rainy days brings in more customers. But then April had only 15 days of rain and had 91 customers. So, in one case, a greater number of rainy days brought in a greater number of customers. But then a smaller number of rainy days also increased the number of customers.

The relationship in the data is weak. In the next section, I show how an XY (Scatter) chart shows the strength or weakness between two sets of data.

I leave you with one observation I think you'll agree with: A store that sells umbrellas will see a strong relationship between rainy days and the number of customers!

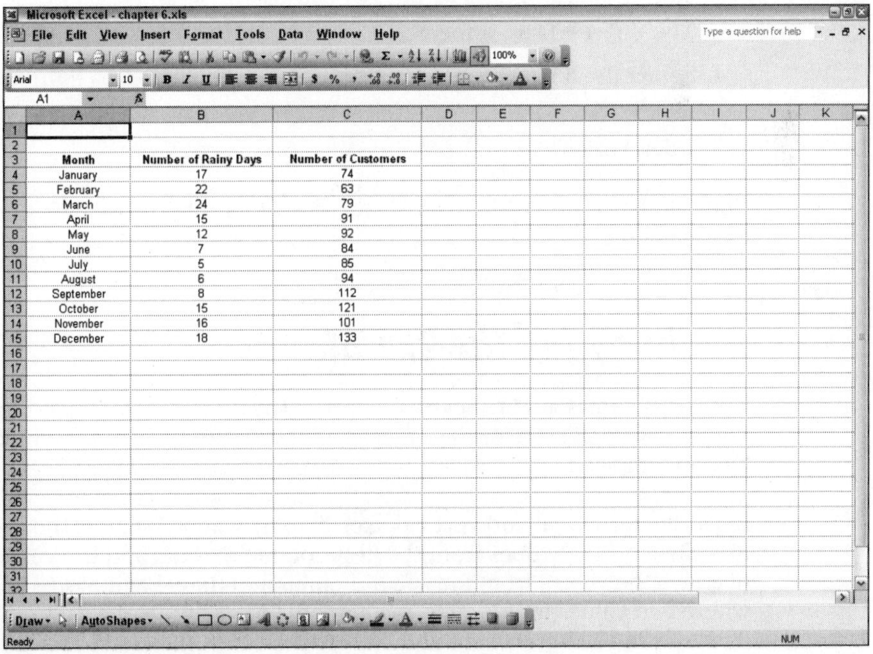

Month	Number of Rainy Days	Number of Customers
January	17	74
February	22	63
March	24	79
April	15	91
May	12	92
June	7	84
July	5	85
August	6	94
September	8	112
October	15	121
November	16	101
December	18	133

Figure 6-2: Analyzing whether the rain affects customer visits.

Laying It Out with XY (Scatter) Charts

XY (Scatter) charts plot points where two values meet. Therefore, XY (Scatter) charts have two value axes and no category axis. When a number of points are plotted, the strength of the relationship becomes apparent by seeing if the plotted points form a trend.

To get a better picture of what I'm talking about, try making an XY (Scatter) chart of your own:

1. **On a worksheet enter two columns of numbers.**

   The examples in Figures 6-1 and 6-2 are perfect. You can copy one of those or create your own. But here's an important point: You only want two columns of data. If you use the data in Figure 6-1, enter just the data from columns A and B. If you use the data from Figure 6-2, enter just the data from columns B and C.

2. **Select the data.**

   You can include the headers.

3. **Click the Chart Wizard button on the Standard toolbar or choose Insert ⇨ Chart.**

   The Chart Wizard appears.

4. **Select the XY (Scatter) chart type, and select the first subtype (Scatter).**

5. **Click Finish.**

Congratulations on making an XY (Scatter) chart! In the following sections, I explain how to make sense of it.

Looking for the trend

Figure 6-3 shows an XY (Scatter) chart of the data from Figure 6-1. Note that I adjusted some of the formatting and added some titles, but the plot of data has not changed.

Both the horizontal and vertical axes display values. That is, the horizontal axis displays the values from the first column of data, and the vertical axis displays the values from the second column of data. Each plotted point is where two values in the same row match. For example, the first row in the data shows 100 letters sent and 12 responses. On the chart, the first plotted point meets where 100 on the horizontal axis meets 12 on the vertical axis.

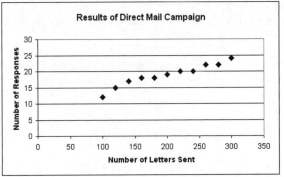

Figure 6-3:
Analyzing
the
relationship
between
mailings and
responses.

A single plotted point is not relevant, but when a batch of points is considered, the strength of the data relationship becomes clear. In Figure 6-3, the plotted points taken together form a discernable line. This indicates a good correlation between the data. And that's not all. The fact that the line is moving up tells that the correlation between the data is a positive one. That means that, as more letters were sent, the number of responses increased. As one set of data values increased, so did the other.

When there is enough correlation in the data to create a noticeable line in an XY (Scatter) chart, the direction of the line tells how the data is related. If the line trends upward, the values in the two data sets move in the same direction. If the line trends downward, the two data sets move in opposite directions. Trendlines are discussed in Chapter 16.

Next, Figure 6-4 shows an XY (Scatter) chart of the data in Figure 6-2. There are two value axes: The horizontal axis is the number of rainy days, and the vertical axis is the number of customers. Each plotted point represents where two values in a row of the data meet.

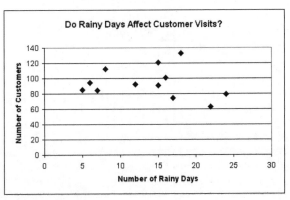

Figure 6-4:
Determining
whether
rain affects
customer
traffic.

In the chart in Figure 6-4, the plotted points are all over the place. There is no trend (that is, no line can be seen) — the points do not line up in any noticeable way.

The conclusion, therefore, is that rainy days have no influence on customer visits. The relationship is weak to the point of being nonexistent.

Changing the points to a line

The XY (Scatter) chart has five subtypes. If you followed the instructions earlier, the Chart Wizard gave you the default subtype that has no lines. Now you'll turn the plotted points into a real line by changing the chart subtype:

1. **Click on the chart once to select it.**

2. **Choose Chart ⇨ Chart Type.**

   The Chart Type dialog box appears.

3. **Select any chart subtype other than the first.**

4. **Click OK.**

The XY (Scatter) chart subtypes that add lines let you select whether to use straight or smoothed lines, and whether to use data markers. These options are all related to formatting and do not affect how the actual data is plotted.

Figure 6-5 shows the same chart as in Figure 6-3 but with the subtype changed to display a line with markers. Applied to this type of strongly related data, the appearance just fills in the line that is already perceived from the plot itself.

Figure 6-5:
Reformatted
to include
a line
and data
markers.

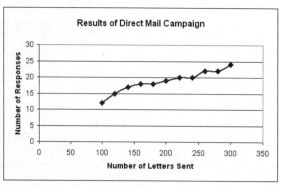

Using Data and Size to Boil Up Bubble Charts

Like XY (Scatter) charts, Bubble charts plot two sets of values, without using a category axis. Bubble charts take this one step further and plot a third set of related values. The third set is represented by the size of the bubbles. Yes, you heard that right. Excel lets you play with bubbles. Excel is fun after all!

Figure 6-6 shows a worksheet with data that relates three facts:

- The length of a movie
- The number of viewers
- How much candy, popcorn, and soda were sold (as total dollars)

In other words, with a given movie length and number of people in the theater, how much is earned on the food and beverages?

This is an interesting question because, during a long movie, some viewers may go to the food stand twice. But if not that many people are watching that long movie, the double visits to the food counter may not add up to all that much.

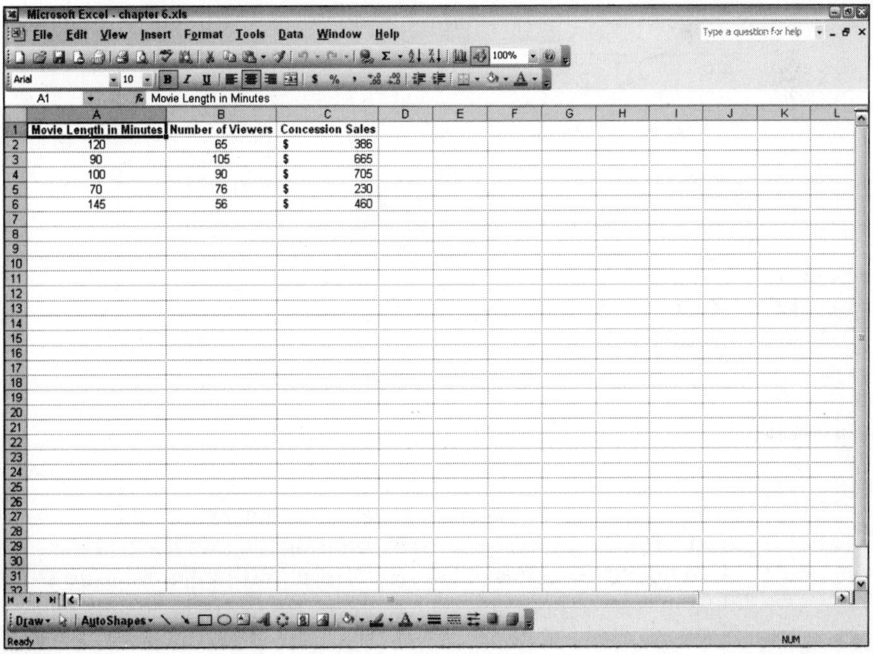

Figure 6-6: Reviewing concession sales at the movies.

On the other hand, if the movie is short, the only sales will be just before the movie starts. But if a lot of people come to the show, that could mean a lot of popcorn is being consumed.

Plotting onto bubbles

In order to create a Bubble chart, you'll need three sets of related data. Here's how to plot a Bubble chart:

1. **On a worksheet, enter three columns of numbers.**

   The example in Figure 6-6 is fine, or you can create your own data.

2. **Select the data.**

   You can include the headers.

3. **Click the Chart Wizard button on the Standard toolbar or choose Insert ⇨ Chart.**

   The Chart Wizard opens.

4. **Select the Bubble chart type, and select the first subtype (Bubble).**

5. **Click Finish.**

   Figure 6-7 shows how my chart looks using the movie data from Figure 6-6.

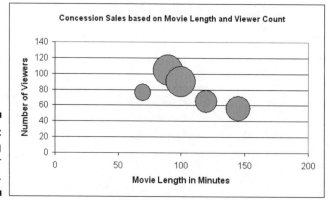

Figure 6-7: Getting bubbly over the movies.

At first, interpreting the chart in Figure 6-7 may seem difficult, but breaking it down into chunks will help. First, ignoring the bubbles and their size, look at the trendline being made. For the most part, there is a downward-sloping line. Therefore, there is *some* correlation in the data. In particular, this is telling you that the longer the movie is, the fewer people come to see it.

Next consider the size of the bubbles. The bubble sizes themselves are the plot of the third column of data — the concession sales. Here, too, is a semi-strong pattern. The short movies with the larger number of viewers have the larger bubbles. Therefore, short movies with larger attendance produces more concession sales compared to longer movies with smaller attendance. The idea that viewers watching a long movie will buy more has not panned out.

Formatting the bubbles

The two value axes can be formatted in standard ways. (I cover this sort of formatting in Chapter 12.) On the other hand, formatting bubbles applies to just Bubble charts, so this is the appropriate place to find out about it:

1. **Right-click directly on a bubble.**

2. **Select Format Data Series from the pop-up menu.**

   The Format Data Series dialog box appears. The Format Data Series dialog box has a number of tabs. Two in particular are of interest here.

3. **Click the Data Labels tab (shown in Figure 6-8).**

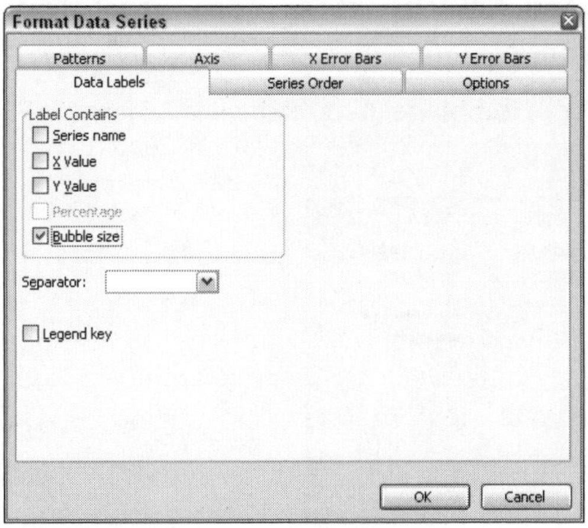

Figure 6-8:
Selecting to show bubble sizes.

4. **Check the Bubble Size check box.**

5. **Click OK.**

   Figure 6-9 shows how the chart appears after selecting to show bubble sizes.

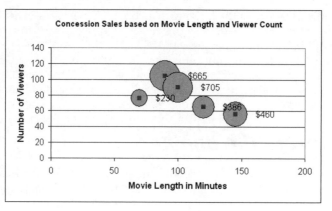

Figure 6-9:
The values
of the third
column now
appear next
to the
bubbles.

In Figure 6-9, the chart shows the concession sales dollar amounts next to the bubbles. This confirms that the bubbles represent the sales data. The larger the amount, the larger the bubble. I think this makes the chart look too busy, but you may require or desire this information on a chart you create. An individual label can be moved around by clicking once on it, letting go of the mouse button, and then clicking on it again. At this point you can drag it around the plot area.

If the Format Data Series dialog box is not open, repeat Steps 1 and 2.

6. Click the Options tab.

There are a number of bubble-related settings, as shown in Figure 6-10.

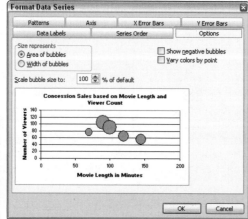

Figure 6-10:
Selecting
bubble
formatting
options.

The best thing to do is experiment with the various settings and see what works best for your chart. Here is a summary of the settings on the Options tab:

What the Setting Is	What It Does
Size Represents	You can select Area of Bubbles or Width of Bubbles. This setting determines the basis of the bubble sizes proportional to the underlying values.
Scale Bubble Size	The overall size can be increased or decreased with this setting. The available range is 0 to 300 percent.
Show Negative Bubbles	Determines whether negative values are visible or hidden.
Vary Colors by Point	Allows each bubble to be plotted with a different color.

TIP

Another formatting option is to change the chart subtype. The Bubble chart has just two subtypes. The only difference is that the second subtype makes the bubbles appear as 3-D spheres — an interesting effect.

Keeping an Eye on It All with Radar Charts

Radar charts do not strictly show the relation of data sets, but their unique design makes them great to show how values tend away from the center. The charts are decidedly different in that the value axis stems from the middle outward to the ends of the categories. The shape of the Radar chart is a function of the number of categories, because each category creates a spike in the design. A way to consider this is that the shape of the design is dependent on the data itself.

Figure 6-11 shows four Radar charts on a worksheet. Each of the four charts has a different number of categories: 3, 4, 5, and 6. This difference creates the change in design among the charts.

Figure 6-12 provides a larger view of one of the Radar charts. There are five categories, so the shape resembles a pentagon. Each series (there are two) covers an area that stretches along each spike to whatever the value is for the category on the spike.

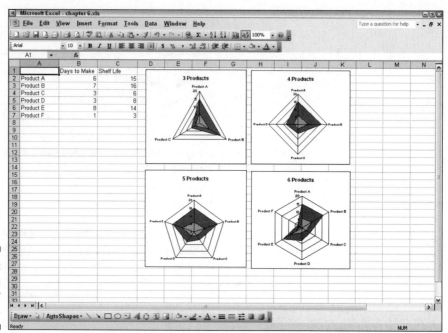

Figure 6-11:
Comparing
Radar
charts.

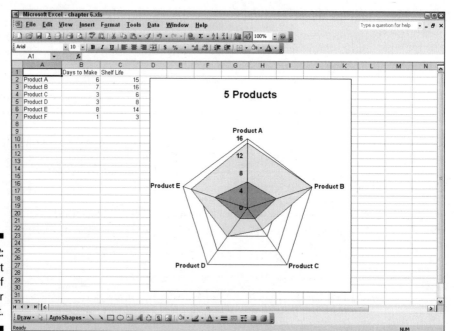

Figure 6-12:
Looking at
the detail of
a Radar
chart.

Creating a Radar chart

It's high time to make a Radar chart, but don't speed through doing this or you may get caught by a radar trap:

1. **Copy the data from columns A through C in Figure 6-12.**

   If you prefer to use your own data, be sure to have a column of categories, such as column A in Figure 6-12.

2. **Also create one or more columns of series data, such as that in columns B and C in Figure 6-12.**

3. **Select the data.**

   You can include the headers.

4. **Click the Chart Wizard button on the Standard toolbar or choose Insert ⇨ Chart.**

   The Chart Wizard appears.

5. **Select the Radar chart type, and select any chart subtype.**

   The chart in Figure 6-12 uses the third chart subtype.

6. **Click Finish.**

You can make formatting changes to the chart as you see fit.

Reordering the series

If you created a Radar chart with the third subtype, you may have inadvertently hidden some data. It happens to everyone — it's a part of the charting life.

In my example, when I first created the Radar chart, only one data series appeared, as shown in Figure 6-13. The series with the larger data points was covering up the series with the smaller data points.

If this happens to you, here's what you need to do:

1. **Right-click anywhere in the middle of the visible data series.**

2. **Select Format Data Series from the pop-up menu.**

   The Format Data Series dialog box appears.

3. **Click the Series Order tab (shown in Figure 6-14).**

4. **Use the Move Up or Move Down buttons to change the order of the series.**

   In this way, the smaller data points can be in front and, therefore, visible.

5. **Click OK.**

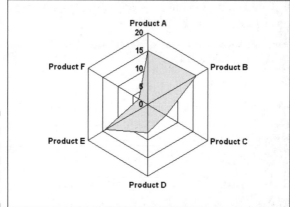

Figure 6-13: Trying to find the missing series.

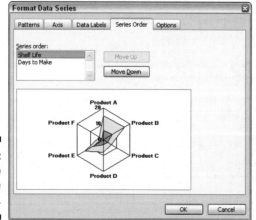

Figure 6-14: Preparing to change the series order.

Seeing Where the Data Lands with Surface Charts

Surface charts are a different breed — of chart, that is! Surface charts display multiple-series data, using the expected category axis and value axis, as well as a third axis that displays the series names. Surface charts are used to show optimum combinations of category and series data.

Chart 1

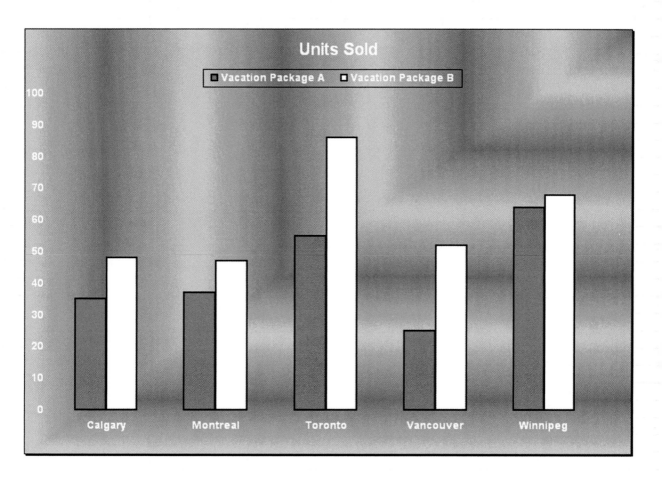

A Column chart. The Brass preset gradient, set with the From Corner shading style is placed in the chart area. All fonts throughout are formatted to white for better contrast against the gradient.

Chart 2

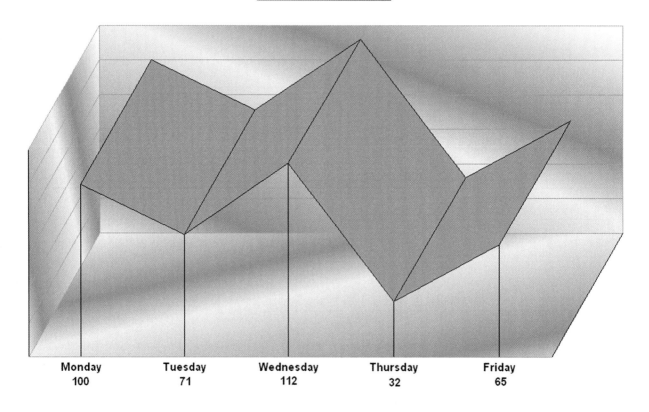

Completed Transactions

| Monday | Tuesday | Wednesday | Thursday | Friday |
| 100 | 71 | 112 | 32 | 65 |

✚ A 3-D Line chart. The elevation is 35. The rotation is 20. The gap depth is 0. The chart depth is 200. Drop lines have been added. The walls and floor have the Silver preset gradient. The gridlines are formatted to the same color as the data series.

Chart 3

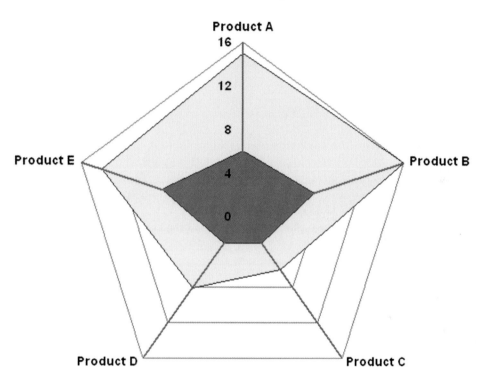

Shelf Life vs. Days in Production

☐ Shelf Life   ■ Days to Make

Product A

Product E

Product B

Product D

Product C

16

12

8

4

0

✚ A filled Radar chart. The two series are formatted with different colors.

Chart 4

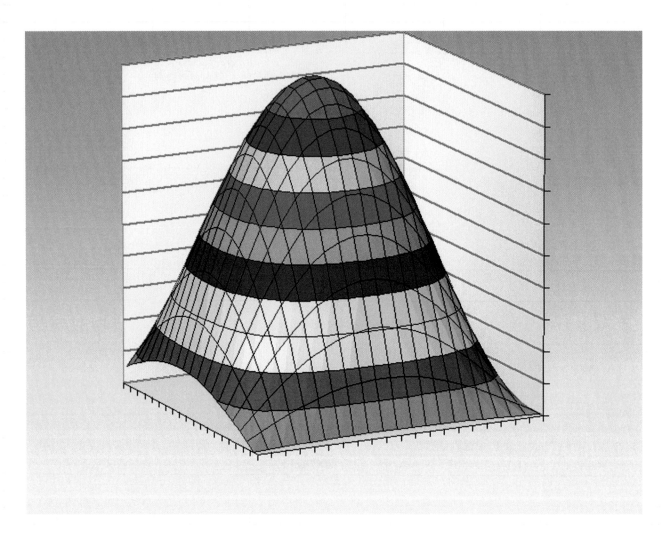

 A Surface chart. The data is based on a formula using sines and cosines. The chart area is formatted with the Daybreak preset gradient. The walls are formatted with a custom gradient.

Chart 5

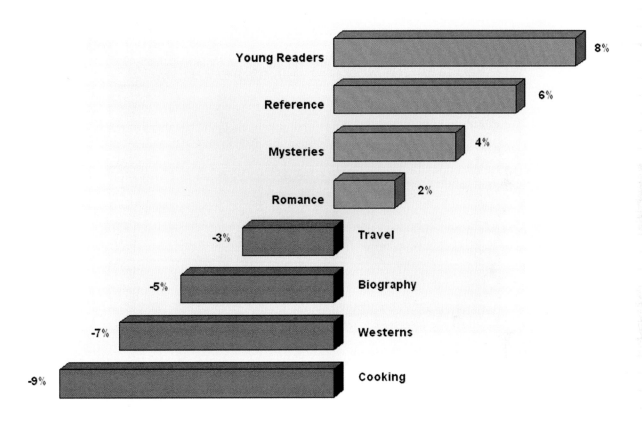

Category Leaders and Losers

A 3-D Bar chart. The source data has positive and negative values. Value data labels are used. Half the bars are individually formatted (the color). The chart area has a custom gradient.

Chart 6

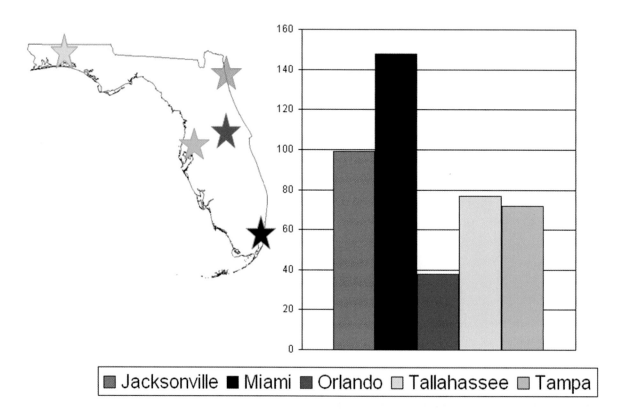

Membership in 2005

☐ Jacksonville ☐ Miami ☐ Orlando ☐ Tallahassee ☐ Tampa

✚ The map of Florida and the stars are inserted graphics.

Chart 7

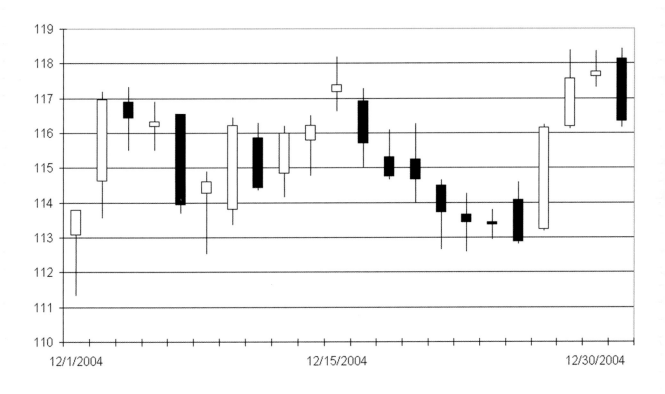

eBay
December 2004

+ A standard Stock chart (with candlesticks).

Chart 8

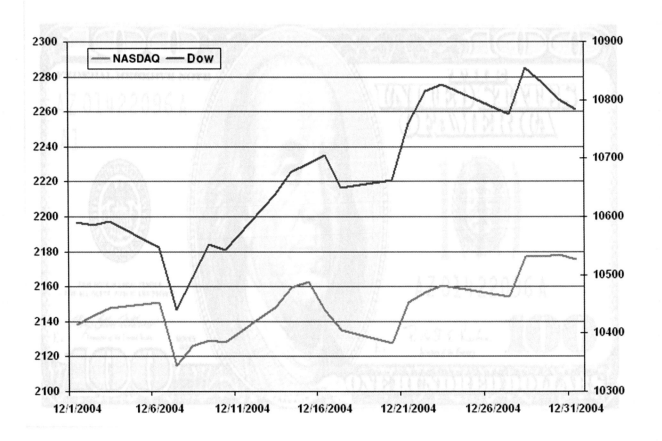

✚ A plot of the Dow and NASDAQ indices, with a picture of a U.S. $100 bill in the chart area. The picture of the $100 bill was set to be 85 percent transparent in an art program, before it was inserted.

Chart 9

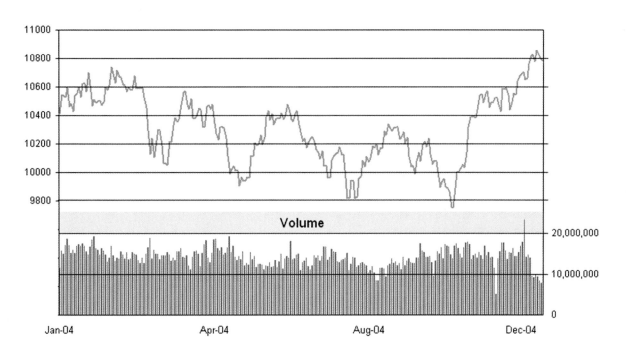

DJIA 2004

✚ A combination chart. The two value axes are scaled such that their values don't meet horizontally, and then white rectangles cover the area of each axis's tick-mark labels that are not needed. In the middle, the word *Volume* is in a text box with a light background.

Chart 10

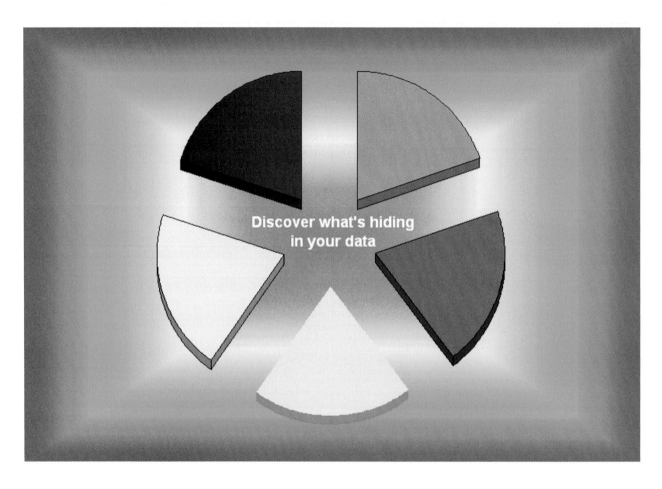

An exploded Pie chart. The chart area is formatted with the preset Rainbow II gradient, using the From Center shading style. The inner text box is formatted to have no fill and no line. The font is formatted to white.

Chart 11

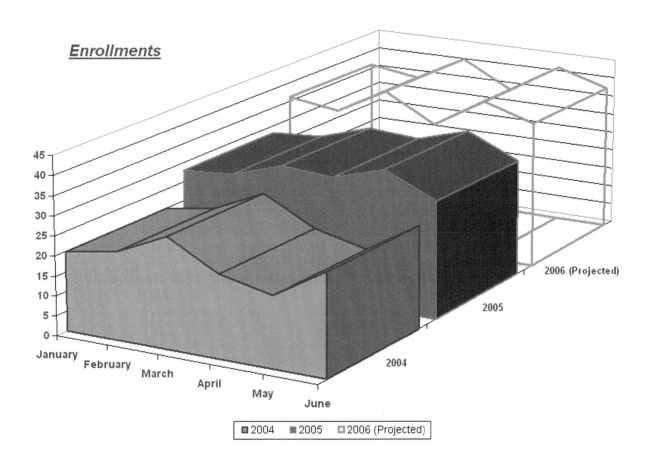

Enrollments

➕ A 3-D Area chart. The area for the last data series (2006) is formatted to None. This gives it the wire-frame appearance.

Chart 12

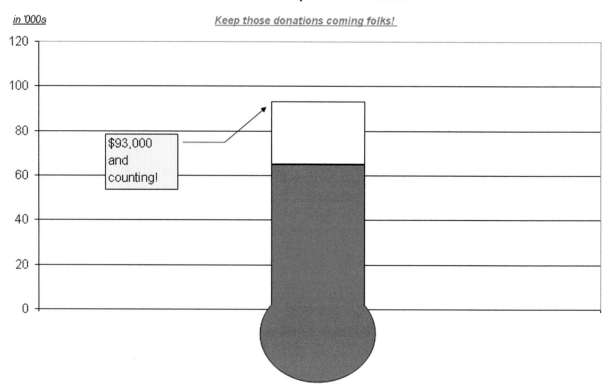

Volunteer Fire Department Donations

in '000s

Keep those donations coming folks!

$93,000 and counting!

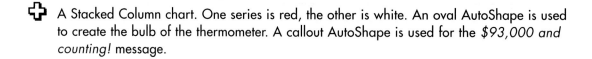

A Stacked Column chart. One series is red, the other is white. An oval AutoShape is used to create the bulb of the thermometer. A callout AutoShape is used for the *$93,000 and counting!* message.

Chart 13

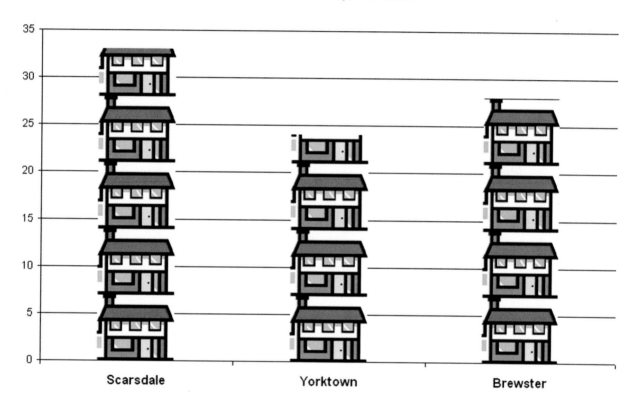

Home Sales 2004, Per Office

✚ A Column chart. A graphic of a house is used to format the data series.

Chart 14

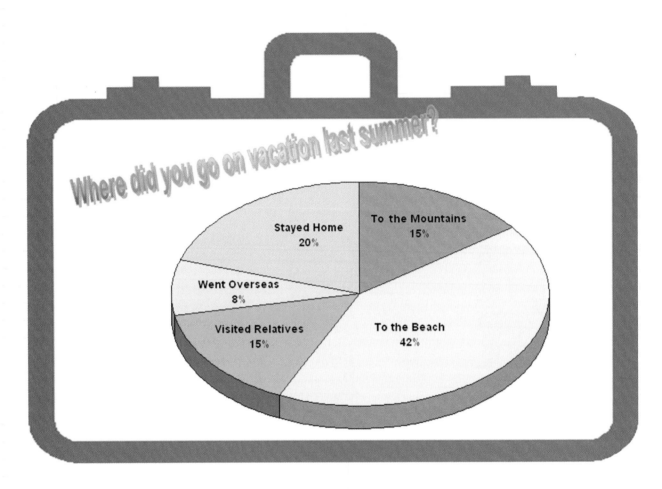

Where did you go on vacation last summer?

- Stayed Home 20%
- To the Mountains 15%
- Went Overseas 8%
- Visited Relatives 15%
- To the Beach 42%

✚ A Pie chart. The chart area has a graphic of a suitcase. Word Art is used.

Chart 15

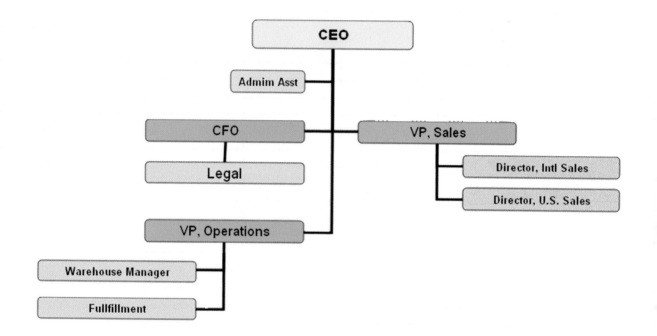

An organization chart.

Chart 16

Action

Planning

Commitment

Decision

 A pyramid diagram.

Think of taking a square and turning it into a box. This process of going from 2-D to 3-D by its very implication creates a third dimension. Three-dimensional objects have width, height, and depth — not that these are terms necessarily used with charts, but I think it helps to understand how some 3-D charts work. So for Surface charts there are:

✔ **The value axis:** Used to encompass the range of values in the data. This is the same as how it is applied in 2-D charts. This can be thought of as the height aspect.

✔ **The category axis:** Used to encompass the categories. This is the same as how it is applied in 2-D charts. This can be thought of as the width aspect.

✔ **The series axis:** This brings the depth aspect to a 3-D chart.

Not all 3-D charts work in the same way. The series axis is not always present in other 3-D chart types.

Plotting by value, not series

To confuse matters, Surface charts do not display the series data points. Instead, they display groupings of the values found in the data. Because a picture says it all, let's create a Surface chart, and you can see for yourself.

First, you need some data. Figure 6-15 shows the data I'm using to make a Surface chart — you can copy mine or create your own. The data must be structured in a certain way. Categories are in the first column. Across a few more columns, but one row higher than the first category, enter headings for the values. Finally, enter data in the cells where the categories intersect with the value column headings.

Here's how to create a Surface chart:

1. **Select the data, including the categories and the headers.**

   In my example this includes the headers <10, 10<=15, and so on, but *not* the Number of Radio Ads text.

2. **Click the Chart Wizard button on the Standard toolbar or choose Insert ➪ Chart.**

   The Chart Wizard opens.

3. **Select the Surface chart type, and select the first subtype (3-D Surface).**

4. **Click Finish.**

   Figure 6-16 shows how my surface chart turned out. Setting aside the fact that the chart needed a little formatting, which I took care of for your viewing pleasure, the immediate uniqueness to the chart is that the plot is by ranges of values. This is evident by the fact that the colors vary by the values along the vertical axis.

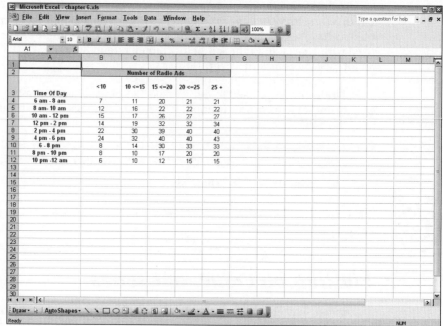

Figure 6-15: Prepping data to make a Surface chart.

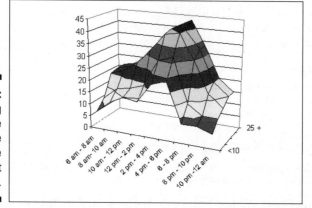

Figure 6-16: Looking at the occurrence of value ranges, not data points.

The number of colors and delineations of the surface are based on the major unit of the value axis. In this case, that number is 5. Increasing this value produces fewer colors, because there will be a smaller number of value delineations. Give it a try:

1. Right-click directly on the value axis itself.

You should see the Format Axis option (see Figure 6-17).

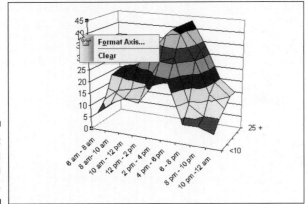

Figure 6-17:
Formatting
the value
axis.

2. **Select the Format Axis option in the pop-up menu.**

   The Format Axis dialog box appears.

3. **Select the Scale tab and change Major Unit to 10, as shown in Figure 6-18.**

   If you used different data than mine, choose a number for the major unit that makes sense for your data. The point is to reduce the number of colors (assuming you have a number of colors showing in your chart), so choose a number that is greater than the current major unit.

   Figure 6-19 shows how my chart now looks.

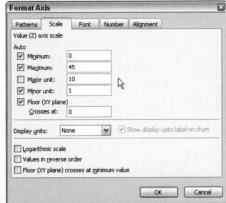

Figure 6-18:
Changing
the major
unit.

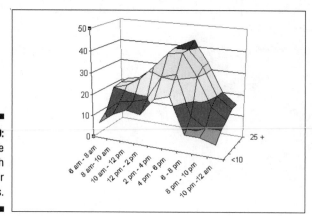

Figure 6-19:
Viewing the
chart with
fewer
colors.

Reviewing Surface chart subtypes

The Surface chart subtypes are not the typical standard and stacked types. There are four surface chart subtypes:

- ✔ **3-D Surface:** Shows trends in values. The chart in Figure 6-19 is a 3-D surface.

- ✔ **Wireframe 3-D Surface:** Same as the 3-D Surface, but without the surface being filled in. The lines remain.

- ✔ **Contour:** A 3-D Surface but positioned such that the view is from above. This removes the aspect of height, while keeping the width and depth perspectives. However, because the chart is positioned in such a way that only two aspects are visible, the appearance is flat.

- ✔ **Wireframe Contour:** Same as Contour, but without the surface being filled in. The lines remain.

Here's how to change the chart to the Contour subtype (the instructions apply to any subtype):

1. **Click on the chart once to select it.**

2. **Choose Chart ⇨ Chart Type.**

   The Chart Type dialog box appears.

3. **Select the Contour subtype — the first subtype in the second row.**

4. **Click OK.**

   Figure 6-20 shows how my chart now looks.

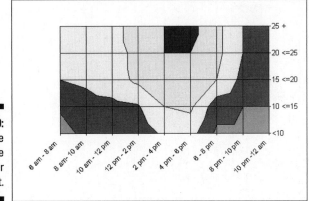

Figure 6-20:
Viewing the
data in the
Contour
format.

Chapter 7

Working With Custom Chart Types

● ●

In This Chapter

▶ Knowing where to find the custom chart types

▶ Creating exciting 3-D charts

▶ Getting artsy with black-and-white charts

▶ Putting colors and textures to work to make interesting charts

● ●

*T*o keep your chart enthusiasm sparked, Excel provides a plateful of custom chart layouts. You add the data and Excel does the rest. These charts run the gamut from retro black-and-white to the easygoing outdoors look. In between, you'll find a bevy of charts such as exploding pies and floating bars.

Just between you and me, there is nothing unique about any of these charts. They all began as standard charts and were let loose into the hands of some creative artists. The result is like a $10,000 makeover. Sure, these are chart types you're familiar with, but I don't think you've ever seen them look this good!

Not all the custom chart types are presented in this chapter. In particular:

✔ Combination charts are discussed in Chapter 17.

✔ The logarithmic chart, which is based on applying a logarithmic value scale, is discussed in Chapter 12.

✔ I've left out a few other charts because the material is repetitious.

Introducing the Custom Chart Types

Step 1 of the Chart Wizard is where you find the custom chart types. Figure 7-1 shows where they're listed.

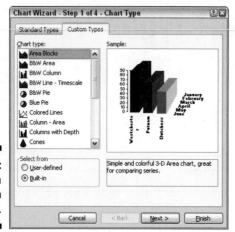

Figure 7-1:
Selecting a
custom
chart type.

A healthy number of custom chart types are available for you to use. Bear in mind, though, that these charts, being of different types, require different layouts of data. So, just to make it easy, I created some data you can use.

If you don't want to use my sample data, I won't take it personally. (I'm good at holding back the tears.) Whether you use my sample data or not, you'll still need *some* data. All that matters is that the data used for Pie charts has one series, and the data used for the other charts has more than one series. (Even *that* is not a strict requirement in all the charts.)

At the bottom of the Custom Types tab, you can select User-Defined or Built-In. I cover user-defined charts in Chapter 18.

Figure 7-2 shows a worksheet with two sets of data. In a nutshell, the top set can be used for the custom Pie charts, and the bottom set of data can be used for all the other custom charts.

Every custom chart presented in this chapter is just a highly formatted version of a standard chart. You can use any appealing look you see in these charts in standard charts. All you need is some mastery of the formatting options.

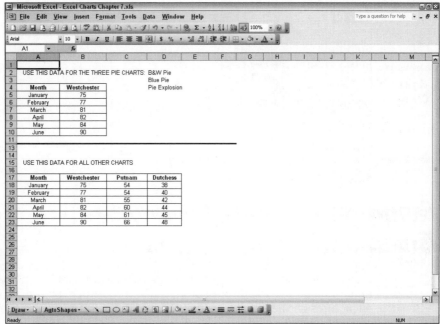

Figure 7-2:
Sample data
for making
custom
charts.

Building Area Blocks

First up is a 3-D Area chart, aptly named Area Blocks. To create this chart, follow these steps:

1. **Enter multiple series data on a worksheet such as that shown at the bottom of Figure 7-2.**

2. **Select the data.**

   You can include the headers.

3. **Click the Chart Wizard button on the Standard toolbar or choose Insert ⇨ Chart.**

   The Chart Wizard opens.

4. **Click the Custom Types tab.**

5. **Select the Area Blocks chart type.**

6. **Click Finish.**

   Figure 7-3 shows how the chart looks. With my example data, the initial appearance shows that both the category and value axes are vertical and the series axis is horizontally in front. This is based on the 3-D settings, which you can, of course, alter.

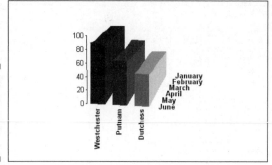

Figure 7-3:
Comparing
series in a
3-D Area
chart.

Going for the Cool Look with Black-and-White Charts

A few of the custom charts provide a black-and-white look — perfect if you don't want to use up all your color ink! (The other day my son printed over 40 pictures off the Internet, and it cost me $28 in ink! At least it was for a school project.)

Creating a black-and-white Area chart

The black-and-white Area chart (named B&W Area) is a stacked, flat Area chart in which the series are formatted with various patterns available in the Fill Effects dialog box (described in Chapter 9). To create the chart:

1. **Enter multiple series data on a worksheet such as that shown in the bottom of Figure 7-2.**

2. **Select the data.**

   You can include the headers.

3. **Click the Chart Wizard button on the Standard toolbar or choose Insert ⇨ Chart.**

   The Chart Wizard opens.

4. **Click the Custom Types tab.**

5. **Select the B&W Area chart type.**

6. **Click Finish.**

   Figure 7-4 shows how the chart looks.

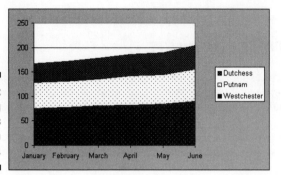

Figure 7-4:
Stacking gray tones in an Area chart.

Switching to a black-and-white Column chart

The custom black-and-white Column chart is interesting to the eye (my eye, anyway). The *chart area* (the background of the chart) is filled with a subtle gradient fill of dark and light gray. The data table appears with this chart, too. To change the Area chart in Figure 7-4 into a Column chart, follow these steps:

1. **Click on the chart once to select it.**

2. **Choose Chart ⇨ Chart Type.**

   The Chart Type dialog box appears.

3. **Click the Custom Types tab.**

4. **Select the B&W Column chart type.**

5. **Click OK.**

   Figure 7-5 shows how the chart looks. This is a 3-D chart but the 3-D effect is not overdone.

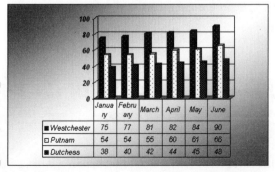

Figure 7-5:
Lining up gray columns.

Converting to a black-and-white Line – Timescale chart

The B&W Line – Timescale chart has a misleading name. The chart isn't a Line chart — it's an Area chart in order to make the best of the gradient formatting. (A gradient cannot appear easily in a line.)

The timescale description means that if the categories are recognized as dates, you have options for how to apply settings on the category scale. (I explain this in Chapter 11.)

To change the Column chart in Figure 7-5 into the B&W Line – Timescale chart, follow these steps:

1. **Click on the chart once to select it.**
2. **Choose Chart ⇨ Chart Type.**

   The Chart Type dialog box appears.
3. **Click the Custom Types tab.**
4. **Select the B&W Line – Timescale chart type.**
5. **Click OK.**

   Figure 7-6 shows how the chart looks.

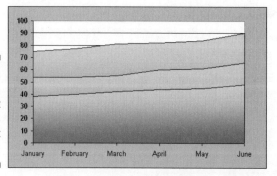

Figure 7-6:
Using an Area chart to provide a gradient effect.

Cooking up a black-and-white Pie chart

The B&W Pie is a simple, flat Pie chart with the slices each set to a different pattern. To create one, follow these steps:

1. **Enter data with categories and a single series on a worksheet, such as that shown in the top of Figure 7-2.**

2. **Select the data.**

   You can include the headers.

3. **Click the Chart Wizard button on the Standard toolbar or choose Insert ⇨ Chart.**

   The Chart Wizard opens.

4. **Click the Custom Types tab.**

5. **Select the B&W Pie chart type.**

6. **Click Finish.**

   Figure 7-7 shows how the chart looks. All in all, a fairly dull-looking chart. Maybe this chart is good when you're stuck reporting some bad news, but you want it to be as low-key as you can make it look.

Figure 7-7:
Displaying a
simple Pie
chart.

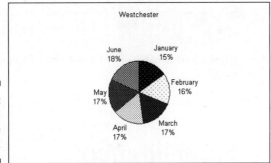

Creating Colorful Charts

The next batch of custom charts is meant to add some color to your output. These are great on the screen but watch out for how much color ink you use when printing!

Making a very colorful pie

The Blue Pie custom chart is a real looker. It has a dazzling background that seems to shine right through the Pie chart. The fact that the pie is exploded helps. Here's how to make a Blue Pie chart:

1. **Enter data with categories and a single series on a worksheet, such as that shown in the top of Figure 7-2.**

2. **Select the data.**

   You can include the headers.

3. **Click the Chart Wizard button on the Standard toolbar or choose Insert ➪ Chart.**

   The Chart Wizard opens.

4. **Click the Custom Types tab.**

5. **Select the Blue Pie chart type.**

6. **Click Finish.**

   Figure 7-8 shows what a good-looking chart this is. Darn, I wish I were an artist. Oh well . . . I'll have to remain content with being a computer nerd.

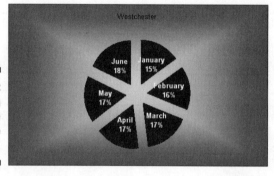

Figure 7-8: Radiating with the Blue Pie chart.

Going for the levitating effect with floating bars

I don't know how they do it, but to me, the bars in the Floating Bars chart really do look like they're adrift on a current. See for yourself! Here's how to make one:

1. **Enter multiple series data on a worksheet such as that shown in the bottom of Figure 7-2.**

2. **Select the data.**

   You can include the headers.

3. **Click the Chart Wizard button on the Standard toolbar or choose Insert ➪ Chart.**

   The Chart Wizard opens.

4. **Click the Custom Types tab.**

5. **Select the Floating Bars chart type.**

6. **Click Finish.**

   Figure 7-9 shows what the Floating Bars chart looks like.

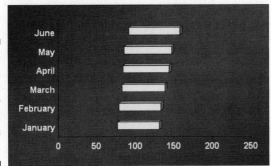

Figure 7-9:
Floating some data while other data remains hidden.

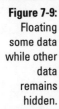

There is a real trick to the chart in Figure 7-9. This is a 3-D Stacked Bar chart, but some of the series have been formatted to be invisible. This is a simple thing actually — you just set both the border and area of a data series to None (this type of formatting is explained in Chapter 13). Leaving the border visible and removing the area may make sense — that would leave an outline. Or you could remove the border and keep the area, which retains a solid bar. In this chart, though, the designers have set both the border and the area to None, except for the second series.

Hiding data is an odd idea. This goes against the grain of using a chart to show something. But if a special effect is what you want, this chart type is a great place to start.

At least two series must be included in a Floating Bars chart, because the first series is invisible. The second series is visible.

Plotting data in the great outdoors

The Outdoor Bars chart type looks like a walk through the woods. The mix of greens and browns is reminiscent of trees and leaves: kind of lush and kind of peaceful. All you need is a tent and some provisions. Here's how to make one of these tranquil charts:

1. **Enter multiple series data on a worksheet such as that shown in the bottom of Figure 7-2.**

2. **Select the data.**

    You can include the headers.

3. **Click the Chart Wizard button on the Standard toolbar or choose Insert ➪ Chart.**

    The Chart Wizard opens.

4. **Click the Custom Types tab.**

5. **Select the Outdoor Bars chart type.**

6. **Click Finish.**

Figure 7-10 shows how my chart appears. Actually, I lightened it up a bit.

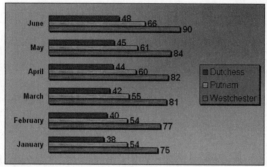

Figure 7-10:
Mixing
nature
and data
together
in a chart.

The two shades of green gradient in the chart area are what gives it a natural feel. A single shade of green would be dull in comparison. My chart has three data series, and each one is formatted with a wood texture. In fact, the three particular textures are oak, medium wood, and walnut. That sounds pretty woodsy to me.

I show you how to apply textures in Chapter 9.

Part III
Formatting Charts

The 5th Wave   By Rich Tennant

FIRED

YOU

"NIFTY CHART, FRANK, BUT NOT ENTIRELY NECESSARY."

In this part . . .

Part III takes the chart experience up a notch or two. In this part, you discover all the formatting techniques and how to work with specific parts of charts. A number of parts are given individual attention, including working with the different axes, working with data series, working with the chart and plot areas, and trying your hand out on 3-D views. You'll see some of the tricks of the trade, such as applying colors to different data points, and using gradients, textures, and patterns. Part III finishes up with a chapter on using shapes and graphics. This opens up a world of possibilities of what you can show in your charts. Impress your friends with what you find here!

Chapter 8

Positioning and Sizing Your Charts

●●

In This Chapter

▶ Placing charts on separate chart sheets

▶ Placing charts on worksheets

▶ Resizing and moving charts

▶ Cutting, copying, and pasting charts

●●

*M*aking charts is most of the work, but that's not all of it. You still have to decide where to put the charts. First, you need to figure out whether to put a chart on a separate chart sheet. That's nice and easy — you don't have to consider anything else, such as the size, or whether other charts, text, or numbers are nearby.

Your other option is to place a chart smack-dab in the middle of a worksheet. You may wonder why anyone would want to do that. Actually, putting a chart in the middle of a worksheet seems to be the preferred way to go. More decisions are involved, such as how large or how small the chart should be, and where on the worksheet it should go. But these options give you the power to align your chart next to supporting information.

The chart location choice is on the last screen (Step 4) of the Chart Wizard. Figure 8-1 shows the last screen of the Chart Wizard. It's interesting to note that of the two choices, the Chart Wizard defaults to placing the chart on a worksheet, not a separate chart sheet. The wizard must know something!

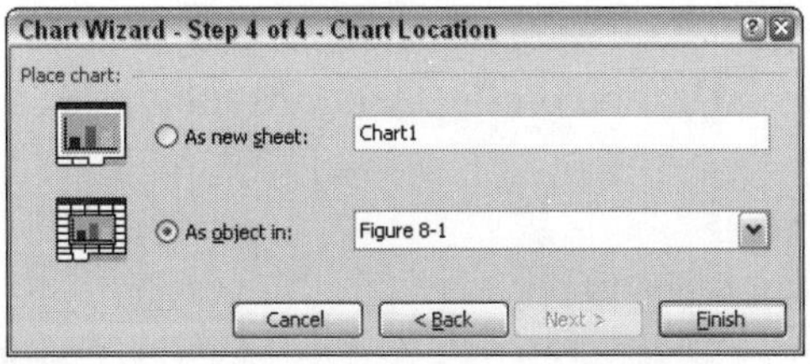

Figure 8-1:
Deciding where to put the chart.

Placing Charts on a Separate Chart Sheet

To place a new chart on a separate chart sheet, you just select the As New Sheet option in the last step of the Chart Wizard. Figure 8-2 shows the selected option in the Chart Wizard.

Figure 8-2:
Selecting
the chart
sheet
option.

You can accept the name supplied by the Chart Wizard, or you can enter your own. The supplied names are functional, such as Chart1, but not specific to your chart or data. Entering your own name isn't a bad idea.

Chart sheets are not the same as worksheets. A chart sheet only displays a chart. There are no cells, and you cannot enter any data on one.

Placing charts on separate chart sheets is great for getting a fast, full-sized chart. Figure 8-3 shows a chart I created.

Note in Figure 8-3 that the chart tab on the bottom is the name entered for the chart sheet. The name of the chart in the last step of the Chart Wizard — whether it's the one supplied by Excel or your own entered name — becomes the sheet name on the tab.

The size of a chart on a chart sheet is just right for printing. The following steps show you what I mean. What you need to start is a chart.

1. **Enter some data on a worksheet.**

    If you want, you can use some good data you want to plot, but for this exercise any old data will do. I'm only trying to point out how to place a chart on a chart sheet.

2. **Click the Chart Wizard button on the Standard toolbar or choose Insert ⇨ Chart.**

    The Chart Wizard opens.

3. **Click the Next button three times.**

4. **In the last step of the Chart Wizard, select the As New Sheet option.**

    If you want, change the name.

5. **Click Finish.**

    You now have a chart on a separate chart sheet.

6. **Click the Print Preview button on the Standard toolbar or choose File ➪ Print Preview.**

   Now you can see how your chart will look when it prints.

You can use the Page Setup feature to make some alterations. While still in Print Preview, click the Setup button. On the Page tab in the Page Setup dialog box, you can set up your chart in either Portrait or Landscape orientation. Figure 8-4 shows how my chart changed from landscape to portrait.

What if you have a chart on a separate chart sheet, but you wish it were placed on a worksheet? Not to fear, the designers of Excel thought of everything. Here's what you do:

1. **If you're still in Print Preview mode, click the Close button.**

2. **Choose Chart ➪ Location, or right-click on the chart and choose Location from the pop-up menu.**

   The Chart Location dialog box appears. It resembles the last step of the Chart Wizard.

3. **Select the As Object In option, and select the worksheet from the drop-down list.**

4. **Click OK.**

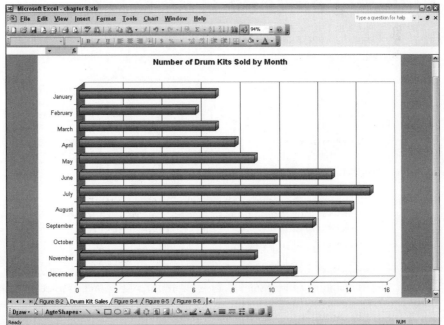

Figure 8-3: Viewing a chart on a chart sheet.

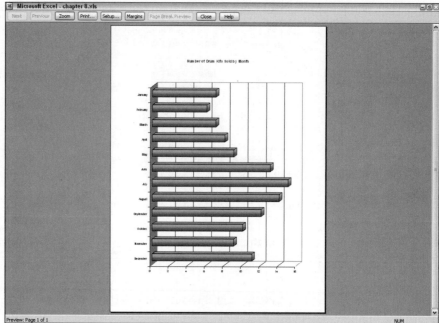

Figure 8-4:
Viewing the
chart in a
different
orientation.

Placing Charts on Worksheets

Placing charts on worksheets has some advantages:

- They can be easily resized.
- They can be strategically placed near related information.
- You can put multiple charts on a worksheet.

The way to place a new chart on a worksheet is to select the As Object In option in the last step of the Chart Wizard. Figure 8-5 shows the selected option in the Chart Wizard.

Charts that are placed on worksheets seem to not have names. Actually, they are named, but the name is irrelevant to placing and manipulating the chart on a worksheet. The chart names do come in handy when using VBA to work with charts.

Figure 8-6 shows one of the reasons placing charts on worksheets is so popular. In Figure 8-6, six charts, one per month, are placed together to convey comprehensive information. Placing charts together in this fashion is possible only with charts placed on worksheets.

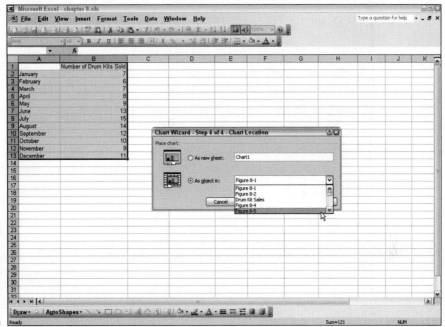

Figure 8-5:
Selecting
to place a
chart on a
worksheet.

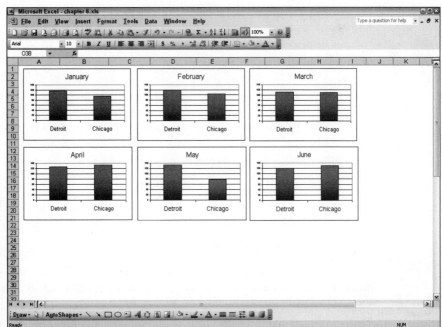

Figure 8-6:
Placing
charts
where
you want
them on a
worksheet.

Here's how to take a chart that is on a worksheet and place it on a separate chart sheet:

1. **Select the chart by clicking on it once.**

2. **Choose Chart ⇨ Location, or right-click on the chart and choose Location from the pop-up menu.**

   The Chart Location dialog box appears. It resembles the last step of the Chart Wizard.

3. **Select the As New Sheet option.**

   You can accept the supplied name or enter one of your own.

4. **Click OK.**

Moving and Resizing Charts

You can easily move and resize charts on a worksheet. You'll find it necessary to do a bit of both of these operations as you work with charts. Here's what you do:

1. **Select a chart.**

   Selecting a chart can be tricky. You want to click on a part of the chart that is empty. If you click on a part of the chart that is not empty — say, for example, on a series line — you select that particular chart component, but not the chart itself.

   The chart area displays handles after it's selected. These are the little black boxes that appear on the top, bottom, sides, and corners of the chart. Figure 8-7 shows how a selected chart appears. Note in Figure 8-7 how the mouse pointer changes shape when placed over one of the handles.

2. **Place the mouse pointer over one of the handles.**

3. **Click and hold down the mouse button.**

4. **Keeping the mouse button pressed, move the mouse to decrease or increase the size of the chart.**

5. **Let go of the mouse button.**

The handles in the corners of a selected chart let you change both the height and width of the chart at the same time. Holding down the Shift key while doing this will maintain the chart's proportions.

Figure 8-8 shows how my chart looks after resizing.

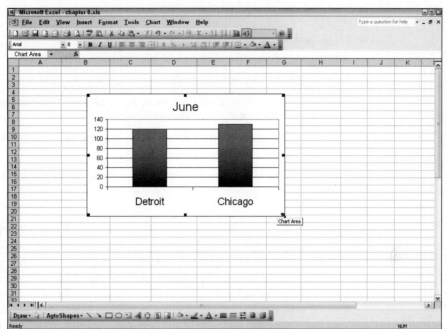

Figure 8-7:
Selecting a
chart before
moving or
resizing.

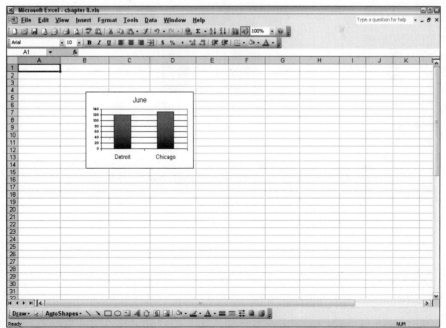

Figure 8-8:
The chart
has been
resized.

Here's how to move a chart:

1. **Click on a chart to select it and keep the mouse button pressed down.**

   Do not click on one of the handles.

2. **With the mouse button still pressed, move the chart by dragging it somewhere else on the worksheet.**

   The mouse pointer changes shape while you do this. Figure 8-9 shows how this looks.

3. **When the chart is where you want it to be, let go of the mouse button.**

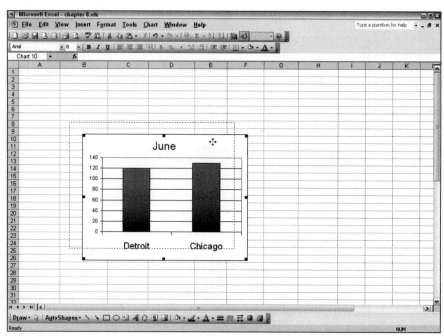

Figure 8-9: Moving a chart.

Copying, Cutting, and Pasting Charts

Charts can be cut, copied, and pasted. This is great because you can quickly make a bunch of identical-looking charts, and then just update where the series data is found. This is how I made the six charts in Figure 8-6 — I created the first chart and then copied it, and pasted it five times. (I hope you don't think I formatted and sized all six charts individually!) All I ended up doing was changing where each chart finds its data.

There is a trick to copying charts that you must know. The chart is selected to copy it, but when you paste, the chart must not be selected. If the chart you copied is still selected when you paste, you'll just be duplicating the existing series — this is *not* what you want.

Here is the correct way to copy and paste a chart:

1. **Select a chart.**

2. **Choose Edit ⇨ Copy to copy the chart.**

   You can instead use any other copy method you're familiar with, such as Ctrl+C.

3. **Here's the important step: Click somewhere on the worksheet.**

   Wherever you click is where the extra chart will appear, so click into a cell that is in the desired location on the worksheet.

4. **Choose Edit ⇨ Paste to paste the new chart into the worksheet.**

   You can instead use any other paste method you're familiar with, such as Ctrl+V.

When pasting a copied chart, make sure the chart that was copied is no longer selected.

Cutting a chart and then pasting it works the same — just replace cutting for copying. You don't have to worry about deselecting the chart — it's no longer there! When you paste it back, it will appear wherever the active cell is.

After copying or cutting a chart, it can be pasted on any worksheet. You aren't limited to pasting it back into the original worksheet. Also, if you want to duplicate a chart on a worksheet, simply hold down the Ctrl key while dragging the chart — a copy is created.

You can create a snapshot of a chart (it becomes a graphic) by holding down the Shift key while choosing Edit ⇨ Copy Picture. When you paste the chart, it's a graphic. (See Chapter 20 for more information.)

Chapter 9

Formatting the Chart Area, Plot Area, and Gridlines

- -

In This Chapter

▶ Understanding the difference between the chart area and the plot area

▶ Using borders

▶ Applying gradients

▶ Using textures and patterns

▶ Inserting a picture into a chart's background

▶ Figuring out how to use gridlines

- -

*O*ne of the goals in making great charts is to ensure they're visually pleasing and easy to read. Many facets of a chart can be formatted to present the data in the best light. In this chapter, I show you how to format the chart area and the plot area. The chart area and plot area are independent of the data. They exist on their own, regardless of what data is being plotted.

Gridlines are included as well in this chapter. Gridlines *are* related to the data in the sense that they're positioned based on the tick marks of the axes. However, their presence slices right through the plot area. Therefore, the formatting of either the plot area or gridlines is best done with consideration of the other.

Figure 9-1 shows a chart with the chart area and plot area defined with labels. Within the plot area, thick gridlines cross left to right.

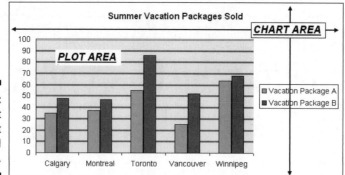

Figure 9-1:
Looking at
the chart
area and
plot area.

✔ The chart area encompasses the entire chart.

✔ The plot area is defined by the height of the vertical axis and the width of the horizontal axis.

In some chart types, the plot area is not as clear to see. For example, a Pie chart does not display axes. The plot area does exist, though. It forms a square such that the sides of the square touch the sides of the pie. Figure 9-2 shows this.

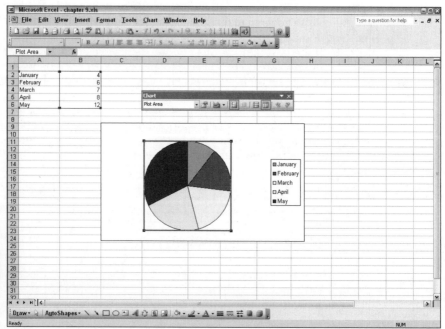

Figure 9-2:
Selecting
the plot
area of a
Pie chart.

To select the plot area of a Pie chart, click in an empty area near but not in the pie itself. An alternative is to select the plot area in the drop-down list on the Chart toolbar, shown in Figure 9-2. You can display the Chart toolbar by choosing View ⇨ Toolbars ⇨ Chart.

The *chart* area has more formatting attributes than the *plot* area. For example, font attributes can be changed in the chart area but not in the plot area.

Working With Borders and Areas

The borders and interior area of both the chart area and the plot area can be formatted. Applying formatting to the interior can lead to a really cool-looking chart, or a really ugly one! Experimenting a bit and trying different formatting settings is worth the time. As a rule of thumb, be sure that the formatting doesn't make it difficult to make sense of the data. ***Remember:*** Formatting should be used to enhance, not distract.

To try out the border and area formatting, you need a chart, of course! So open up a workbook and find a chart you've previously made, or you can create a new one.

The Format Chart Area dialog box is where formatting attributes are set. There are two ways to display the Format Chart Area dialog box:

 ✔ Right-click once on the *chart area* (any blank area of the chart between the plot area and the edge of the chart). From the pop-up menu, select Format Chart Area.

 ✔ Click anywhere on the chart to select it. From the Chart toolbar, select Chart Area. Then click on the Format button on the Chart toolbar (this is the button with a picture of a hand holding a piece of paper, as shown in Figure 9-3).

The title bar of the format dialog box will display either Format Plot Area or Format Chart Area depending on which chart object is selected.

Laying it on with borders

Figure 9-4 shows a chart in which the chart area has been selected and the Format Chart Area dialog box is displayed. In the Format Chart Area dialog box, the Patterns tab is on top.

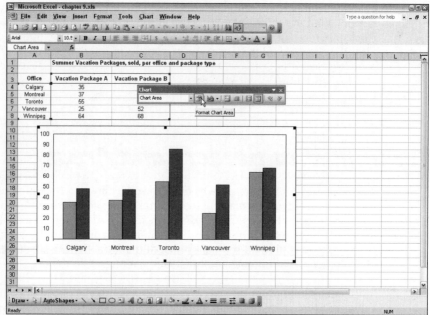

Figure 9-3:
Using the
Chart
toolbar to
open the
Format
Chart Area
dialog box.

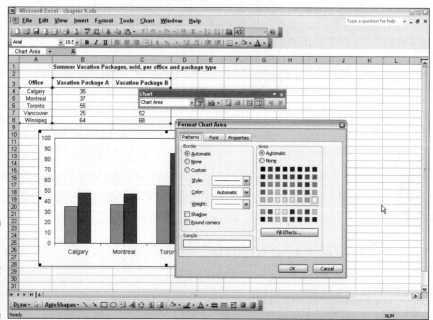

Figure 9-4:
Displaying
the Format
Chart Area
dialog box.

In the left side of the Patterns tab are options for formatting the border. There are three major options:

✔ **Automatic:** This is the default. Excel decides how to apply the border. The standard is a thin black border around the chart. The chart in Figure 9-4 has a thin black border around the chart.

✔ **None:** Selecting this removes any border.

✔ **Custom:** This lets you control the style, color, and weight of the border. Selections for each of these custom attributes are made by clicking on the associated arrow, which opens a drop-down list of choices:

- **Style:** You can select from among a solid line, and various dotted, dashed, and patterned lines. Figure 9-5 shows the available choices.

- **Color:** The border line can be any color available on the color palette, shown in Figure 9-6.

- **Weight:** The border line can be thin, thick, or in between. Figure 9-7 shows the list of choices

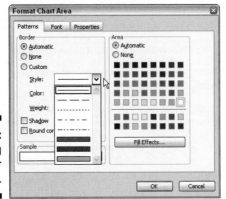

Figure 9-5: Selecting the border line style.

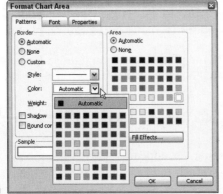

Figure 9-6: Choosing a color for the border.

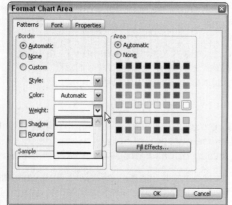

Figure 9-7:
Selecting a
weight for
the border.

It's time to try apply border formatting on your chart. Here's what you can do:

1. **Right-click once on the chart area and select Format Chart Area from the pop-up menu.**

   The Format Chart Area dialog box appears.

2. **If necessary, click on the Patterns tab to bring it to the top.**

3. **In the left side of the tab, select the Custom option and experiment with different styles, colors, and weights.**

   You have to click OK each time to see how your selections look, and then reopen the Format Chart Area dialog box to make further changes.

   There are two additional settings for the chart area border — Shadow and Round corners. These options only appear for the chart area; they don't appear when formatting the plot area.

Figure 9-8 shows my chart in which I selected to have a shadow effect applied to the border. To make the shadow effect easy to see, I removed the gridlines from the underlying worksheet. The gridlines on the worksheet are not the same as the gridlines on a chart. To remove the worksheet gridlines, I chose Tools ➪ Options and unchecked the Gridlines check box on the View tab.

Applying border formatting to the plot area is completed in the same way. The plot area has to be selected and the formatting settings are made in the Format Plot Area dialog box:

1. **Right-click once on the plot area and select Format Plot Area from the pop-up menu.**

   The Format Plot Area dialog box appears.

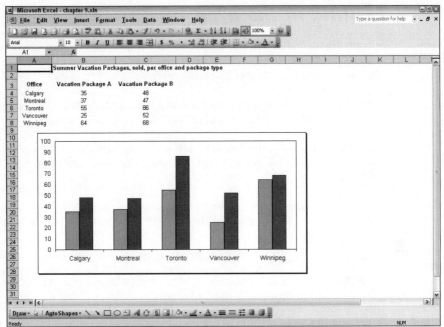

Figure 9-8:
Adding a
shadow to
the chart's
border.

2. If necessary, click on the Patterns tab to bring it to the top.

3. In the left side of the tab, select the Custom option and experiment with different styles, colors, and weights.

You'll have to click OK each time to see how your selections look, and then reopen the Format Plot Area dialog box to make further changes.

Figure 9-9 shows how I applied short dashes to the plot area border on my charts. I also selected a thick weight so the dashes will show up well.

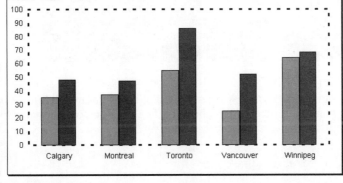

Figure 9-9:
Giving the
plot area a
heavy
dashed
border.

Filling in the area

Applying formatting to the interior of the chart area or plot area makes for some really exciting charts! It's not just that colors can be inserted into these areas, but also gradients, patterns, textures, and pictures.

What you can do with all these choices is mind-boggling. Well, at least it boggles *my* mind — maybe yours will just get a little rattled.

On the right side of the Patterns tab in the Format Chart Area dialog box, shown in Figure 9-4, are settings to format the area. First, you have three options:

- **Automatic** lets Excel decide how the area should appear. Generally passive colors such as white or gray are applied when the setting is Automatic.
- **None,** of course, removes any formatting.
- Many colors are available in the **color palette.** Whatever color is selected is applied as a solid color.

Figure 9-10 shows a chart in which solid colors have been selected for both the chart area and the plot area. The chart area has been given a dark color, and the font has been set to a light color. Font settings are discussed in the "Applying Font Attributes" section later in this chapter.

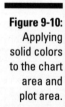

Figure 9-10:
Applying solid colors to the chart area and plot area.

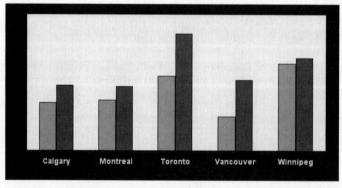

On the right side of the Patterns tab in Figure 9-4 is the Fill Effects button. Clicking on this button opens the Fill Effects dialog box, shown in Figure 9-11.

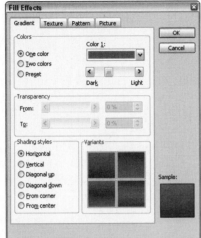

Figure 9-11:
Using the
Fill Effects
dialog box.

The Fill Effects dialog box has four tabs, each of which is covered in the following sections. Within these tabs are ways to provide superb formatting to your charts.

Going for the wow effect with gradients

Gradients are blends of colors. To make a gradient, lighter and darker hues of a single color may be blended together, or two distinct colors may be blended. You have control over the positioning of the colors when you use a gradient.

In Figure 9-11, the Gradient tab is on top in the Fill Effects dialog box. You have a few key areas to discover:

- ✔ **Colors:** In the colors frame, you can select one color, two colors, or a preset gradient pattern:

  - When the One Color option is selected, a slider control appears underneath where you selected the single color, allowing you to mix light and dark hues of the color. Refer to Figure 9-11 for such a setting.

  - When the Two Colors option is selected, the slider control is replaced with a second color-selection drop-down list. Figure 9-12 shows how two colors are selected.

  - The Preset option presents a list of predesigned gradients. There are some pretty catchy gradients in here, including ones that use more than two colors. For example there are two rainbow gradients. Figure 9-13 shows how to select a preset gradient.

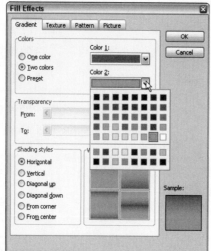

Figure 9-12:
Selecting a
two-color
gradient.

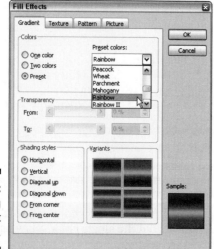

Figure 9-13:
Viewing
the preset
gradients.

✓ **Transparency:** Unfortunately, this feature is not available in the Windows edition of Excel, but it does work in the Mac version of Excel. However, if you're handy with an art program, you may know how to make your graphics part transparent in the first place.

✓ **Shading Styles:** This is a key part of using gradients. By applying the direction of the gradient, you can make some very interesting effects. You can have the gradient appear from the sides, from the center, horizontal, vertical, and so on.

✔ **Variants:** The variants are based on the colors and shading style. This is where you select variations on how to apply the gradient. For example, when selecting to have a two-color gradient start from the center, you can select which color is in the center, and which is in the periphery.

Here's how to create a gradient:

1. **Select either the plot area or the chart area by right-clicking on it.**

2. **From the pop-up menu, select to display the Format dialog box.**

   The Format dialog box appears.

3. **Click the Fill Effects button.**

   The Fill Effects dialog box appears.

4. **On the Gradient tab, experiment with different settings of Colors, Shading Styles, and Variants.**

   When you've made selections, click OK to see how the chart is formatted. You'll have to reopen the Format dialog box to make further selections.

Figure 9-14 shows my chart with the chart area formatted with a two-color gradient. The shading style is From Center. The font color and colors of the series (the columns) have also been changed to work well with the colors of the gradient.

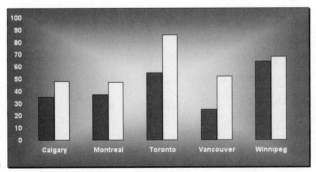

Figure 9-14:
Applying a
gradient
effect.

Making a theme with textures

In the Fill Effects dialog box is a tab for textures. Figure 9-15 shows the Texture tab.

The textures are pictures of paper, wood, fabric, and other items that have a textural appearance. There are a number of interesting textures, including sand, denim, granite, oak, and woven mat. To apply a texture, first select it by clicking on it, and then click OK twice.

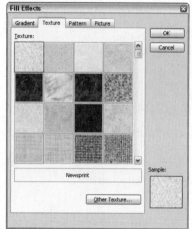

Figure 9-15:
Selecting a
texture.

But wait — there's more! You can use a custom texture. Clicking on the Other Texture button opens the Select Texture dialog box, in which you can select a graphics file. The graphic becomes the texture in the chart.

A custom texture works best when the selected graphic is *seamless*. This means that when the graphic is repeated (also known as *tiling*), the result is a larger graphic that appears as a single cohesive unit, although it's made up of a repeating smaller graphic.

Figure 9-16 shows a custom texture file, named `eclipse.bmp`, being selected in the Select Texture dialog box.

Figure 9-16:
Selecting
a graphic
file as the
source for
a texture.

Figure 9-17 shows the how the `eclipse.bmp` file has been incorporated into the chart area, thereby setting the texture to span the full dimensions of the chart.

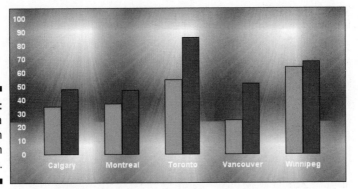

Figure 9-17:
Viewing a
chart with
a custom
texture.

Creating contrast with patterns

Patterns are mixes of two colors in dots, stripes, bricks, and other symmetrical arrangements. Patterns are similar to gradients, in that you can select two colors; however, patterns differ in the fact that the two colors are not blended. Instead, with patterns, one color becomes the background, and the other color becomes the pattern.

Figure 9-18 shows the Pattern tab in the Fill Effects dialog box. You have several preconfigured patterns to choose from. One of the colors is being selected from the drop-down of palette colors.

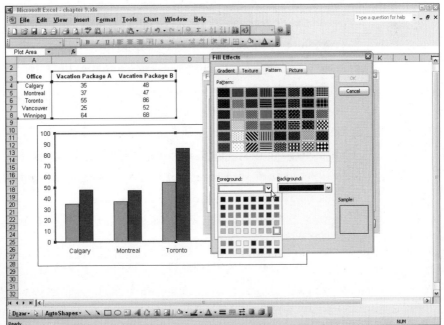

Figure 9-18:
Creating a
pattern.

Figure 9-19 shows a chart with just the plot area filled in with a pattern. The chart area remains empty.

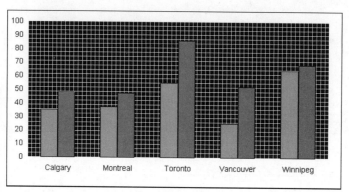

Figure 9-19:
Placing a
pattern in
the plot
area.

Customizing it all with pictures

You can put a picture into the chart area or plot area. The method is to select a graphic file on your system and the picture becomes the background of the chart area or plot area.

Be sure to use a picture that doesn't make reading the chart difficult.

Here's how to put a picture in the chart area:

1. **Select the chart area by right-clicking on it.**
2. **From the pop-up menu, select to display the Format dialog box.**
3. **If necessary, click the Pattern tab to bring it to the top.**
4. **Click the Fill Effects button.**

    The Fill Effects dialog box appears.

5. **On the Picture tab, click the Select Picture button.**

    The Select Picture dialog box, shown in Figure 9-20, appears.

5. **Browse through your computer to a desired graphic and click Insert.**
6. **Click OK twice to close the other dialog boxes.**

    Figure 9-21 shows how my chart looks with a picture of rapids in the background.

Figure 9-20:
Selecting a
picture for
the chart (or
plot) area.

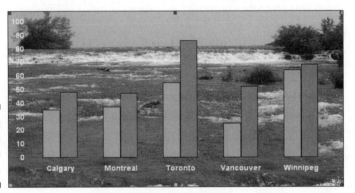

Figure 9-21:
Viewing a
picture in
the chart.

Applying Font Attributes

Font settings can be applied globally to all text in a chart by applying changes
to the chart area font settings. Any font changes applied to the chart area will
universally set the text of the series labels, axes labels, legend, and titles to
all have the font attributes that you select. By contrast, to set the font for just
one item, such as the legend, you would set the font properties of the item in
its own Format dialog box.

Figure 9-22 shows the Font tab of the Format Chart Area dialog box. On the
tab are all the standard font settings, including the font itself, the font style
(italic, bold), the font size, and the effects (such as strikethrough). You can
select the font color and the background effect.

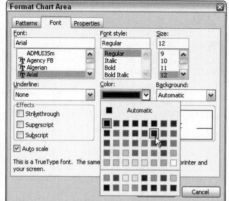

Figure 9-22:
Setting font
attributes.

After you select the font attributes and click OK, all text throughout the chart is formatted the same. Figure 9-23 shows how all the text on my chart has been formatted to appear the same.

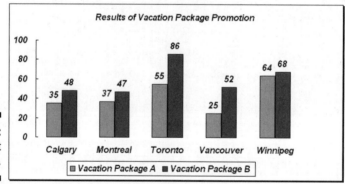

Figure 9-23:
Uniform text
formatting.

If you want to have all the text in the chart appear the same, use the font settings for the chart area to apply the formatting to all text. This technique also makes it easy to have most of the text appear the same and have the text for one or two items appear different. First, format all the text together using the chart area font settings, and then adjust the font settings for the individual item(s).

Here's how to set the chart area font settings:

1. **Select the chart area by right-clicking on it.**

2. **From the pop-up menu, select to display the Format dialog box.**

3. **If necessary, click the Font tab to bring it to the top.**

4. **Select the desired font settings.**

5. **Click OK.**

Applying font formatting to the chart area will not affect text in AutoShapes and other graphics. Only core chart items reflect font settings made in the Format Chart Area dialog box.

The Background font setting has three choices: Automatic, Transparent, and Opaque. The Automatic setting leaves it up to Excel how to handle the font background. The Transparent and Opaque settings are important when using a gradient, texture, pattern, or picture in the chart (or plot) area, so I'll give you a closer look at them.

Figure 9-24 shows my chart formatted with the Parchment texture background. On the Font tab of the Format Chart Area dialog box, the font background is being set to Opaque.

Figure 9-25 shows the effect of the opaque setting. The text backgrounds are dark and solid. I changed the font color to white so the text will be visible against the dark background. The point is that the backgrounds sit on top of the texture in the chart area. This makes the text stand out, in a bold way — which may be an effect you're looking for.

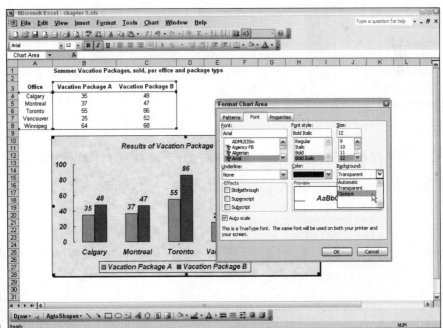

Figure 9-24: Applying an opaque font background.

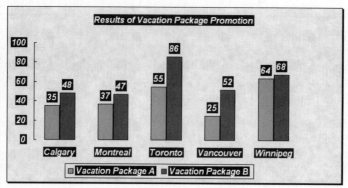

Figure 9-25:
You can use
an opaque
font back-
ground for
a dramatic
effect.

Figure 9-26 shows how the font appears when the background is set to Transparent. For this example, I changed the font color back to black. The text sits pleasingly on the textured background.

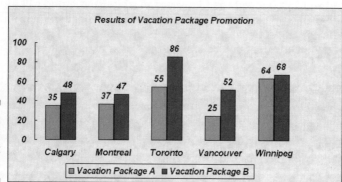

Figure 9-26:
Text with a
transparent
background.

Setting Moving and Sizing Properties

On the Properties tab in the Format Chart Area dialog box are settings that control how a chart is resized or moved as the underlying worksheet rows and columns are manipulated. For example, say your chart sits on a work-sheet in a such a way that it spans column C. If you change the width of column C, should your chart also change width? Never thought of this intriguing problem before? Well, not to fret: The wonderful designers of Excel have given this issue lots of thought.

Figure 9-27 shows the Format Chart Area dialog box with the Properties tab on top. You have three object positioning options:

✔ **Move and Size with Cells:** When row heights or columns widths are changed, or rows or columns are added or deleted, the chart moves and resizes accordingly. So, for example, if you add three new columns in a part of the worksheet where your chart is, the chart becomes wider.

✔ **Move but Don't Size with Cells:** The position of the chart changes as rows or columns are added, deleted, or resized, but the chart size remains the same.

✔ **Don't Move or Size with Cells:** The chart position and size are unaffected by changes in the underlying worksheet.

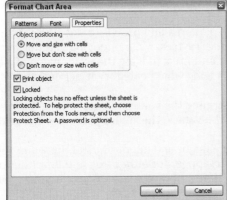

Figure 9-27:
Choosing how a chart moves and resizes with changes on the worksheet.

The best way to understand how these settings work is to try it yourself. Here's how:

1. **Select the chart area by right-clicking on it.**

2. **From the pop-up menu, select to display the Format dialog box.**

3. **If necessary, click the Properties tab to bring it to the top.**

4. **Select one of the object positioning options.**

5. **Click OK.**

6. **Make changes to the underlying worksheet.**

   Try adding and deleting rows and columns, as well as resizing rows and columns. See how the dimensions and placement of your chart are affected.

7. **Repeat Steps 2 through 4 to try the other object positioning settings.**

On the Properties tab are two check boxes:

✔ **Print Object:** Indicates whether the chart will print when the worksheet is sent to the printer. When Print object is checked, the chart will appear in the output.

✔ **Locked:** Applies protection to the chart. This feature works the same way that cell protection works. With the check box set to locked, the chart cannot be manipulated when worksheet protection is on. You set worksheet protection by choosing Tools ⇨ Protection ⇨ Protect Sheet. (For more information on protection, turn to the Excel Help system.)

Working With Gridlines

Gridlines cross through the plot area and provide a line of sight for the delineations of the value and category axes. Most often, it's just the value axis that spawns gridlines across the plot area; judging the exact value of a data point is often more difficult than seeing which category it belongs to.

Gridlines are helpful to determine the values of data points. If the series are already formatted to show the values, there's no point in using gridlines.

Gridlines are anchored to the major and minor units of the value and category axes. You can set gridlines to appear for either axis and for either or both of the major and minor units. Here's how to set gridlines for your chart:

1. **Select the chart.**

2. **Choose Chart ⇨ Chart Options.**

   The Chart Options dialog box appears.

3. **Click the Gridlines tab.**

4. **Check the desired gridlines and click OK.**

Figure 9-28 shows the Gridlines tab of the Chart Options dialog box. Selections are being made to display gridlines for the major units of both the category and value axes.

Gridlines do not apply to Pie or Doughnut charts. Some 3-D charts can display gridlines for three axes: value, category, and series.

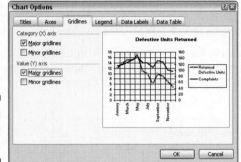

Figure 9-28:
Selecting
gridlines.

Figure 9-29 shows how the gridlines appear in the plot area of the chart.

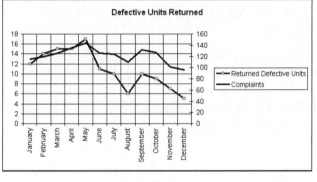

Figure 9-29:
Using
gridlines
to follow
values and
categories.

Right-clicking on a gridline displays a pop-up menu with two choices:

✔ **Clear:** One option is to clear the gridlines (see Figure 9-30). Selecting this removes the gridlines from the plot area. To have them appear again, select the chart, and choose Chart ➪ Chart Options to set them within the Chart Options dialog box.

✔ **Format Gridlines:** The Format Gridlines option on the pop-up menu opens the Format Gridlines dialog box. There are two tabs in the dialog box: Patterns and Scale.

　　• **Patterns tab (see Figure 9-31):** On the Patterns tab, when you select the Custom option, you can format the style, color, and weight of the gridlines, which is helpful because the gridlines need to enhance the series data and not obscure the data. Throw in a background gradient, texture, pattern, or picture, and providing proper formatting to the gridlines becomes even more of an issue.

- **Scale tab:** The Scale tab in the Format Gridlines dialog box provides access to setting the values of the major and minor units of the axis. (These settings are covered in Chapters 11 and 12.)

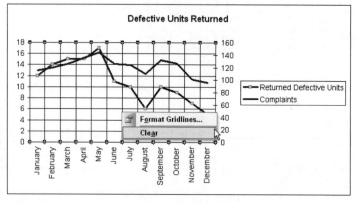

Figure 9-30:
Working with gridlines directly in the plot area.

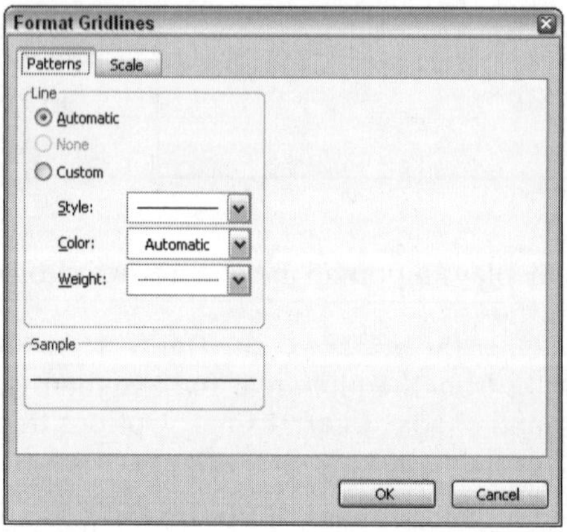

Figure 9-31:
Setting format options for the gridlines.

Chapter 10

Formatting the Axes' Patterns, Font, Number Format, and Alignment

- -

In This Chapter

▶ Formatting axes' lines

▶ Using tick marks and tick-mark labels

▶ Formatting the font of an axis

▶ Using number formatting

▶ Aligning text along an axis

- -

M ost chart types display data plotted on the coordinates of the value and category axes. The values and categories themselves typically are shown in the chart. To make the best of their appearance, it's important to know how to format them. This chapter discusses various formatting attributes that you apply to the axes.

Some 3-D charts have a third axis, for the series. This z-axis also can be formatted in the ways described in this chapter.

Scale settings of the axes are made based on the data. These are discussed in Chapters 11 and 12. This chapter focuses on formatting that is applicable regardless of the data.

Axis formatting changes are made in the Format Axis dialog box. To open the dialog box, right-click directly on an axis and choose Format Axis from the pop-up menu, as shown in Figure 10-1.

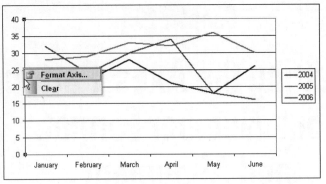

Figure 10-1:
Opening the
Format Axis
dialog box.

The Format Axis dialog box (shown in Figure 10-2) has various tabs. This chapter discusses four of them: Patterns, Font, Number, and Alignment.

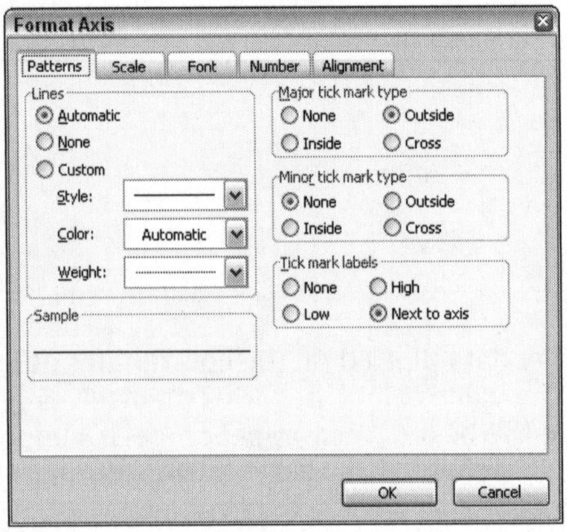

Figure 10-2:
Reviewing
the Format
Axis dialog
box.

Applying Settings in the Patterns Tab

The Patterns tab is where you can control two distinct types of formatting: the style, color, and weight of the axis line; and the application of tick marks and tick-mark labels.

Changing the axis line style, color, and weight

In the Lines section of the Patterns tab are three options:

✔ **Automatic:** Choosing this option lets Excel decide the best way to format the axis line, usually as a thin black line.

✔ **None:** Choosing this option removes the axis line. The line can be absent and yet the tick-mark labels can still be visible. (I fill you in on tick-mark labels in the next section.) *Note:* Selecting the None option for the Axis line allows the tick-mark labels to still appear, but not the tick marks themselves.

✔ **Custom:** Choosing this option lets you control the style, color, and weight of the axis line.

Figure 10-3 shows how the chart appears with no value axis line. The tick-mark labels have been left visible, but the line is not there. Also note that the border of the plot area has been set to None. The plot area border occupies the same space as the axis line. If the plot area border were left intact, it would make it seem as though the axis line were visible.

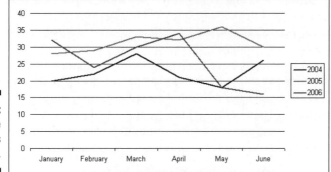

Figure 10-3:
The value
axis line is
set to None.

The appearance of an axis line is less important than the tick-mark labels, perhaps. What's important is that the data is understood. Although axis lines are usually visible, a case could be made that removing them lessens a chart's clutter.

Applying tick-mark types and labels

Tick marks and tick-mark labels help convey the meaning of a chart. Without some indicator of what is being presented, a chart is not worth its salt. The tick marks provide the guide to delineations of the values on the value axis, or the categories on the category axis. The tick-mark labels tell you what the values or categories actually are.

You don't need to use tick-mark labels if the information is presented in some other way. A common option is to have the values and/or categories appear with the actual data points. In this case, the tick-mark labels serve no purpose.

On the Patterns tab (refer to Figure 10-2) are three groups of settings for the tick marks and tick-mark labels:

🡒 **Major Tick Mark Type:** This is where you set the placement of marks along the axis line, coinciding with the major scale unit.

🡒 **Minor Tick Mark Type:** This is where you set the placement of marks along the axis line, coinciding with the minor scale unit.

The major and minor scale units are set on the Scale tab, discussed in Chapters 11 and 12.

The settings for both the major and minor tick marks have four options of where to be placed: None, Inside, Outside, and Cross. The None setting removes the tick marks. The other three settings indicate the placement relative to the axis line. For example, a Cross setting means that the tick marks straddle the axis line, a bit inside and outside.

Figure 10-4 shows how the placement settings work. The value axis tick marks are set to Outside, and the category axis tick marks are set to Inside. The gridlines have been intentionally removed to make the tick-mark settings visible on their own merit (the gridlines would reach to the axis lines making the tick-mark placement less obvious).

🡒 **Tick Mark Labels:** The actual values and category names can be placed in three different positions, or left out altogether. The four settings, as shown in Figure 10-2 are

• **None:** Tick-mark labels are not displayed.

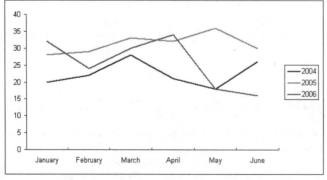

Figure 10-4:
Viewing
tick-mark
placements.

- **Low:** For a vertical axis, the tick-mark labels are displayed to the left of the plot area. For a horizontal axis, the tick-mark labels are displayed at the bottom of the plot area.

- **High:** For a vertical axis, the tick-mark labels are displayed to the right of the plot area. For a horizontal axis, the tick-mark labels are displayed at the top of the plot area. Figure 10-5 shows a chart in which the value tick marks are set to the right and the category tick marks are set to the top.

- **Next to Axis:** This setting keeps the tick-mark labels next to the axis. The usefulness of this setting is only apparent when an axis is not situated on the side or bottom of a chart. Figure 10-6 shows a chart in which the value axis crosses through a midpoint of the categories. The tick-mark labels are kept next to the axis.

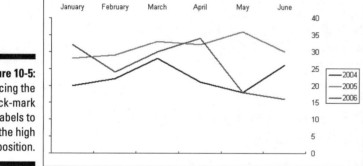

Figure 10-5:
Placing the
tick-mark
labels to
the high
position.

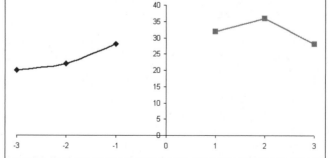

Figure 10-6:
Keeping
tick-mark
labels next
to the axis.

In Chapters 11 and 12, I fill you in on placing the axis line within the plot area.

Here's how to work with tick marks and tick-mark labels:

1. **In a chart of your choice, right-click on an axis.**

   It doesn't matter if it's the value or category axis.

2. **Choose Format Axis from the pop-up menu.**

   The Format Axis dialog box appears.

3. **If necessary, click on the Patterns tab to bring it to the top.**

4. **Select different settings of the major tick marks, minor tick marks, and tick-mark labels.**

   To see how the settings look, click OK.

   Repeat Steps 1 through 4 to try different settings.

Adjusting the Font Settings

Font formatting for an individual axis is done on the Font tab in the Format Axis dialog box. To open the dialog box and make changes to the font, follow these steps:

1. **In a chart of your choice, right-click on an axis.**

   It doesn't matter if it's the value or category axis.

2. **Choose Format Axis from the pop-up menu.**

   The Format Axis dialog box appears.

3. **If necessary, click the Font tab to bring it to the top.**

4. **Select different font settings and click OK.**

   Repeat Steps 1 through 4 to try different settings. The selected font settings are applied to just the single axis. The other axis or axes can be formatted in the same way.

Note the Auto Sale check box. When checked, the font size is enlarged or reduced as the chart is resized. When unchecked the font size remains unchanged as the chart is resized.

Figure 10-7 shows a chart in which the category axis font is being formatted.

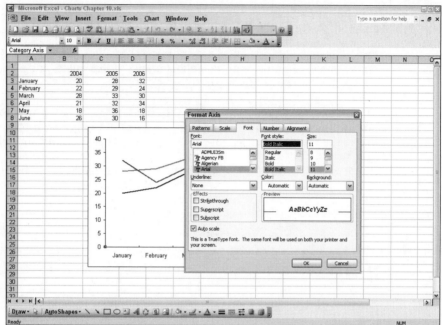

Figure 10-7:
Applying
font
formatting.

Figure 10-8 shows the chart after the category axis font is formatted to be bold and italic. Being able to apply font formatting individually to each axis ensures that the best readability of the tick-mark labels can be attained.

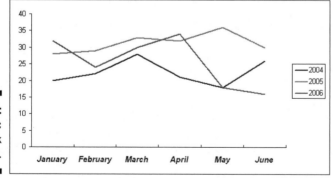

Figure 10-8:
Bold italic
tick-mark
labels.

Specifying the Number Format

Left to its own devices, Excel may not present values correctly. The numbers on the value axis may require decimal points, dollar signs, and so on. No one knows the data better than you (I hope!).

Numerical values are formatted on the Number tab in the Format Axis dialog box. Although this tab is available to any axis type, using it with the value axis makes the most sense, because this is the axis that presents numeric values.

Figure 10-9 shows a chart in which the value axis numbers are being formatted as currency.

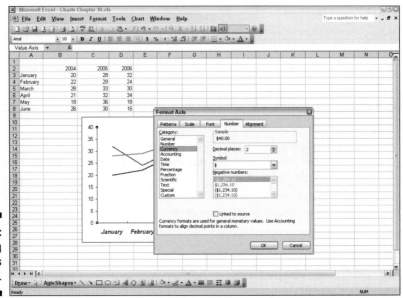

Figure 10-9: Formatting numbers as currency.

Note the Linked to Source check box. When this is checked, the formatting of the underlying cells (the series data) is forced onto the axis tick-mark labels, which is useful to ensure formatting is correct but only matters when formatting is applied to the cells in the first place.

In Figure 10-9, the underlying cells are in the General format. Assuming the chart should reflect the numbers as currency, and then making sure the Linked to Source check box is unchecked, is key to overriding the general setting. Figure 10-10 illustrates this situation. The value axis tick marks are now formatted as currency even though the cells that hold the series data are not.

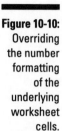

Figure 10-10:
Overriding
the number
formatting
of the
underlying
worksheet
cells.

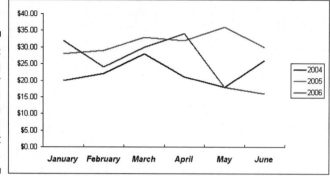

When the Link to Source check box is checked, the formatting of the first series in the series order is the formatting applied to the tick-mark labels.

Here's how to change the number formatting:

1. **In a chart of your choice, right-click on the value axis.**

2. **Choose Format Axis from the pop-up menu.**

   The Format Axis dialog box appears.

3. **If necessary, click the Number tab to bring it to the top.**

4. **Select different category, decimal, and other settings, and click OK.**

   Repeat Steps 1 through 4 to try different number format settings.

Working with Text Alignment

Having control over how text is aligned along an axis really helps to make the best of the chart space. There is only so much room on a chart, and good design protocol dictates the avoidance of a cluttered and cramped appearance.

Figure 10-11 shows a chart in which the categories are dates. The dates are situated at the bottom of the chart and are aligned on their sides. This makes the dates a little hard to read.

Another issue with the dates in Figure 10-11 is that the vertical placement takes up room. Figure 10-12 shows the how the text can be aligned. On the Alignment tab in the Format Axis dialog box, the text is aligned so that it appears at a slant — specifically, at a 45-degree angle.

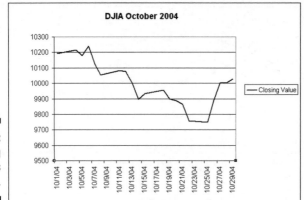

Figure 10-11:
Reading
sideways
dates.

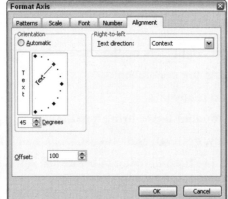

Figure 10-12:
Adjusting
the text
alignment.

Figure 10-13 shows the result of the alignment change. The dates are a bit easier to read.

The axis text alignment in Figure 10-13 is an improvement, but perhaps even more can be done. The next step is to make the dates appear horizontal, as normal text. The problem, though, is that there are too many dates, and if made horizontal, the dates will overlap each other.

Chapter 11 discusses how to work with the number of categories appearing along the axis. For now, just know that I've changed the scale settings to display the labels for every seventh day. Therefore, setting the text to a horizontal alignment will work. Figure 10-14 shows the text being aligned to 0 degrees.

Figure 10-15 shows how the aligned text now looks. The chart has gained a bit of space (in other words, the plot area has expanded, making the chart easier to read). The fact that the category dates are set to display every seventh date not only helps clean up the appearance, it makes sense: When a time-based series is presented, it's often in order to see the trend of the line, not to study in minutiae every data point.

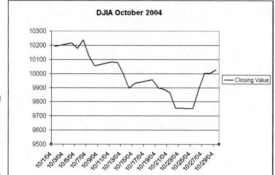

Figure 10-13:
Making the dates easier to read.

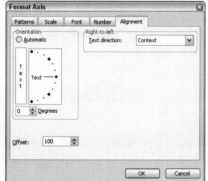

Figure 10-14:
Making the text alignment.

On the Alignment tab of the Format Axis dialog box, shown in Figure 10-14, are a few different settings:

- ✔ **Orientation:** This settings is the key setting of the text angle. When the Automatic option is selected, Excel decides how to align the text. Otherwise, you can enter a degree amount, or use the small up/down arrows to dial up a degree amount. Alternatively, you can drag the gauge handle to the desired angle.

- ✔ **Offset:** This setting determines how close the text is to the axis line. The possible settings are from 0 through 1,000. The lower the setting, the closer the text is to the axis line.

- ✔ **Right-to-Left:** This settings lets you choose how text is read. For example, Hebrew, Arabic, and other languages are read from right-to-left.

There are three settings in the drop down: Context, Left-to-Right, and Right-to-Left. This setting can be ignored because Excel senses the language of the text and treats it accordingly.

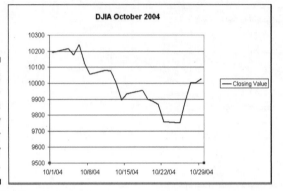

Figure 10-15:
The tick-mark labels are few in number and easy to read.

Here's how to use the text-alignment features:

1. **In a chart of your choice, right-click on the value axis.**

2. **Choose Format Axis from the pop-up menu.**

   The Format Axis dialog box appears.

3. **If necessary, click on the Alignment tab to bring it to the top.**

4. **Select an angle and offset.**

   To select an angle, you can enter a number in the Degrees entry box, or use the small up/down buttons to find the desired angle. Figure 10-16 show how the mouse can be used to drag the gauge to the desired angle.

5. **Click OK to see the formatting.**

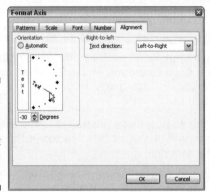

Figure 10-16:
Dragging the gauge to select the angle for the text.

Chapter 11

Working With the Category-Axis Scale Settings

*T*he delineations along the category axis let you know what is being plotted. Knowing that a value is 10 or 100 or 1,000 isn't enough; you also need to know what the value is a measure of. Categories give values meaning.

Selecting category-axis settings can be a tricky business. If you select to show too many categories labels, they may be unreadable. If you select to display too few category labels, your viewers may be confused about where particular values fall within the realm of the data.

Sometimes the number of categories within the data is just right for displaying all the category labels — but not always. In this chapter, I show how to manage the pesky category axis and get it to support your chart in the best way possible.

First, though, keep in mind that there are two variations of the category axis. Categories can be (and often are) time-based. For example, the value of an investment may be plotted, and the chart shows how the investment did each day for the month. The flip side is an axis that contains non-time-based categories.

Figure 11-1 shows the Scale tab of the Format Axis dialog box when working with time-based data. Particular options are unique to working with this type of data. For example, selecting the base unit (as days, months, or years) is an option only seen when the underlying data has time-based categories.

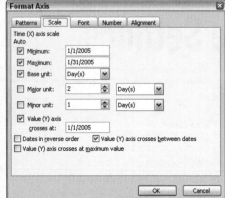

Figure 11-1:
Working with time-based category scale settings.

When working with dates as the category labels, Excel will plot the data in the correct sequential date order, even if the source data is not sorted by date.

Figure 11-2 shows the alternative Scale tab. When the data is not categorized as time-scale, the options are simpler. You just have to decide how many category labels will appear.

Figure 11-2:
Reviewing the scale settings for non-time-based categories.

The two versions of the Scale tab share some common settings. I address these common settings first; then I move on to the variations.

Selecting the Category Axis Type

When you create a chart, Excel figures out the best way to present the categories — time-scale or not. You can override Excel, if you want. Here's how to override the setting:

1. **Select your chart.**

2. **Choose Chart ⇨ Chart Options.**

   The Chart Options dialog box appears.

3. **Click on the Axes tab to bring it to the top.**

   Figure 11-3 shows where the settings for the category axis can be set.

4. **If you want, try a different setting.**

5. **Click OK to close the dialog box.**

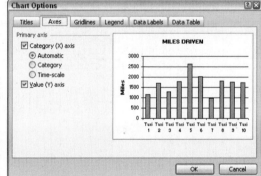

Figure 11-3: Where to change the category axis type.

For your chart, the category axis may be set to Automatic. The three possible settings are

- ✓ **Automatic:** Excel makes a guess as to whether the categories are time-based.

- ✓ **Category:** The categories are not to be treated as time-based.

- ✓ **Time-Scale:** The categories are to be treated as time-based.

Besides selecting the option of how the category axis is used, the Category (X) Axis check box controls whether the axis is visible. Keep it checked to keep the category axis on the chart.

Note that you can change the category type even if it doesn't make sense. For example, the chart in Figure 11-2 doesn't use time-based categories. In fact, the categories are named Taxi1, Taxi2, and so on. I can't imagine how this can be considered any type of time-based category labeling. Even so, you can select the option to make it time-based. Figure 11-4 shows how I've set a category to be time-based even though it doesn't make sense to do so. The categories become nonsense dates.

On the other hand, changing a time-based chart so that it uses a non-time-based category axis may make a lot of sense. Figure 11-5 shows a plot of the Dow Jones Industrial Average (DJIA) for the beginning of October 2004. Although there are no category dates for October 2, 3, 9, or 10, these dates appear as categories and seem to have plotted data to boot!

In fact, Excel just connects the series line from one plotted point to the next, and the nonexistent categories, now visible on the category axis, seem to relate to a value. For example, there are category labels for October 2 and 3, even though they don't exist in the source data. (October 2 and 3 was the weekend — the market was closed.) On the chart, the series line goes from the point for October 1 to the point for October 4. By doing this, it appears that October 2 and 3 have values. I don't think we should have Excel create data!

By changing the way the category axis is treated — from Time-Scale (or Automatic) to Category — the nonexistent dates will disappear from the category axis. The Axes tab in the Chart Options dialog box (refer to Figure 11-3) is where you make this change. By selecting the Category option, the chart is presented without the nonexistent dates, as shown in Figure 11-6.

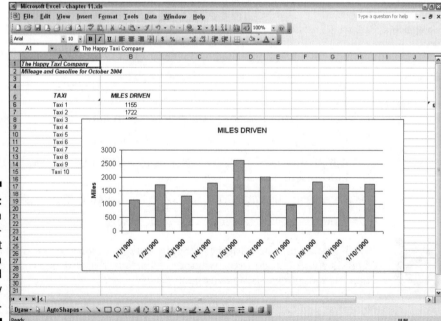

Figure 11-4: Changing a non-time-based chart to use a time-based category axis.

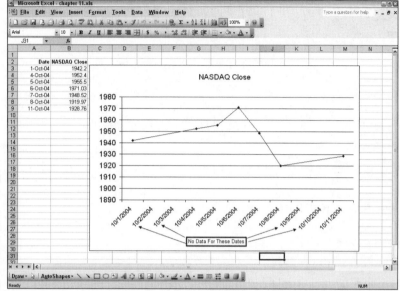

Figure 11-5:
How non-existent dates have been plotted.

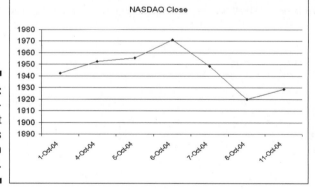

Figure 11-6:
The non-existent dates have been removed.

In summary, having time-based data be treated as non-time-based data may seem odd. In charts such as this, the choice of how to handle "gaps" in the time-based categories is subjective. If the number of gaps in the sequence is significant, switching to a category-based category axis may be necessary.

Plotting time-based data on a Category type axis (instead of a time-scale axis) sometimes makes sense. But plotting non-time-based categories on a Time-Scale type category axis never makes sense.

Selecting the Category Where the Value Axis Crosses

Usually the category axis and the value axis each line up against the border of the plot area. For Line and Column charts, the bottom of the plot area is where the category axis appears, and the left edge of the plot area is where the value axis goes. This configuration is the opposite in Bar charts: The categories are on the side, and the values are on the bottom.

Regardless of which way the axes are configured, certain settings allow you to decide where the value axis crosses the category axis — that is, at which category. Left alone, the value axis actually crosses at category 1, which effectively is the left side of the plot area.

Having the value axis cross at a specific category

You can specify at which category the value axis will cross. The setting works the same whether plotting with a time-scale or non-time-scale category axis. Figure 11-7 shows an example of setting the value axis in the middle of the plot area.

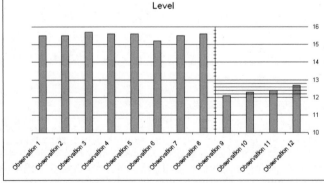

Figure 11-7: Moving the value axis into the middle of the plot area.

The data that's plotted in the chart in Figure 11-7 has a noticeable change in the last few data points. As a group, they range a little differently from the rest of the data. So I moved the value axis to where these data points are and added some formatting and lines to accentuate this portion of the data. By the way the lines were drawn using the Line tool on the Drawing toolbar, which I explain in Chapter 15.

Figure 11-8 shows how I set the value axis to cross at the ninth category.

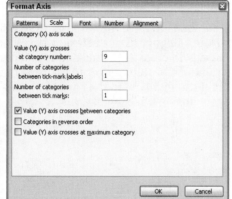

In addition, I made the following changes:

✔ For the value axis, I set Tick-Mark Labels to High (on the Patterns tab of the Format Axis dialog box). This moves the tick-mark labels to the right axis (leaving the tick-mark labels next to the axis obscures the plotted data).

✔ Also for the value axis, I set the Minor Tick-Mark type to Cross (also on the Patterns tab of the Format Axis dialog box).

✔ I drew lines that extended for the minor tick marks to the right border of the plot area, to give a more accurate guide to the data in this section.

Here's how to set which category the value axis crosses at:

1. **Double-click on the category axis of your chart.**

   The Format Axis dialog box appears.

2. **Click the Scale tab to bring it to the top.**

3. **Enter a number in the Value (Y) Axis Crosses At Category Number box.**

   Enter a 1 or greater. If you enter a number that is greater than the number of categories, this just forces the value axis to the right side (or to the top in a Bar chart). If the category axis is set to time-scale instead of entering a category number, you'll enter a date-based value that falls within the range of categories.

4. **Click OK.**

Setting to have the value axis cross at a specific category is conceptually the same, whether using time-scale data or not. With time-scale data you enter which date the value axis should cross at. With non-time-scale data, you enter the actual category number.

Setting the value axis to cross at the maximum category

One of the options on the Scale tab is to have the value axis cross at the maximum category. Whether the category axis is category-based or time-scale-based, setting the value axis to cross at the maximum category simply moves the value axis to the right of the plot area, or to the top of the plot area for a Bar chart. Figure 11-9 shows where in the Format Axis dialog box to set the value axis to cross at the maximum category. Just a simple click in a check box is all it takes!

Figure 11-9:
Selecting to have the value axis cross at the maximum category.

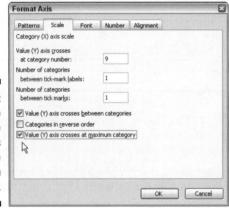

The Scale tab on the Format Axis dialog box differs in appearance when the category axis is time-scale-based, but the setting to have the value axis cross at the maximum category is the same.

Setting the value axis to cross between categories

A category axis option is how to plot data values at the category tick marks. On the Scale tab is the Value (Y) Axis Crosses Between Categories check box. This controls whether data is plotted between categories or lined up with the category tick marks. Wanting the data to line up with the tick marks may seem like a no-brainer, but hold off on your conclusion until I show you the difference!

First, referring to Figure 11-9, you'll see the check box for setting whether the values are plotted between categories. Figure 11-10 shows how a chart appears when the check box is checked.

When the Value (Y) Axis Crosses Between Categories check box is unchecked, the data points shift. Figure 11-11 shows how this appears.

The chart in Figure 11-11 looks a little odd, don't you think? The data points (columns, in this case) at the first and last categories are cut in half. Nothing is particularly wrong here — it's just an odd formatting twist.

Figure 11-10:
Plotting values between categories.

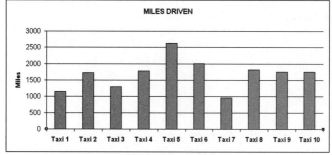

Figure 11-11:
Lining up plotted values with the category tick marks.

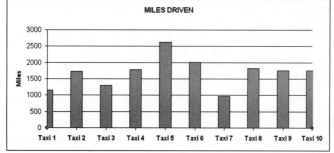

Reversing the Order of the Categories

On the Scale tab, you have the option to reverse the way the categories appear along the axis. This feature is great, because the alternative would be to re-sort the source data and re-create the chart.

Figure 11-12 shows where the Categories in Reverse Order check box is on the Scale tab.

Figure 11-13 shows the result of reversing the categories. In the chart, the left-most category label is Taxi 10 and the rightmost category label is Taxi 1. Also, the vertical axis has shifted to the right of the plot area. This is because true to its setting, the value axis is crossing at the first category. The placement of the value axis can be changed as described in the "Selecting the Category Where the Values Axis Crosses" section, earlier in this chapter.

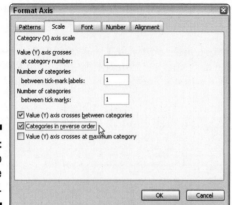

Figure 11-12:
Preparing to
reverse the
categories.

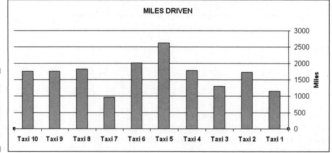

Figure 11-13:
Reviewing
the reversed
categories.

Being able to reverse the categories is a useful feature. Your categories may not be such that they have to go in a certain order. Having the option to reverse them provides an additional formatting option.

Working With Time-Based Categories

Categories are often time-based. For example, charting the performance of a stock involves plotting the value of the stock at different periods (usually daily). Or, as another example, tracking sales over the course of a year means plotting the tally of sales at a periodic period, such as each month.

To facilitate using time-based categories, Excel presents certain scale options. The following sections discuss each of these.

When making selections in the Format Axis dialog box, make sure the Auto check box is unchecked for the selection you're setting. If left checked, Excel will ignore your settings and use ones Excel deems to be the best choice.

Setting the base unit

When a chart contains dates for categories, the Scale tab in the Format Axis dialog box has a setting for the base unit. When your chart was created, Excel determined the initial setting of the base unit.

Figure 11-14 shows a Line chart of General Electric (GE) stock for the six-month period of July 2004 through December 2004. Stock prices are daily. The line is a continuous plot of daily values.

Figure 11-15 shows the Format Axis dialog box with the Scale tab on top. The Base Unit setting originally defaulted to Day(s) but is being changed to Month(s).

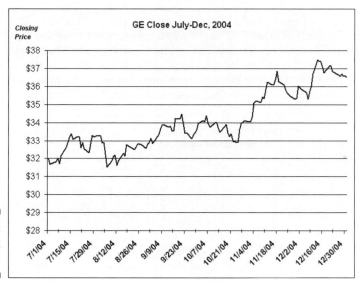

Figure 11-14: Daily stock price data.

Figure 11-16 shows the result of selecting Month(s) as the base unit for daily data. The chart plot is decidedly different but nonetheless serves to visually summarize the daily data into monthly plots.

How dates are used in charts

When the categories are dates, Excel automatically sets the category axis to be time-scale-based. The base unit becomes one of days, months, or years. Excel determines the smallest interval found among the dates and sets the base unit accordingly. Hours, minutes, and seconds are not plotted with a time-scale axis.

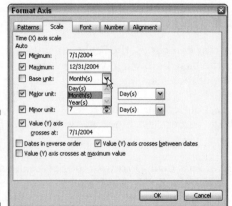

Figure 11-15:
Changing
the time-
scale base
unit.

The chart in Figure 11-16 is actually great at quickly showing facts about the data. The vertical lines over each month category label are sized by the lowest and highest values of the month. The horizontal connecting lines start and end based on the values for the particular last and first day of preceding and succeeding months. For example, the line between September and October originates from the value for September 30 and ends on the value for October 1.

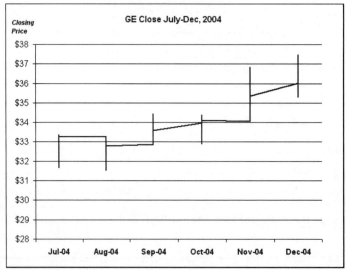

Figure 11-16:
Daily data
summarized
into a
monthly plot.

Setting the minimum and maximum dates

Even though a chart may reference source data of a given range of dates, you can change the range of dates used by the category axis to a smaller subset of dates. To do this, follow these steps:

1. **On a chart in which the category axis is time-scale-based, double-click the category axis.**

   The Format Axis dialog box appears.

2. **Click the Scale tab to bring it to the top.**

3. **Enter a new date in the Minimum and/or Maximum entry boxes.**

4. **Click OK to close the dialog box.**

The chart in Figure 11-17 is based on six months of daily source data, July 1, 2004, through December 31, 2004. The Format Axis dialog box is open and the Minimum and Maximum dates are being changed to plot just September 1 through September 15.

Figure 11-18 shows the chart with the new range of dates along the category axis.

Using the Minimum and Maximum settings to override the range of dates provides an easy way to focus the chart on a key subset of data.

Even though the range of dates along the category axis has been changed, the chart title still states the full range of dates. Eyeballing a chart after making changes, to see if all the labels make sense, is always a good idea.

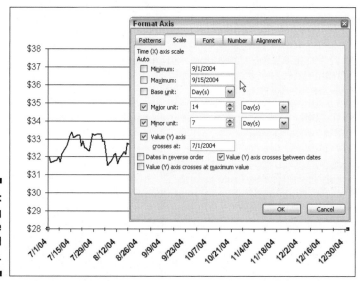

Figure 11-17:
Changing
the range
of plotted
dates.

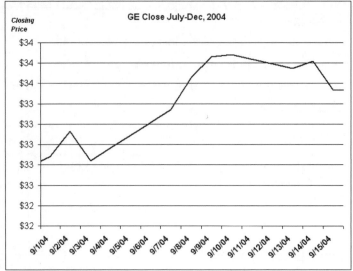

Figure 11-18:
Viewing the
new range
of category
dates.

Selecting the major and minor units

The Major Unit and Minor Unit settings control how tick marks and tick-mark labels are displayed along the category axis. The major unit on a time-scale category axis sets an interval of days (or months or years) as a pattern for how many of the category dates to display.

Figure 11-19 shows the Major Unit setting being set to 28 days. The Minor Unit setting is set to 7 days.

Figure 11-20 shows how the dates now appear along the category axis. The dates (the tick-mark labels) and the major tick marks themselves are spaced at an interval of 28 days.

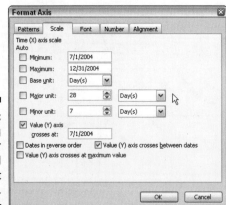

Figure 11-19:
Changing
the Major
Unit and
Minor Unit
settings.

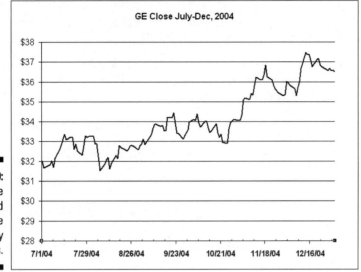

GE Close July-Dec, 2004

Figure 11-20:
Viewing the
updated
dates on the
category
axis.

In the chart in Figure 11-20, the Major Tick-Mark Type is set to Outside and the Minor Tick-Mark Type is set to Inside. The settings are made on the Patterns tab of the Format Axis dialog box.

Working With Non-Time-Based Categories

With charts that are not built on a time-scale category axis, the Scale options are simpler. There are no minimum or maximum settings. Whereas, with dates, selecting a new range to use is feasible, this would be difficult to do with any other type of category labeling, because the category labels are probably not sequential in nature when not time-based.

Also there are no settings for the Major and Minor units. However, there are settings that let you control how many tick marks and tick-mark labels appear along the category axis.

Setting the number of categories between tick-mark labels

The interval of how many category labels to display is set with the Number of Categories Between Tick-Mark Labels setting. This setting establishes the interval of category labels to display. For example, if there are 12 categories and the Number of Categories Between Tick-Mark Labels is set to 2, six category labels will be displayed. The interval, therefore, is 2.

Figure 11-21 shows a chart for which the Number of Category Tick-Mark Labels is being set to 2. As is evident on the chart, each category is displayed prior to the setting being changed.

After the setting is completed, the chart displays half of the category labels — which doesn't quite make sense (see Figure 11-22). Removing some of the category labels hasn't made the chart more understandable; in fact, it leaves out vital information — it isn't known what the half of the columns shown represent.

Displaying less than all the category labels on a non-time-scale chart rarely makes sense. The only reasonable time to do so would be when there are a large number of categories and displaying all the category labels isn't feasible.

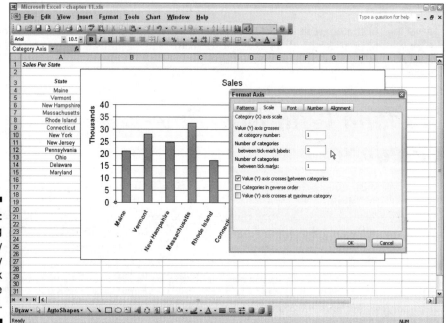

Figure 11-21: Changing how many category tick-mark labels are displayed.

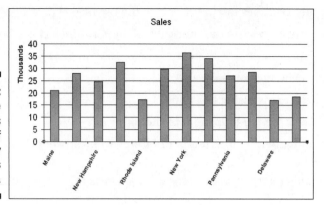

Setting the number of categories between tick marks

Adjusting the Number of Categories Between Tick Marks is a useful formatting option that can enhance the visual appeal of your chart. The tick marks, situated as the small lines along the axis, are placed in between each category when the setting is 1. Adjusting the setting to a higher number is a way to visually group categories together. Refer to Figure 11-21 to see where this setting is on the Scale tab.

Figure 11-23 shows a chart in which the Number of Categories Between Tick Marks has been set to 3. Major gridlines for the category axis are also set to be visible.

The use of tick marks and gridlines in the chart in Figure 11-23 doesn't particularly make sense for these state categories, but with certain categories in your data, adjusting the Number of Categories Between Tick Marks may very well provide interesting formatting options.

Why not try these settings on one of your charts? Here's what you do:

1. **Create a chart or open an Excel file with a chart you already made.**

   This should be a chart in which the categories are not time-based.

2. **Click once on the chart to select it.**

3. **Choose Chart ⇨ Chart Options.**

   The Chart Options dialog box appears.

4. **Click the Gridlines tab to bring it to the top (see Figure 11-24).**

5. **Under Category (X) Axis, check the Major Gridlines check box.**

6. **Click OK.**

7. **Double-click the category axis.**

   The Format Axis dialog box appears.

8. **Click the Scale tab to bring it to the top.**

9. **Enter a number for the Number of Categories Between Tick Marks setting.**

   This number should be greater than 1 and less than the number of categories.

10. **Click OK to see how your chart came out.**

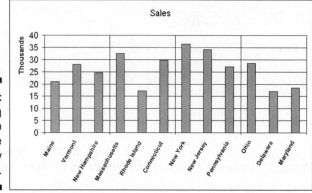

Figure 11-23:
Using gridlines to accentuate category groupings.

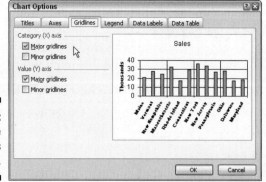

Figure 11-24:
The Gridlines tab.

Chapter 12

Working With the Value-Axis Scale Settings

- -

- -

Scale settings are arguably the most important attributes for an axis. Whereas other settings, such as the font and the alignment, are based on formatting, scale settings are based on the data itself.

In most charts, the value axis runs vertically on the left side of the plot area. This is certainly the case in a Line chart — values are vertical on the left, and categories are horizontal on the bottom. This arrangement is true also for Column charts, Area charts, and Scatter charts. Bar charts, which are like Column charts flipped on their side, have the placement of the axes reversed. On a Bar chart, the value axis runs horizontal along the bottom of the plot area.

Wherever the value axis might be, the scale settings control how data is plotted. In particular, the minimum and maximum settings create the range within the plot area in which the data values are placed. Altering these settings changes how the series data appears. This will all become clear as you read the chapter.

First things first — let's display the Format Axis dialog box and have a look at the scale settings. Here's what you do:

1. **Open or create a chart that has a value axis.**

   For ease of getting through the concepts in this chapter, use a Line, Bar, or Column chart.

2. **Right-click on the value axis, as shown in Figure 12-1.**

   If your chart type is Line or Column, the value axis is vertically situated on the left of the plot area. If your chart type is Bar, the value axis is horizontally situated along the bottom of the plot area.

3. **Click Format Axis in the pop-up menu.**

   The Format Axis dialog box appears.

4. **Click the Scale tab (shown in Figure 12-2) to bring it to the top.**

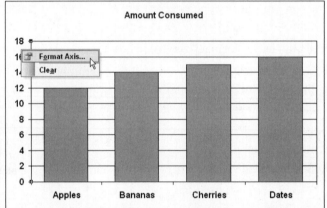

Figure 12-1:
Right-clicking the value axis.

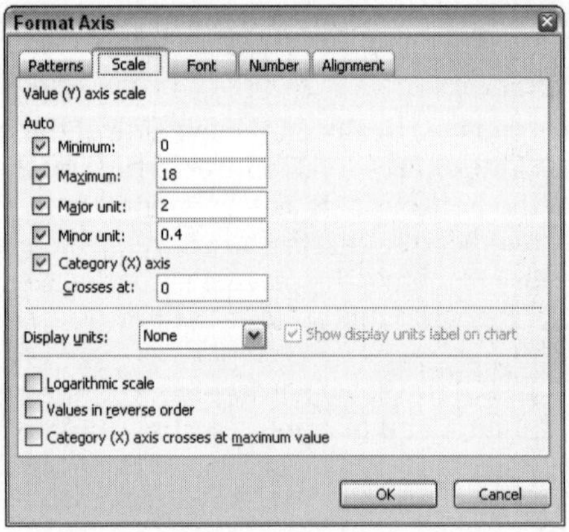

Figure 12-2:
The Format Axis dialog box.

Setting the Minimum and Maximum Values

The value axis encompasses the range amongst which the series data is plotted. For example, a data point with a value of 30 is plotted wherever 30 is within the value axis range. If the range is not wide enough to include 30, the data point will not be shown. That's a no-no.

The values in my sample chart in Figure 12-1 are as follows:

Fruit	Value
Apples	12
Bananas	14
Cherries	15
Dates	16

Let's say that, for some unfathomable reason, I decide to change the axis range to have a minimum of 14. What will happen to my apples and bananas? In the Format Axis dialog box, I've changed the minimum to 14, as shown in Figure 12-3.

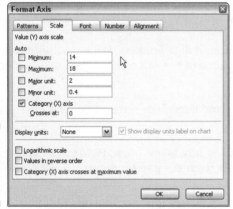

Figure 12-3: Changing the minimum setting.

You can uncheck the Auto check boxes next to the Minimum, Maximum, Major Unit, and Minor Unit. This prevents Excel from overriding your selections.

Figure 12-4 shows the result of this setting change. A couple of things occurred:

✔ The apples and bananas are not plotted, because their values don't fall in the range.

✔ The columns for the cherries and dates look smaller.

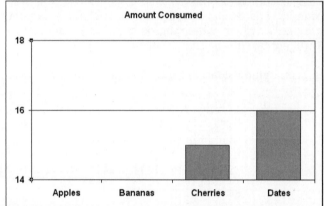

Figure 12-4:
The
changed
data plot.

The fact that the cherries and dates columns look smaller makes sense because the range of values along the axis has been narrowed. The way the columns looked in my chart in Figure 12-1 is based on a range of 0 to 18. So cherries and dates, respectively at 15 and 16, covered the majority of the area. The chart in Figure 12-4 has a value axis range of 14 to 18. Cherries, at 15, cover just 25 percent of the range, and dates cover 50 percent.

Scale settings affect how plotted data appears. Data can appear larger or smaller depending on the range of the value axis, which makes it critical to consider the value range.

Try changing the minimum and maximum settings on your chart. Here's what to do:

1. **If the Format Axis dialog box is not open, right-click on the value axis and select Format Axis from the pop-up menu, or just double-click on the axis.**

   The Format Axis dialog box appears.

2. **Click the Scale tab so that it's on top.**

3. **The minimum and maximum settings will already be filled in, but change one or both and uncheck the Auto check boxes.**

4. **Click OK to close the dialog box and see the change.**

Note that the Major Unit and Minor Unit settings affect the display. They don't alter the range of values, but they do serve as the basis for the gridlines and tick marks. I explain this concept in the following section.

Declaring the Major Unit and Minor Unit Tick Marks

Gridlines are helpful to perceive a more accurate position at which a data point is plotted. Although you can display values at the data points, doing so is often not feasible because of the *number* of data points. Instead, gridlines and tick marks are the way to go.

Chapters 9 and 10 introduce gridlines and tick marks. Here is where they come together in how they're set. In Figure 12-3, settings are being entered into the Format Axis dialog box. This includes the major and minor units — which are set, respectively, at 2 and 0.4. The chart in Figure 12-4 shows that the gridlines occur at each multiple of 2. This is the direct effect of the major unit setting of 2. Figure 12-5 shows the Format Axis dialog box with the Patterns tab on top. The settings on the Patterns tab cause the display of major gridlines and the absence of minor gridlines and minor tick marks.

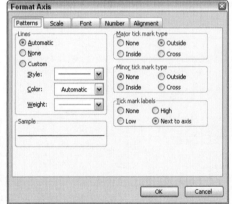

Figure 12-5:
Reviewing
tick-mark
settings.

Major Tick Mark Type is set to Outside and Minor Tick Mark Type is set None. Also, gridlines are set to be visible. This is set on the Gridlines tab in the Chart Options dialog box. Use the Chart ➪ Chart Options menu to display the dialog box.

It's time to make a change. In my chart, I'm resetting the major unit to 0.5. Figure 12-6 shows where I make this change on the Scale tab in the Format Axis dialog box.

Note also in Figure 12-6 that I changed the minor unit to 0.1. Next, on the Patterns tab, I've changed Minor Tick-Mark Type to Cross (see Figure 12-7).

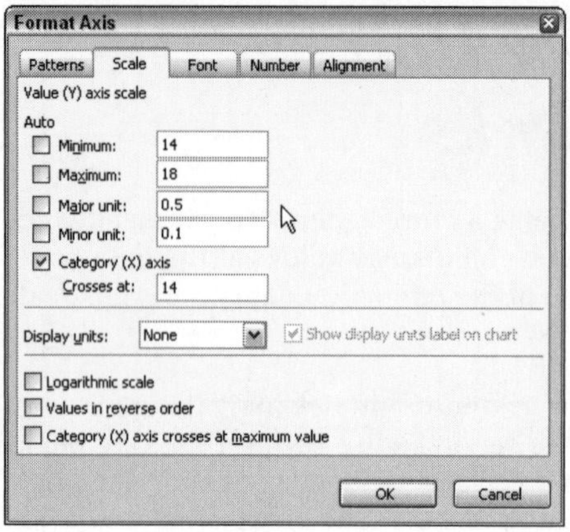

Figure 12-6:
Resetting
the Major
Unit setting.

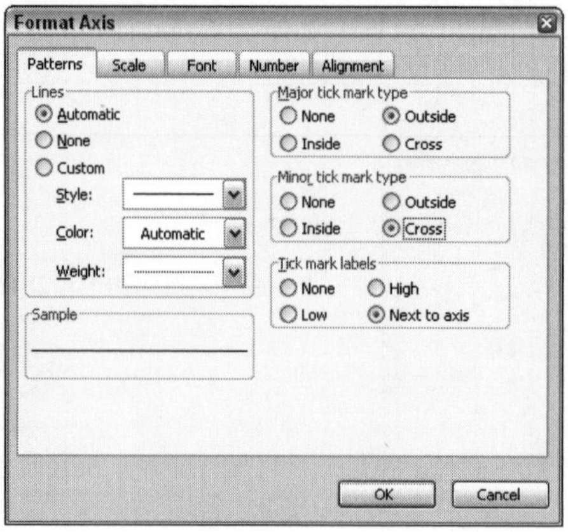

Figure 12-7:
Selecting
to display
minor unit
tick marks.

Figure 12-8 shows the result of these settings. There are more gridlines, occurring at each multiple of the major unit. Also, there are tick marks at each 0.1 multiple.

Try adjusting the major unit, minor unit, and tick mark settings on your chart. Here's how:

1. **If the Format Axis dialog box is not open, right-click on the value axis and select Format Axis from the pop-up menu, or just double-click the axis.**

   The Format Axis Dialog box appears.

2. **Click the Scale tab to bring it to the top.**

3. **Enter a setting for the major unit.**

   This number should be smaller than the range of the minimum and maximum settings. For example, if the minimum is 0 and the maximum is 10, the major unit should be a number less than 10.

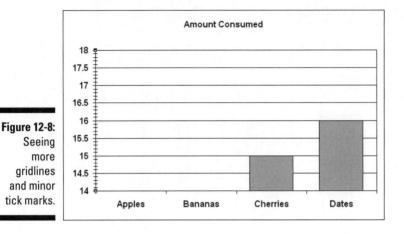

Figure 12-8:
Seeing
more
gridlines
and minor
tick marks.

4. **Enter a setting for the minor unit.**

   This number cannot be larger than the major unit. It's okay to have it be the same number as the major unit, but this serves no purpose. The minor unit should be less than the major unit.

5. **Click the Patterns tab to bring it to the top.**

6. **Make selections on how to display the major tick-mark type and the minor tick-mark type.**

7. **Click OK to close the dialog box and see the results.**

Selecting the Value Where the Category Axis Crosses

Typically, the category axis is situated along the border of the plot area. For a Line or Column chart, this is the bottom of the plot area. For a Bar chart, the category axis is on the left side of the plot area.

Selecting where to have the category axis cross

You may need to move the category axis into the plot area. Often, the reason is because there is a mix of positive and negative data values. Figure 12-9 shows a chart that was generated using the Chart Wizard. The source data contains positive and negative values. The Chart Wizard has situated the category axis where 0 is located. This makes sense, but the category tick-mark labels are a problem.

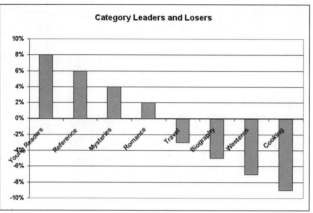

Figure 12-9:
Where
the Chart
Wizard
placed the
category
axis.

The series data in the chart in Figure 12-9 falls both above and below 0. The columns take up room above and below 0, and having the category axis sit in the middle of the plot area makes it possible for the bars to be situated in both directions.

You have some options on how to handle the category labels:

✔ **Select not to display category tick-mark labels.**

✔ **Select not to display category tick-mark labels and instead elect to display category name data labels.** (This is set on the Data Labels tab in the Chart Options dialog box. Choose Chart ➪ Chart Options to display the dialog box.) Figure 12-10 shows how this configuration looks. This option isn't bad. Using series data labels instead of category tick-marks labels makes it easier to see the actual category names, especially if the gridlines are removed.

✔ **Change the Category Axis Crosses At setting.**

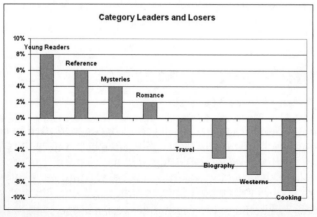

Figure 12-10:
Turning off
category
tick-mark
labels and
turning on
series data
labels.

Figure 12-11 shows where on the Scale tab to change the value where the category axis is situated along the range of values of the value axis. In this example, the value is being changed to the lowest value. In other words, the category axis will cross at the minimum value of the value axis — at the bottom. The value in this case is –0.1. This is a chart that displays percentages, so there are decimal values in the data. A value of –0.1 becomes –10% on the chart.

Figure 12-11:
Changing
the value
where the
category
axis
crosses.

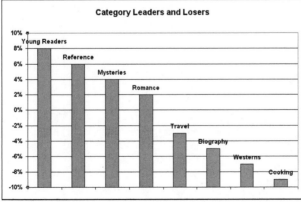

Figure 12-12 shows the result of setting the cross value for the category axis. The chart has a few serious issues:

Figure 12-12:
Reviewing
the chart
after
changing
where the
category
axis
crosses.

> ✔ **The data points that are positive values now are plotted in columns that start at the bottom value of –10%.** Before changing the category axis, the positive values started from 0.

> ✔ **The negative data points start at the bottom value of –10% and their columns finish at their respective values.** However, this is backwards. The columns should cover space between 0 and their respective values.

> ✔ **The size of the columns of the negative data points has been reversed.** In Figure 12-10, for example, the Travel column took up the least amount of space, and the Cooking column took up the most space. In Figure 12-12, the opposite is true.

All is not lost! You can still turn this chart into a useful vehicle to convey information. Here's what to do:

1. **Prepare a Column chart based on data with some positive and negative values.**

2. **Double-click the value axis.**

   The Format Axis dialog box appears.

3. **Click the Scale tab to bring it to the top.**

4. **In the Category (X) Axis Crosses At field, enter the same value that appears in the Minimum box.**

5. **Make sure the check box next to Category (X) Axis Crosses At is unchecked.**

6. **Click OK.**

   Your chart should now be similar to the one in Figure 12-12 (that is, the columns originate from the bottom of the plot area).

7. **Right-click directly on a column.**

   A pop-up menu appears (see Figure 12-13).

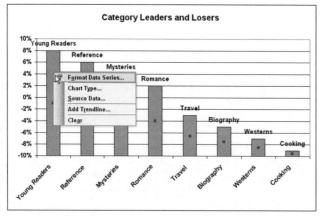

Figure 12-13:
Preparing to
format the
data series.

8. **Select Format Data Series from the pop-up menu.**

   The Format Data Series dialog box appears.

9. **Click the Data Labels tab to bring it to the top (see Figure 12-14).**

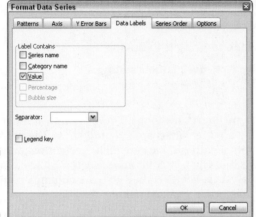

Figure 12-14:
The Data
Labels tab.

10. **Under Label Contains, check Value, but not Series Name or Category Name (see Figure 12-14).**

11. **Click OK.**

12. **Optionally, format the data labels themselves by double-clicking on one to open the Format Data Labels dialog box. Click on the Number tab to bring it to the top, and then select a format (see Figure 12-15).**

    In my example, I selected Percentage because I'm working with percentage-based data.

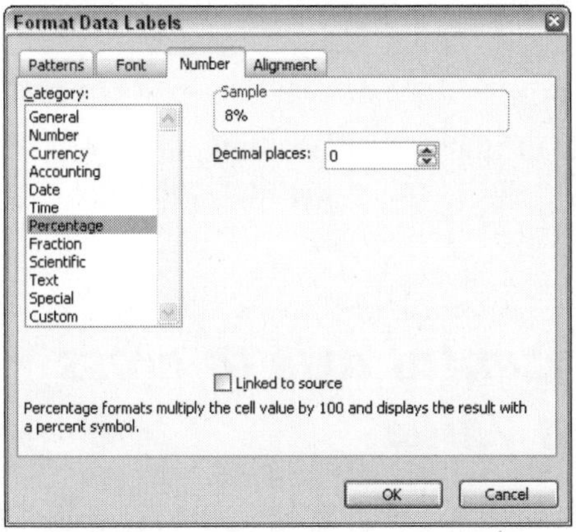

Figure 12-15:
Formatting
the data
labels.

13. **Click OK.**

    The chart now displays the values in the data labels.

14. **Clear the gridlines by right-clicking directly on one, and then selecting Clear from the pop-up menu.**

15. **Double-click on the value axis.**

    The Format Axis dialog box appears.

16. **Click the Patterns tab to bring it to the top.**

17. **Select None for the Tick-Mark Labels setting.**

18. **Click OK.**

Figure 12-16 shows how my chart now looks. There are no values showing along the value axis. Instead, the values are situated above the columns. Although the positive and negative values are all in upright columns, having the values makes it clear that the last columns are actually based on negative values. Comparative analysis is achieved because the columns diminish in size from the largest value to the smallest value.

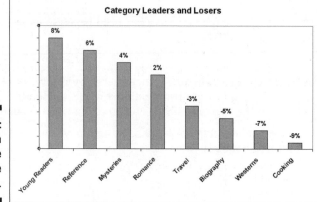

Figure 12-16:
Giving a
comparative
sense to the
data points.

This chart can be formatted further to have the columns based on negative values be formatted in a different color. Formatting individual data points is covered in Chapter 13.

Forcing the horizontal axis to cross at the maximum value

One of the options on the Scale tab is to have the category axis cross at the maximum value. In the previous section, I show you how to manually set the category axis to cross at the minimum value. Having the category axis cross at the maximum value is as easy as a checking a check box.

Figure 12-17 shows where this check box is on the Scale tab of the Format Axis dialog box.

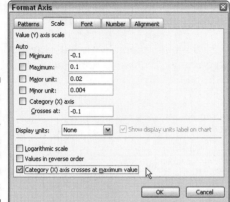

Figure 12-17:
Having the
category
axis cross
at the
maximum
value.

There is no automatic setting to have the category axis cross at the minimum value — you have to set it yourself.

Figure 12-18 shows my chart with the category axis crossing at the maximum value. The chart certainly has an interesting look to it, but is it useful? It may be, with proper labeling and formatting.

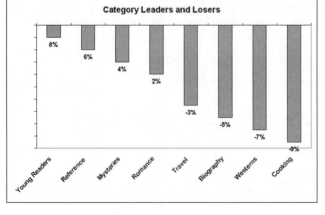

Figure 12-18:
Showing
plotted
values
when the
category
axis crosses
at the top.

Choosing the Display Units

On the Scale tab is an option to select how the values are formatted as a multiple of their true value. When plotting large numbers — in the hundreds, thousands, millions, or even larger — it is best to not display the large values along the value axis. They would simply take up a lot of room.

Instead, the large numbers are represented by a smaller number of digits, with a qualifier stating how the numbers are to be interpreted.

Figure 12-19 shows a chart with large numbers on the value axis. Although they could be formatted with commas, that would only increase the amount of room they occupy.

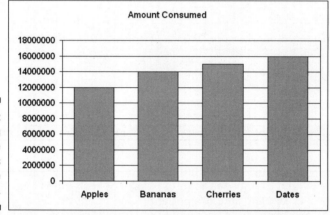

Figure 12-19:
Displaying
large
numbers
along the
value axis.

Excel to the rescue! Figure 12-20 shows where on the Scale tab of the Format Axis dialog box to select how the numbers are to be interpreted.

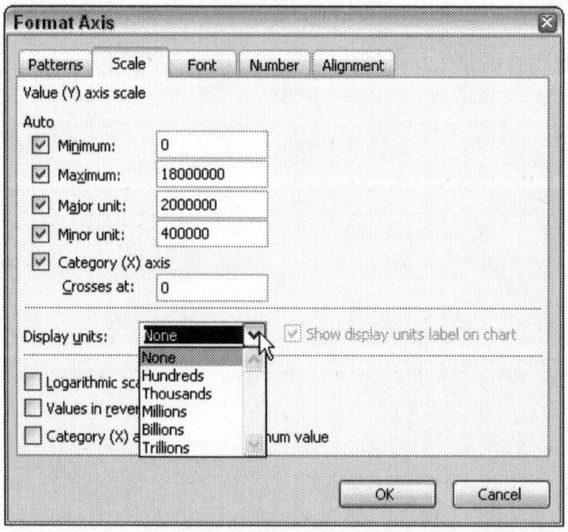

Figure 12-20:
Selecting
how large
numbers
should be
displayed.

In the Display Units drop-down list are a handful of choices: None, Hundreds, Thousands, Millions, Billions, and Trillions. Hmm, you can use some really big numbers here! Figure 12-21 shows the result of selecting to display units as millions. Excel displays the numbers in such a way that they have effectively been divided by the selected unit label. The Show Display Units Label on Chart check box is used to have the actual unit name appear next to the axis.

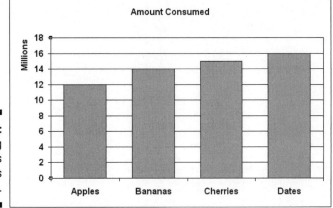

Amount Consumed

Figure 12-21:
Displaying
the numbers
as millions
of units.

If Show Display Units Label on Chart is left unchecked, you can always add a label later as inserted text. Also a custom number format can be applied to the axis. This is done on the Number tab. See the Excel Help system for information on custom number formats.

Applying a Logarithmic Scale

A logarithmic scale is useful when plotting values that fall in a wide range. Instead of values being flattened in some areas of the chart, a log scale treats the range of the value scale in powers of 10. That is, the scale starts at 1; the next major unit is 10; the next is 100; the next is 1,000; and so on. This scale plots data in a decidedly different manner.

Figure 12-22 shows the Scale tab and where to check to use a logarithmic scale.

Figure 12-23 shows two Line charts that plot the same source data. Most of the data on the upper chart is unseen, because it remains flat along the bottom of the plot area — until there are values that can appear higher based on the value axis range. By contrast, the lower chart presents all the data, by using a logarithmic scale.

You can put any multiple of 10 as the major unit when using a logarithmic scale. For example, using a major unit of 1,000 causes the scale to increase in powers of 1,000. The first value is 1; then 1,000; then 1,000,000; and so on.

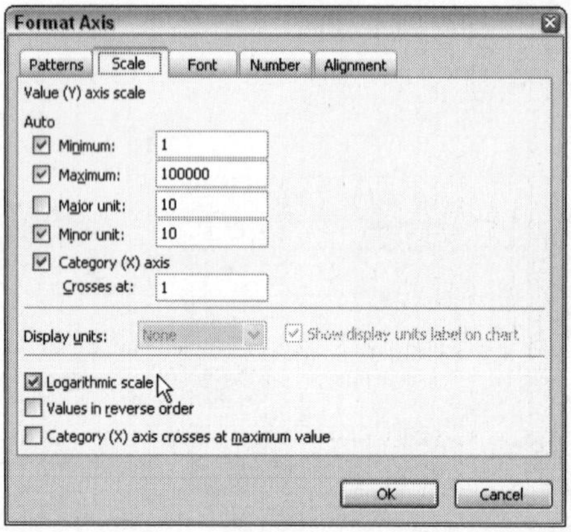

Figure 12-22:
Using a
logarithmic
scale.

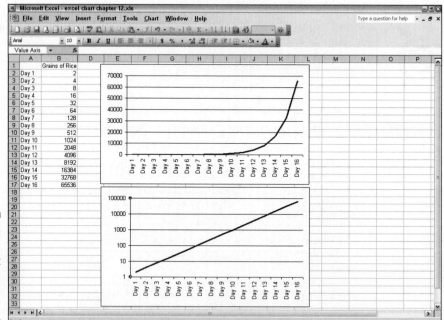

Figure 12-23:
Comparing
a straight
plot with a
logarithmic
plot.

Displaying the Values in Reverse Order

On the Scale tab you have the option to have the range of values appear in reverse order, which is a useful formatting option. Figure 12-24 shows a Bar chart with the Format Axis dialog box open with the Scale tab on top. Recall that a Bar chart has its value axis along the bottom. In the dialog box, the option to reverse the values is being set.

Figure 12-25 shows the result of reversing the values. The bars now plot from right to left, which could be a desired formatting technique.

Figure 12-26 shows an example of how reversed values can be useful. The chart in Figure 12-26 is a Combination chart (explained in greater detail in Chapter 17). In a nutshell, this particular chart compares terminations and registrations for the same time period. Each set of data is presented on its own set of bars. By plotting one of the sets in reverse order, the two sets fit on one chart without overlapping each other.

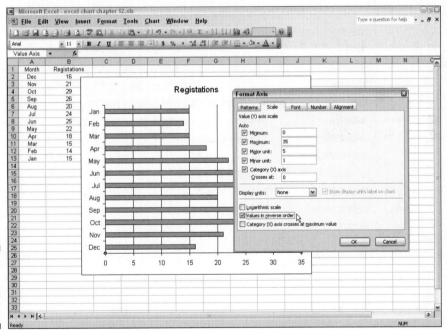

Figure 12-24:
Reversing
the values
on the axis.

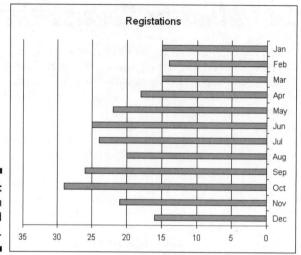

Figure 12-25:
A chart with reversed axis values.

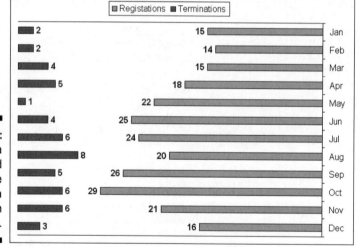

Figure 12-26:
Using a reversed value order in a Combination chart.

Chapter 13

Formatting the Data Series

● ●

In This Chapter

▶ Formatting line styles and using markers

▶ Apply formatting to individual data points

▶ Using high-low lines, up-down bars, and drop lines

▶ Formatting the border and area

▶ Using overlap and gap-width settings

▶ Placing series lines on stacked charts

● ●

A good amount of chart formatting is applied to the chart as a whole. Formatting the chart area or the plot area provides attributes that are not related or dependent or drawn from individual data. Formatting an axis does involve the data, but even so, it may involve generally all the data.

In contrast, formatting a data series involves, well, just the individual data series! Some charts have a single data series, and others have multiple series. Figure 13-1 shows a line chart with three data series; each line is a series.

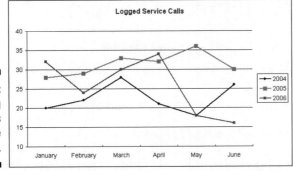

Figure 13-1:
Plotting
three series
in a line
chart.

With three lines on a chart, you need some way to differentiate among the lines. You do this with color, line weight, line style, and *markers* (little shapes — such as squares, circles, or triangles — that are placed at each data point in a plotted line). With the use of these visual aids, the appearance of each series is unique.

Not all chart types support markers. In chart types that use lines (Line, Scatter, and Radar charts), using markers is an option. In chart types that plot the data point in a way that covers area, such as Column or Bar charts, the data series are formatted with borders and interior colors, gradients, and so on. In this chapter, I show you how to format both types of data series, as well as how to format Pie and Doughnut charts, and more!

Formatting the Data Series for Line, XY (Scatter), and Radar Charts

Line, XY (Scatter), and Radar chart types all use lines as the means to connect data points. Each data series line can be individually formatted. The data points themselves can be formatted with markers.

Changing the line style, color, and weight

There are three formatting attributes used to distinguish lines from each other:

- **Style:** Solid, dashed, and so forth
- **Color:** Selected from a palette
- **Weight:** Thin, medium, thick, and so forth

Figure 13-2 shows a Line chart in which the data series format options are presented in the Format Data Series dialog box.

In the left side of the Patterns tab is where line attributes are set. You'll find three options near the top:

- **Automatic:** Excel formats the data series line.
- **None:** The line is not shown in the chart (although the data points themselves can still be visible).
- **Custom:** You set the style, color, and weight of the line.

Here's how to format a series line:

1. **Create a Line (or Scatter or Radar) chart, or open a workbook that has a chart that uses lines.**

2. **Double-click directly on one of the lines.**

   The Format Data Series dialog box appears.

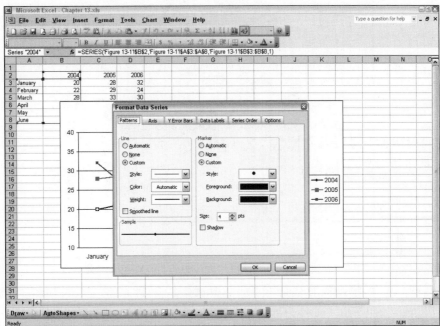

Figure 13-2:
Formatting
options for
a line.

If the Format Data Point dialog box opened instead, that means you may have performed two successive single clicks, instead of one double-click. Close the dialog box and try again double-clicking on a line.

3. **Click the Patterns tab to bring it to the top, if it isn't already.**

4. **Select the Custom option in the Line section on the left side of the Patterns tab.**

5. **Make selections of style, color, and weight.**

   Figure 13-3 shows where I'm selecting to change the color of a line.

6. **Click OK to close the dialog box and complete the change.**

Make sure each line is formatted in a unique way or else you won't be able to tell which line belongs to which data series.

Note that there is a formatting option to smooth out a line. In the Format Data Series dialog box is the Smoothed Line check box. Figure 13-4 shows the result of selecting a smoothed line. Compare the line in Figure 13-4 with the one in Figure 13-1.

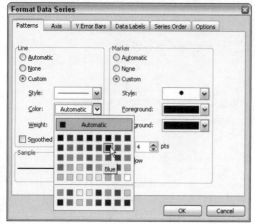

Figure 13-3:
Changing
the color of
a series line.

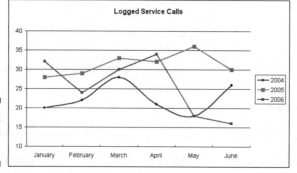

Figure 13-4:
Smoothing
a line.

Changing the marker style, foreground, and background

If you want, you can use markers to emphasize the actual data points. If you don't use them, the data points will appear as simple points and won't stand out at all along the line. If the line is formatted to not be visible, the data points can be seen.

On the other hand, when a line is used (which is more often than not), using markers helps make the data points stand out.

You format markers in the right side of the Patterns tab of the Format Series dialog box. As you can see in Figure 13-2, the right side of the tab has the Marker section. In it are three options:

✔ **Automatic:** Excel formats the marker.

✔ **None:** The marker is not used.

✔ **Custom:** You set the style, foreground color, background color, size, and shadow for the marker.

The marker styles are presented in a drop-down list. Figure 13-5 shows a marker style being selected.

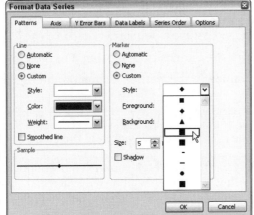

Figure 13-5:
Selecting a
marker
style.

Some of the marker styles have a character, such as a cross. The foreground color sets the color for the character. The background color sets the color for the marker itself. In Figure 13-6, I purposely selected a marker style with a cross character, formatted to white. The background of the marker is set to black, and I set the size to an overwhelming 20. You wouldn't typically set the marker to such a large size, but I've done so here in the hope that you can see the white cross on black.

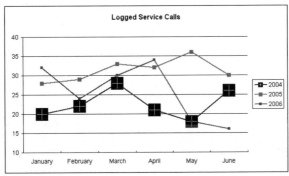

Figure 13-6:
Viewing a
marker's
foreground
and
background
colors.

All three data series in the chart in Figure 13-1 have markers.

Here's how to format a marker:

1. **Create a Line (or Scatter or Radar) chart, or open a workbook that has a chart that uses lines.**

2. **Double-click directly on one of the lines.**

   This opens the Format Data Series dialog box.

   If the Format Data Point dialog box opened instead, that means you may have performed two successive single clicks, instead of one double-click. Close the dialog box and try again double-clicking on a line.

3. **If it isn't on top, click the Patterns tab to bring it to the top.**

4. **Select the Custom option in the Marker section on the right side of the Patterns tab.**

5. **Make selections of style, foreground, background, size, and shadow.**

6. **Click OK to close the dialog box and complete the change.**

Although in the preceding instructions I tell you to avoid working on a single data point, working on a single data point can be quite useful. I cover it in the "Formatting Individual Data Points" section later in this chapter.

Using high-low lines to emphasize the highest and lowest values per category

On a Line chart with multiple series, high-low lines can be used to point out the range covered between the highest and lowest values per category. Figure 13-7 shows a Line chart in which high-low lines have been used.

High-low lines are an option only on Line charts.

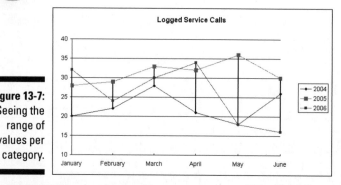

Figure 13-7: Seeing the range of values per category.

The high-low lines make it easy to garner a couple of facts about the chart in Figure 13-7:

- ✔ March shows the smallest range of values, and this coincides with the highest value in the 2004 series. This piece of information could be relevant.

- ✔ May has the largest range of values, and yet this occurs when the 2006 series is *not* at its lowest (2006 is lowest in June). You may draw the conclusion that the large range is more likely caused by the high value for the 2005 series, more than for the low value of the 2006 series. This type of information could be relevant.

High-low lines are set on the Options tab of the Format Data Series dialog box. Here's how to set high-low lines:

1. **Create a Line chart with multiple series, or open a workbook that has one.**

2. **Double-click on a series line.**

   The Format Data Series dialog box appears.

3. **Click on the Options tab to bring it to the top.**

   Figure 13-8 shows what the Options tab looks like.

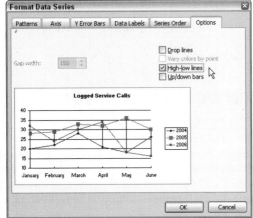

Figure 13-8:
The Options
tab.

4. **Check the High-Low Lines check box.**

5. **Click OK to close the dialog box and see the change in the chart.**

You can format high-low lines. To do this, follow these steps:

1. **Double-click directly on one of the high-low lines.**

   The Format High-Low Lines dialog box, shown in Figure 13-9, appears.

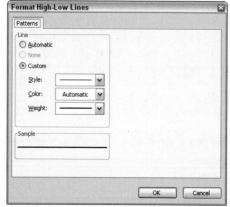

2. **Select the Custom option and change any of the style, color, or weight settings.**

3. **Click OK to close the dialog box and see the changes on the chart.**

To remove the high-low lines, right-click on one of them and then select Clear from the pop-up menu.

Using up-down bars to accentuate the first and last series

On a Line chart with multiple series, you can use up-down bars to show the range between the first and last series, at each category. With three or more series, it isn't necessarily clear which of the series are the first and last. The up-down bars traverse the space between the first and last series, so there is no doubt where these two series are.

Up-down bars are only an option on Line charts.

Up-down bars have been set in the chart in Figure 13-10. The bars have a certain width and a certain color. The bars, at each category, connect the 2004 series with the 2006 series. For January, February, March, and April, the bars are white. In May, the 2004 and 2006 value is the same and no bar is present. For June, the bar is black. When the last series, at any given category, has a higher value than the first series, the bar is white. In June, the 2006 value is lower than the 2004 value, resulting in a black bar.

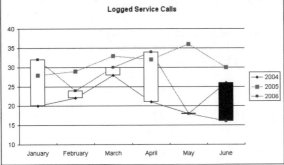

Figure 13-10:
Using up-down bars to connect the first and last series.

Here's how to use up-down bars:

1. **Create a Line chart with multiple series, or open a workbook that has one.**

2. **Double-click on a series line.**

   The Format Data Series dialog box, shown in Figure 13-11, appears.

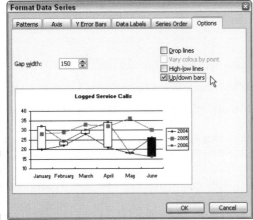

Figure 13-11:
Using up-down bars.

3. **Click on the Options tab to bring it to the top.**

4. **Check the Up/Down Bars check box.**

   When you do this, the Gap Width setting becomes available. The Gap Width setting controls how much space is between the bars. A higher value increases the space, which shrinks the bars. A smaller value decreases the space, which widens the bars.

5. **You can select a Gap Width value (0 to 500) or just leave it as is.**

6. **Click OK to close the dialog box and see the change in the chart.**

You can format up-down bars, but there is a twist. You format the up bars (the white ones) separately from the down bars (the black ones). For example, here's how to format the up bars:

1. **Double-click directly on one of the up bars.**

   The Format Up Bars dialog box, shown in Figure 13-12, appears.

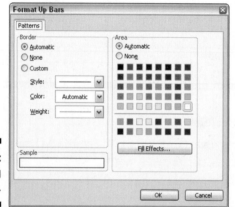

Figure 13-12: Formatting the up bars.

2. **Make any desired changes to the border and/or the area.**

   Clicking the Fill Effects button leads to further formatting options.

3. **Click OK to close the dialog box and see the changes on the chart.**

To remove the up-down bars, right-click on one of them and then select Clear from the pop-up menu.

Formatting the Data Series for Bar, Column, and Area Charts

The data points in Bar, Column, and Area charts all take up an area of space, so these data point types have a border and an interior area that you can format.

Changing the border style, color, and weight

Figure 13-13 shows the Format Data Series dialog box opened over a column chart. On the Patterns tab of the dialog box are two sections: Border and Area.

There are three formatting attributes that you can apply to borders:

- **Style:** Solid, dashed, and so forth
- **Color:** Selected from a palette
- **Weight:** Thin, medium, thick, and so forth

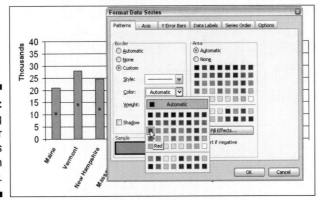

Figure 13-13:
Formatting
the border
of the series
in a Column
chart.

In Figure 13-13, the border for the data series is being formatted to a thick solid red line. Figure 13-14 shows how the chart looks after the border formatting is applied.

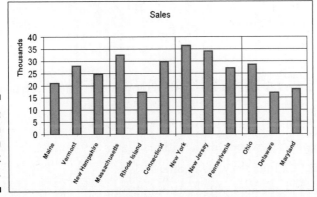

Figure 13-14:
The data
series with
a thick
border.

Here's how to format the border of a data series:

1. **Double-click directly on a data series,** or right-click and choose Format Data Series.

   The Format Data Series dialog box appears.

2. **If it isn't on top, click the Patterns tab to bring it to the top.**

3. **Select the Custom option in the Border section on the left side of the Patterns tab.**

4. **Make selections of style, color, and weight.**

5. **Click OK to close the dialog box and see the changes on the chart.**

Formatting the data series area

The area of the data points have more formatting options:

✔ **Automatic:** Excel provides the formatting.

✔ **None:** The area of the data points is empty (although the border may still be present). Figure 13-15 shows how the chart looks with the thick border but empty data-point areas.

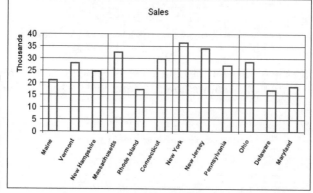

Figure 13-15: Presenting data points with no area and a thick border.

✔ **Solid Color:** Clicking on one of the colors in the palette on the Patterns tab fills the area of the data points with that color.

✔ **Gradient:** Fills the area with either a predesigned or a custom gradient.

✔ **Texture:** Fills the area with a texture.

✔ **Pattern:** Fills the area with a pattern.

✔ **Picture:** Fills the area with a custom picture.

Clicking the Fill Effects button leads to where gradients, textures, patterns, and pictures are set. See Chapter 9 for a complete discussion on how to use gradients, textures, patterns, and pictures.

Figure 13-16 shows where a gradient is being applied to the data series area. The Fill Effects dialog box opens when you click the Fill Effects button in the Format Data Series dialog box.

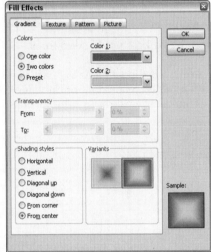

Figure 13-16: Setting a gradient.

Figure 13-17 shows the chart in which the data series area is formatted with a gradient.

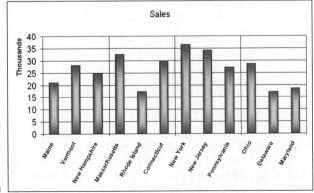

Figure 13-17: Viewing the gradient.

Here's how to format the area of a data series:

1. **Double-click directly on a data series.**

   The Format Data Series dialog box appears.

2. **Click the Patterns tab to bring it to the top, if it isn't already.**

3. **On the right side of the Patterns tab, select a solid color from the palette, or click the Fill Effects button to set a gradient, texture, pattern, or picture.**

4. **Click OK to close the dialog box and see the changes on the chart.**

   If you opened the Fill Effects dialog box, you'll need to click OK twice.

Just one more for the show: Figure 13-18 shows an Area chart in which the series area has been filled in with a picture. The data point values wind lower and lower to support the point of the chart — showing where your money goes.

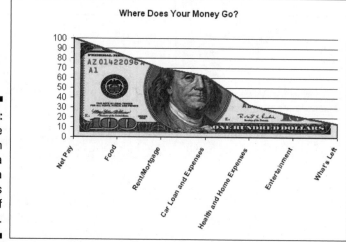

Figure 13-18:
You can use
a picture in
the data
series area
to stress
the point of
the chart.

Adjusting the overlap and gap width on Bar and Column charts

In Bar and Column charts, you can control the placement and size of the bars or columns. Figure 13-19 shows a Bar chart in which the Format Data Series dialog box is open with the Options tab on top. This is where the overlap and gap width are set:

✔ **Overlap:** Controls how the bars or columns from multiple series, at the categories, are placed relative to each other. Overlap only has an effect with multiple series. The possible value for this setting is –100 to 100.

✔ **Gap Width:** Controls how much space is between columns or bars, at different categories. The possible value for this setting is 0 to 500. A larger number means more space is between the bars or columns, resulting in them being narrower.

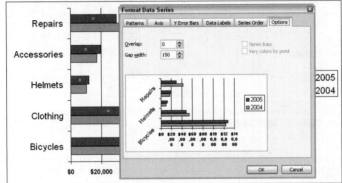

Figure 13-19:
Setting the overlap and gap width.

Figure 13-20 shows four charts that are identical other than the overlap and gap width:

Chart	Overlap	Gap Width
A	0	150
B	–50	150
C	50	150
D	0	0

Here's how to set overlap and gap width:

1. **On a Bar or Column chart, double-click directly on a bar or column.**

   The Format Data Series dialog box appears.

2. **Click the Options tab to bring it to the top.**

3. **Enter settings for the overlap and/or the gap width.**

4. **Click OK to close the dialog box and see the changes on the chart.**

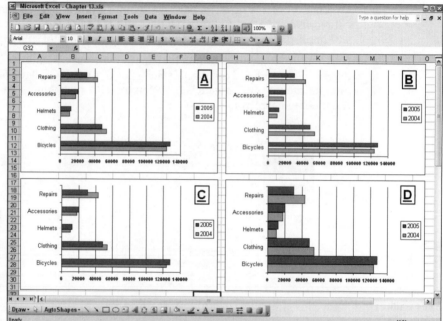

Figure 13-20:
Comparing
overlap and
gap width
on four
charts.

Formatting Individual Data Points

Excel provides a nice feature of allowing individual data points to be separately
formatted. This feature is really useful, because it lets you highlight key elements of your data. Also, for most chart types, you can check a box that simply
applies a different color to each data point. No fuss, no muss — simple as 1-2-3.

Working with individual data points

Figure 13-21 shows a Bar chart in which just one bar is selected. You can tell
this because it's the only bar with handles (little black boxes) around it.

Selecting and formatting an individual data point marker takes a little mouse
finesse. Here's how you do it:

1. **Click once on a data point.**

2. **Wait a moment and then click on it again.**

   You're waiting in between clicks to avoid a double-click.

3. **When the single data point is selected, double-click it.**

   The Format Data Point dialog box appears.

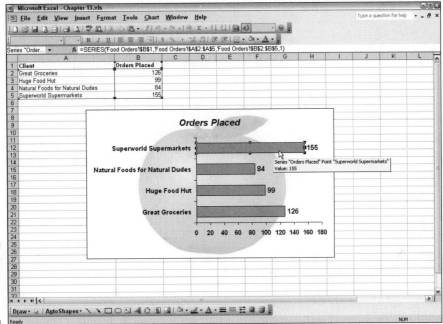

4. **Click the Patterns tab to bring it to the top.**

5. **Make any desired formatting changes.**

6. **Click OK to close the dialog box and see the changes on the chart.**

Figure 13-22 shows the Format Data Point dialog box in which a new color is being selected for the individual data point, as well as a border.

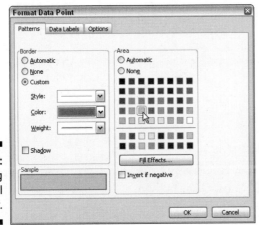

Figure 13-23 shows the change in the individual bar.

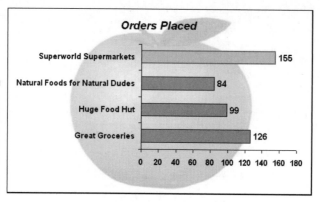

Figure 13-23:
The chart with an individually formatted data point.

Varying colors by point

Another option to differentiate data points is to simply let Excel apply a different color to each point. This option is available in the Format Data Series dialog box:

1. **Double-click a data series to open the Format Data Series dialog box.**

2. **Click the Options tab to bring it to the top.**

3. **Check the Vary Colors by Point check box (see Figure 13-24).**

4. **Click OK to close the dialog box and see the changes in the chart.**

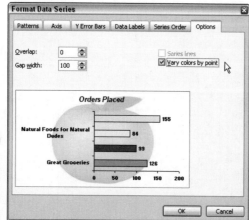

Figure 13-24:
Varying the colors of the data points.

Figure 13-25 shows how the chart looks with different data-point colors.

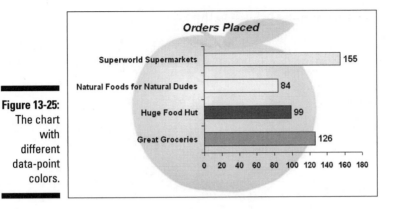

Figure 13-25:
The chart
with
different
data-point
colors.

Using Formatting Line Options

There are a couple of line treatments that help focus on data values in certain types of charts. *Drop lines* work by placing a line from the data point to the category. They're available for Line and Area charts. *Series lines* are lines that connect the data points in stacked charts.

Applying drop lines

Figure 13-26 shows an Area chart in which drop lines have been applied. The lines extend from the data points in the topmost series down to the category axis.

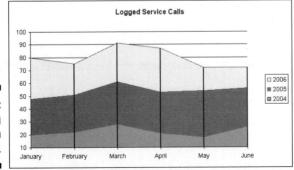

Figure 13-26:
Viewing
drop lines in
a chart.

Here's how to use drop lines:

1. In a Line chart or Area chart, double-click a series.

The Format Data Series dialog box appears.

2. **Click the Options tab to bring it to the top.**

3. **Check the Drop Lines check box, as shown in Figure 13-27.**

4. **Click OK to close the dialog box and see the changes on the chart.**

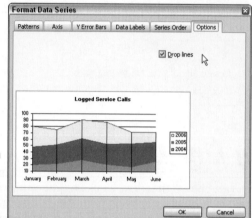

Figure 13-27:
Using drop
lines.

You can format a drop line by right-clicking on it and selecting to open the Format Drop Lines dialog box.

Using series lines

Series lines are a formatting option available only with stacked Bar and Column charts. Their purpose is to emphasize the range of values among the stacked series at each category.

Here's how to make a series line:

1. **Create a stacked Bar or Column chart, or open a workbook that has one.**

2. **Double-click on a series point.**

   The Format Data Series dialog box appears.

3. **Click the Options tab to bring it to the top.**

4. **Check the Series lines check box (see Figure 13-28).**

5. **Click OK to close the dialog box and see the changes in the chart.**

Figure 13-29 shows how my chart looks with series lines.

You can format a series line by right-clicking on it and selecting to open the Format Series Lines dialog box.

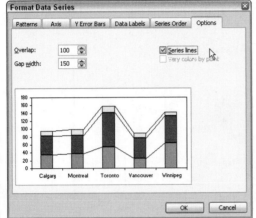

Figure 13-28: Selecting to use series lines.

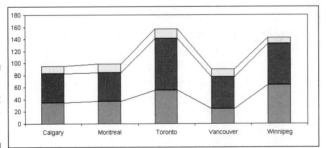

Figure 13-29: The chart with series lines.

Series lines are an option only on stacked Bar and Column charts.

Formatting Pie Charts and Doughnut Charts

Pie charts and Doughnut charts are similar — after all, they're both named after desserts! What's more, you can separate the individual data points into separate slices.

Not only can the data points (markers) in Pie charts and Doughnut charts be individually formatted (see the "Formatting Individual Data Points" section, earlier in this chapter), but they can also be individually placed.

Moving individual slices

Figure 13-30 shows a Pie chart in which one individual data point (a slice) has been selected. Clicking once on the slice selects the whole pie. Clicking a second time on the slice selects just the slice.

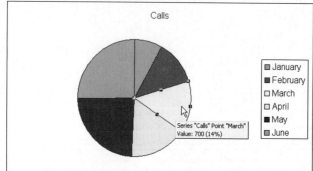

Figure 13-30:
Selecting
a single
pie slice.

After the slice is selected, you can move it by clicking once on it, holding down the mouse button, and dragging the slice out from the center. Figure 13-31 shows this being done.

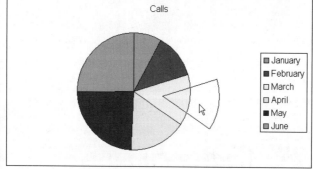

Figure 13-31:
Dragging a
pie slice
away from
the center.

After you release the mouse button, the slice is in a new location, as shown in Figure 13-32.

You can independently place each slice in a new location, as shown in Figure 13-33.

The pie slices can only be moved away from or back toward the center. You cannot arbitrarily move the slices around the plot area or chart area.

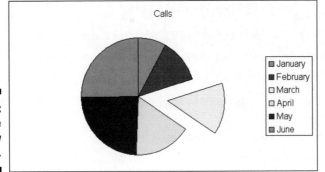

Figure 13-32:
The slice
in a new
location.

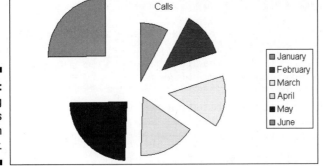

Figure 13-33:
Spreading
the slices
away from
the center.

You can also move individual slices in Doughnut charts. Figure 13-34 shows a Doughnut chart in which an individual data point has been moved away from the center.

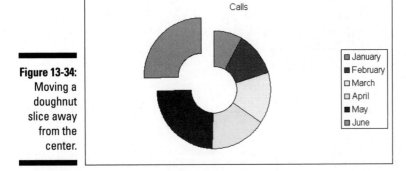

Figure 13-34:
Moving a
doughnut
slice away
from the
center.

Here's how to move individual pie or doughnut slices:

1. **On a Pie or Doughnut chart, click once on a data point.**

2. **Wait a moment and then click on the data point again.**

   You're waiting in between clicks to avoid a double-click.

3. **When the single data point is selected, click on it and hold down the mouse button.**

4. **Drag the slice away from or toward the center.**

5. **Release the mouse button.**

Rotating the Pie or Doughnut

A formatting option is available for Pie and Doughnut charts to rotate the chart by setting the angle of the first slice. The setting does not change any angles of the slices relative to each other — it just lets you position the sequence of slices along the circumference.

Here's how to rotate a Pie or Doughnut chart:

1. **On a Pie or Doughnut chart, double-click on a data point.**

   The Format Data Series dialog box appears.

2. **Click the Options tab to bring it to the top.**

3. **Select a value for the Angle of First Slice.**

   Possible values are between 0 and 360 — in other words, the full rotation of a circle.

4. **Click OK to close the dialog box and see the change in the chart.**

When formatting a Doughnut chart, you can also specify how large the doughnut hole is. The possible values are from 10 percent (a very small hole) to 90 percent (a very large hole).

Chapter 14

Working With 3-D Views

*Y*ou have to admit it — 3-D charts look *really* cool! That said, they do occasionally have a bad reputation for distorting the facts. In this chapter, I tell you a bit about that distortion. But I also show you how to master 3-D charts and twist them into works of art that do the data justice.

Working with 3-D charts really just requires a basic understanding of height, width, and depth. Along the way, I show you how to rotate and set the elevation for a chart. 3-D charts have a few other settings as well. Figure 14-1 shows the 3-D View dialog box, in which you can change the 3-D settings. You can access that dialog box by selecting a chart and choosing Chart ➪ 3-D View.

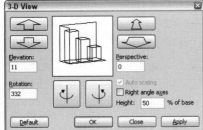

Figure 14-1:
The
3-D View
dialog box.

The 3-D View menu item is only available when the selected chart is a 3-D chart. If the 3-D View menu item is disabled, first change the chart type to a 3-D type by choosing Chart ➪ Chart Type.

Not all chart types are available in a 3-D subtype, and not all charts that are available in 3-D have all the same settings. Table 14-1 lists the charts that have 3-D subtypes. Note that the Cylinder, Cone, and Pyramid chart types are not included in Table 14-1 even though they have 3-D subtypes, because they're just variations of Bar and Column charts.

The Apply button in the 3-D View dialog box lets you see how your settings affect the chart without having to close the dialog box.

Table 14-1	Chart Types That Support 3-D Views
Chart Type	*3-D Adjustable Settings*
Column	Elevation, rotation, perspective, right-angle axes, height percent of base
Bar	Elevation, rotation, height percent of base
Line	Elevation, rotation, perspective, right-angle axes, height percent of base
Area	Elevation, rotation, perspective, right-angle axes, height percent of base
Pie	Elevation, rotation, height percent of base
Surface	Elevation, rotation, perspective, right-angle axes, height percent of base

Bubble charts have a subtype that gives the bubbles a 3-D effect. This is not the same as a 3-D chart.

The types of settings that are applicable to 3-D charts are summarized in Table 14-2.

Table 14-2	3-D Attributes	
Setting	*What It Does*	*Possible Values*
Elevation	Adjusts the over and under view.	–90 to 90 for Column, Line, Area, and Surface charts; 0 to 44 for Bar charts; 10 to 80 for Pie charts.
Rotation	Adjusts the left and right view.	0 to 360 for Column, Line, Pie, Area, and Surface charts; 0 to 44 for Bar charts.

Setting	What It Does	Possible Values
Perspective	Controls the effect of the closer part of a chart appearing larger and the farther part of a chart appearing smaller. This effect could be an enhancement or a detriment to the appearance of a chart, depending on how the effect appears given the settings for the other 3-D attributes.	0 to 100 for Column, Line, Area, and Surface charts. The effect is not available for Bar or Pie charts.
Right-Angle Axes	Overrides the perspective effect and forces the x-axis and y-axis to meet at a right angle. When the Right-Angle Axes box is checked, the option to set perspective is not visible.	As a check box, available for Column, Line, Area, and Surface charts.
Height % of Base	Controls the height of the 3-D data series. The setting works by gauging the height of the series as a percentage of the base of the chart floor or plot area.	5 to 500 for Bar, Column, Line, Pie, Area, and Surface charts.
Auto Scaling	Overrides the Height % of Base setting. When applied, Excel adjusts the height and width ratio.	As a check box, available for Column, Bar, Line, Area, and Surface charts.

Raising and Lowering a Chart's Elevation

The elevation setting formats the vertical view of a 3-D chart. For most 3-D charts, the range of –90 to 90 allows you to literally look at a chart straight up from the bottom to straight down from the top, or anywhere in between. Figure 14-2 shows four charts that plot the same data. The elevation is different in each chart, while all other settings are identical.

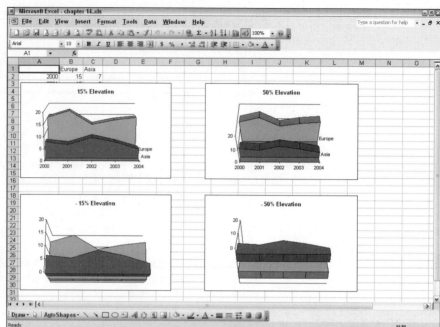

Figure 14-2:
Reviewing
different
elevation
settings.

The four charts in Figure 14-2 are respectively set at 15% elevation, 50% elevation, –15% elevation, and –50% elevation. The two charts on the right side of Figure 14-2 (50% and –50%) show the view on the way to being completely over or under — as a 90% or –90% setting would do. The chart in Figure 14-3 gets close to that. In Figure 14-3, the chart is at a 75% elevation, which is almost like looking straight down at the chart.

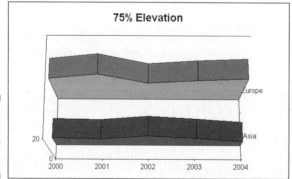

Figure 14-3:
Taking a
high view
of a chart.

Bar and Pie charts do not have a full range of settings to turn a chart from top to bottom. Figure 14-4 shows elevation variations for a Pie chart.

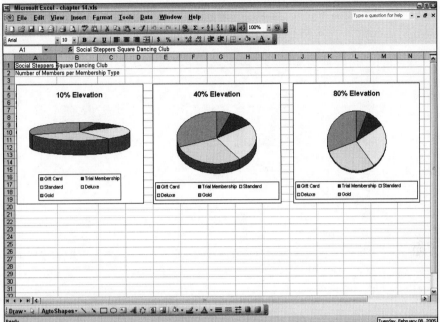

Figure 14-4:
Looking at
Pie chart
elevations.

Here's how to adjust the elevation of a 3-D chart:

1. **Create and select a 3-D chart, or open a workbook with a 3-D chart and select it.**

2. **Choose Chart ⇨ 3-D View.**

   The 3-D View dialog box appears.

3. **Adjust the elevation setting.**

   Refer to Table 14-2 to see which values can be used.

4. **Click OK to close the dialog box and see the change in the chart.**

Rotating a Chart

Rotating a chart moves it left or right. A complete 360 degrees of rotation is available for all 3-D charts, except the Bar chart. Figure 14-5 shows a chart formatted with different rotation settings.

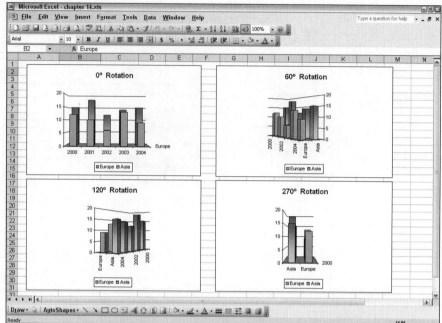

Figure 14-5:
You can
rotate your
chart left
or right.

The charts in Figure 14-5 respectively have 0 degrees rotation, 60 degrees rotation, 120 degrees rotation, and 270 degrees rotation. Here are some important points to consider:

✔ The 0-degree rotation view is acceptable because the frontmost series is smaller than the series behind it. If this weren't the case, the series in the back would not be seen. (An adjustment of the elevation or changing the series order could compensate for this.)

✔ The 60-degree rotation view serves this data well because both series are easy to see.

✔ The 120-degree view hides most of the lesser-valued series. This is not a good situation.

✔ The 270-degree view does not create a conflict of the two series, but instead makes seeing all the data points within each individual series possible. Even adding a change to the elevation setting will not help much.

Rotation values of 0 degrees, 90 degrees, 180 degrees, and 270 degrees often obscure data.

Figure 14-6 shows a mix of rotation and elevation that work together to present the two series. The rotation is set at 10 degrees — more or less a nudge away from looking at the data flat on. The elevation is set at 25%.

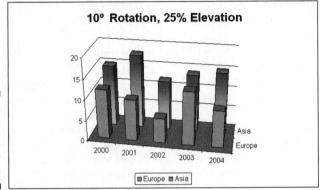

Here's how to adjust the rotation of a 3-D chart:

1. **Create and select a 3-D chart, or open a workbook with a 3-D chart and select it.**

2. **Choose Chart ⇨ 3-D View.**

   The 3-D View dialog box appears.

3. **Adjust the rotation setting.**

   Refer to Table 14-2 to see which values can be used.

4. **Click OK to close the dialog box and see the change in the chart.**

Although you can adjust the rotation of a Pie chart, the effect does nothing other than to spin the pie around; it doesn't make it any easier or harder to see data slices.

Adjusting the Perspective

Picture a classic example of the perspective effect: parallel lines that seem to come together in the distance.

Perspective provides charts with an effect of objects that are closer appearing larger and those that are farther away appearing smaller; in other words, perspective can add depth to a chart. This, of course, simulates the way you see things out in the world. Charts don't necessarily need this treatment, but it is available for you to use.

Figure 14-7 shows the same Column chart plotted twice. All settings are the same except for perspective:

- ✔ The chart on the left has a perspective setting of 0. All the columns are the same size, and there is no perception of depth.

- ✔ The chart on the right has a perspective setting of 100 (the maximum setting). The columns seem to shrink in size, looking from front to back.

The charts in Figure 14-7 show the perspective as applied to a series of data points (the columns). Figure 14-8 shows another example of perspective. The same Line chart is plotted twice. The chart on the left has a low perspective setting of 30. The chart on the right has a full perspective setting of 100. The lines in the chart on the right seem to be heading slightly toward each other. This is a common depth perception, such as when railway tracks seem to converge in the distance.

The use of perspective can work against you. As shown in Figure 14-7, the use of perspective makes it seem that the data points are not equal in value, although in fact they're identical.

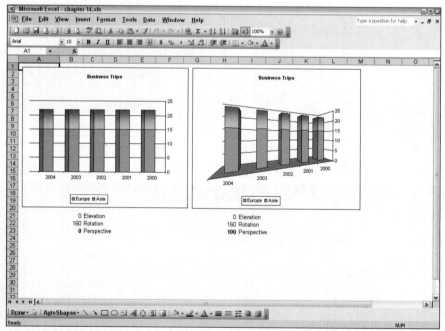

Figure 14-7: Comparing perspective settings on a Column chart.

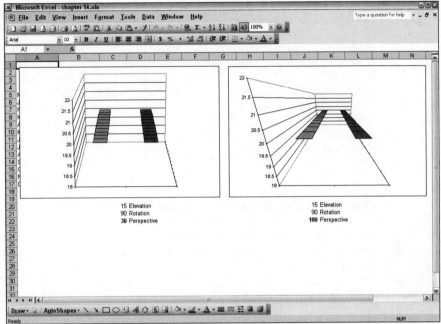

Figure 14-8:
Comparing
perspective
settings on
a Line chart.

Here's how to adjust the perspective of a 3-D chart:

1. **Create and select a 3-D chart, or open a workbook with a 3-D chart and select it.**

2. **Choose Chart ➪ 3-D View.**

   The 3-D View dialog box appears.

3. **Adjust the perspective setting.**

   Refer to Table 14-2 to see which values can be used.

4. **Click OK to close the dialog box and see the change in the chart.**

Forcing Right-Angle Axes

In the 3-D View dialog box is a check box to force Right-Angle Axes. When this box is checked, the X and Y axes are realigned to a right angle. Also, the ability to adjust perspective is disabled. Perspective often distorts the axes, so forcing a right angle to the axes, and using perspective, are mutually exclusive. That is, you can use one or the other.

Applying Scaling

Scaling controls the height of 3-D charts. However the scaling does not strictly control height in a vacuum. Instead, the setting is of the ratio between the height of the chart and the size of the chart's base. There isn't actually a part of a chart strictly named the base; instead, it's often the *floor* of the chart. (You can easily see the floor of the chart in Figure 14-6 — it's the gray area underneath the columns.) Even this is not consistent; for example Pie charts do not have a floor yet still have a scaling setting that involves the base. Just think of the base as the "bottom" of the chart.

Adjusting scaling manually

You can manually set scaling whenever the Auto Scaling check box is cleared. Then, a value between 5 and 500 can be entered — that's a big range of values to choose from.

In the 3-D View dialog box, the actual setting is Height % of Base. The value that goes in this entry box is the manual scaling percentage (the ratio of wall size to floor size).

Figure 14-9 shows the same chart four times but with differing scaling values: 20%, 50%, 100%, and 200%. You can eyeball how the values appear. In each chart, take a look at the size of the base and the height of the sides of the charts (known as the *walls*). You should be able to get a sense that the scaling percentage matches the ratio of wall to floor (or base). That is, for example, the 20% chart shows walls that are 20% the size of the floor.

Figure 14-10 gives another example of manual scaling, this time with a Pie chart. The chart is presented four times with differing scale values: 5%, 100%, 200%, and 500%. Manual scaling is a useful attribute to apply to 3-D Pie charts, because you can really shape the pie from a pancake to a large cylinder.

Here's how to manually set the scaling of a 3-D chart:

1. **Create and select a 3-D chart, or open a workbook with a 3-D chart and select it.**

2. **Choose Chart ⇨ 3-D View.**

   The 3-D View dialog box appears.

3. **Enter a value between 5 and 500 in the Height % of Base entry box.**

4. **Click OK to close the dialog box and see the change in the chart.**

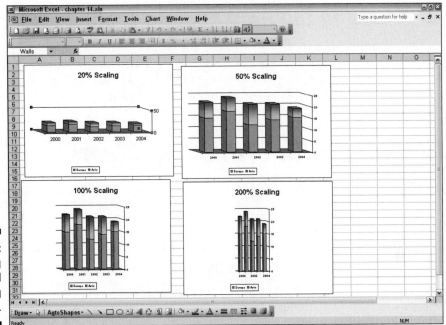

Figure 14-9:
Viewing
manual
scaling
settings.

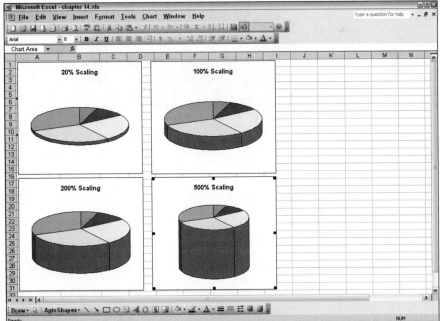

Figure 14-10:
Different
scale
settings
applied to a
Pie chart.

Using the Auto Scaling feature

When the Auto Scaling check box is checked, Excel determines a scaling percentage. This value is not presented in the Height % of Base entry box. Auto scaling is only enabled when the Right-Angle Axes check box is checked. *Note:* Auto Scaling is not an option for Pie charts.

Working With Walls and Floors

For the most part, 3-D charts have walls and floors. The walls are the sides of the chart, and the floor is the bottom. Walls and floors can be formatted. Follow along on a chart of your own as I show you how to format it:

1. **Create a 3-D chart, or open a workbook with a 3-D chart.**

2. **Right-click on a wall of the chart.**

   A pop-up menu appears, as shown in Figure 14-11.

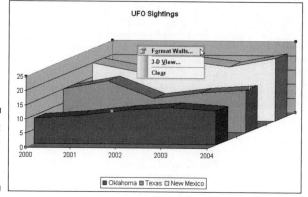

Figure 14-11: Preparing to format the walls.

3. **Select Format Walls from the pop-up menu.**

   The Format Walls dialog box, shown in Figure 14-12, appears.

4. **Select any desired formatting settings.**

5. **Click OK to close the dialog box and see the formatting.**

Figure 14-13 shows how my chart came out. I opted to format the walls with a gradient. Clicking on the Fill Effects button on the Format Walls dialog box had opened the Fill Effects dialog box, in which I selected the gradient. Also, I formatted the floor with a solid color.

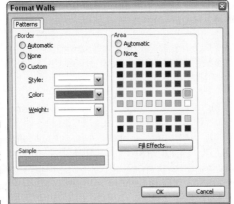

Figure 14-12:
The Format
Walls
dialog box.

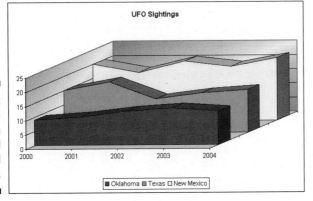

Figure 14-13:
Viewing the
chart with
formatted
walls and
floor.

The floor is formatted in the same way as the walls.

Adjusting 3-D Series Options

Some 3-D settings are found on the Options tab of the Format Series dialog box. The Gap Depth, Gap Width, and Chart Depth settings appear on the tab when working with a 3-D chart. Also, the chart type determines which of these settings is available. For example, 3-D Bar and Column charts have all three settings; 3-D Line charts and 3-D Area charts have Gap Depth and Chart Depth settings, but no Gap Width setting; and 3-D Pie charts have none of the settings.

Figure 14-14 shows the same chart four times. Various 3-D settings have been applied to each, but most notable is the Gap Width setting. The area data points have varying width. This is accomplished by raising or lowering the gap width, which does not actually alter the data points, but instead alters the amount of space between the data points.

The four charts in Figure 14-14 also have differing amounts of chart depth. The effect of chart depth is more subtle (that is, it generally just flattens a 3-D chart). Figure 14-15 shows this effect.

The three 3-D Line charts in Figure 14-15 have all the same parameters, except for the difference in the Chart Depth setting. From left to right, the chart depth is 100, 200, and 300. From left to right, each chart is becoming progressively flatter (that is, the height of the plot area is shrinking). Also, the width of the lines is increasing. This is not occurring because of any width setting, but rather because there is interaction between the various 3-D settings.

Often, a 3-D setting will seem to affect other chart attributes. A balance of settings, formatting, and some experimenting are needed to create the best-looking 3-D charts.

In Figure 14-16 are four 3-D bar charts that all plot the same data. The gap width and gap depth are the same in all the charts:

- The gap width is 5.
- The gap depth is 0.

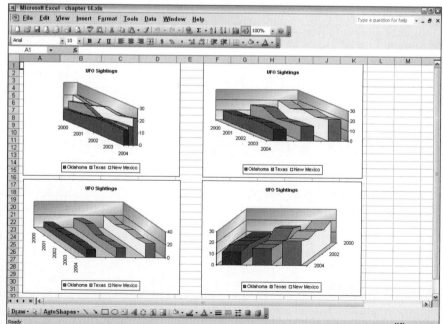

Figure 14-14:
Viewing various settings of Chart Depth and Gap Width.

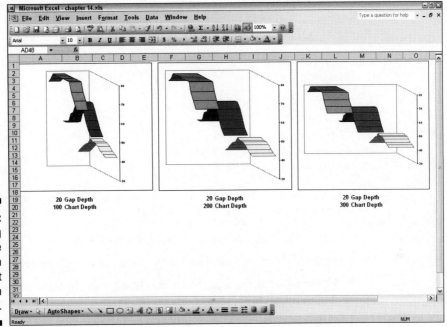

Figure 14-15:
Viewing
three line
charts with
different
Chart Depth
values.

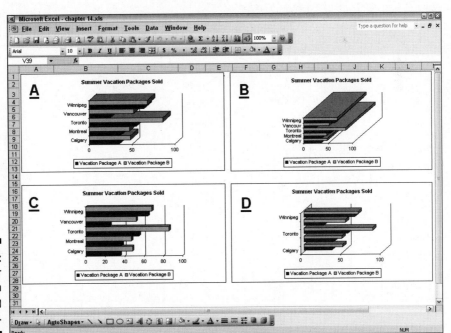

Figure 14-16:
Viewing Bar
charts with
varying
chart depth.

Each chart in Figure 14-16 has a different Chart Depth setting:

Chart	Chart Depth
A	500
B	1800
C	50
D	200

Not all series options are presented here. See Chapter 13 for other series options that are not pertinent for 3-D charts.

The best way to understand the interaction of the 3-D series option settings is to experiment! Here's how to work with the settings:

1. **Create a 3-D chart, or open a workbook with a 3-D chart.**

2. **Double-click directly on a series line, bar, column, or area.**

3. **Enter various values into the Chart Depth, Gap Depth, and Gap Width settings (not all settings may be available).**

4. **Click OK to close the dialog box and see the change in the chart.**

Chapter 15

Using AutoShapes and Graphics

In This Chapter

- Using the Drawing toolbar
- Placing AutoShapes in a chart
- Inserting arrows
- Figuring out how shapes and objects are stacked
- Placing text on a chart
- Inserting Word Art
- Searching for and inserting clip art
- Placing a photograph on a chart

Customizing charts is a great thing because it helps one chart look different from another. Really, why should my chart and your chart look alike? I don't mean the data, of course, but the chart elements — the look and feel of the chart.

This reasoning applies to items such as a company's logo, the name of a manager, other important information, and even visual aids, such as arrows. You can insert all these into an Excel chart. You have a batch of drawing tools at your disposal, and you can insert photographs and external art files. These goodies give you ways to make your charts look grand.

Most of the drawing tools and other features discussed in this chapter are found on the Drawing toolbar, shown in Figure 15-1. To display the toolbar, choose View ➪ Tools ➪ Drawing, or click the Drawing icon on the Standard toolbar.

Figure 15-1: Displaying the Drawing toolbar.

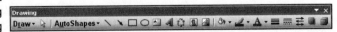

Inserting AutoShapes

The AutoShapes button on the Drawing toolbar leads to lists of shapes. There are many shapes, categorized as: Lines, Connectors, Basic Shapes, Block Arrows, Flowcharts, Stars and Banners, and Callouts. There is even a menu item for finding More AutoShapes. Figure 15-2 shows how a star is being selected to use on the chart.

Try this out for yourself. Here's how:

1. **If the Drawing toolbar is not visible, choose View ⇨ Tools ⇨ Drawing to display the toolbar.**

2. **Click the AutoShapes button and select a shape.**

   You can also choose Insert ⇨ Picture ⇨ AutoShapes to display the AutoShapes toolbar, from which you can insert AutoShapes.

   When you select a shape, the mouse pointer changes to a small cross.

3. **On the chart, click and hold down the mouse button.**

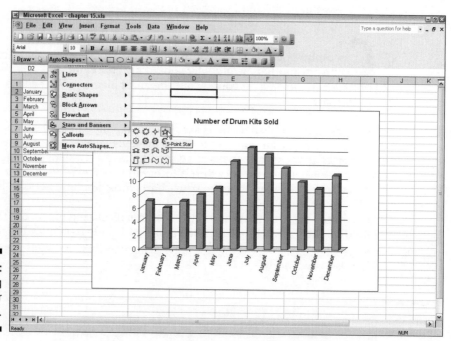

Figure 15-2:
Selecting
a star
AutoShape.

4. **Drag the mouse diagonally and the shape appears and resizes as you draw it.**

   Figure 15-3 shows how I drew a star on my chart.

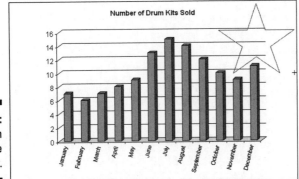

Number of Drum Kits Sold

Figure 15-3:
Drawing an
AutoShape
on the chart.

5. **Release the mouse button.**

   The shape fills with the default color.

You can format AutoShapes. Here's how:

1. **Double-click the AutoShape.**

   The Format AutoShape dialog box appears.

2. **Click the Colors and Lines tab to bring it to the top.**

3. **Make selections for the Fill and Line formats.**

   Figure 15-4 shows the selections I made to fill the star's area with a 50 percent transparent light blue, with a heavy red border.

4. **Click OK to close the dialog box and see the changes on the chart.**

Figure 15-5 shows the completed formatting of the AutoShape.

Holding down the Shift key while drawing an AutoShape keeps the shape's dimensions proportional.

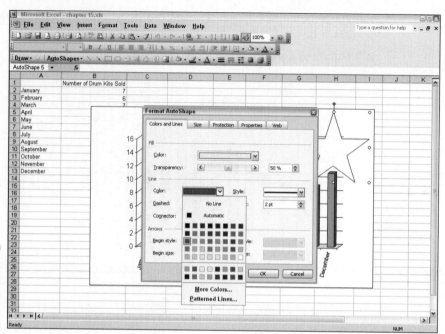

Figure 15-4:
Formatting
the
AutoShape.

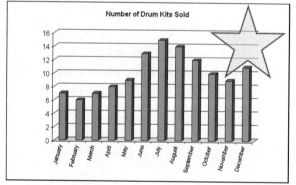

Figure 15-5:
The
formatted
AutoShape
on the chart.

Using Lines and Arrows

Lines and arrows are great for pointing things out. Figure 15-6 shows where to find the Arrow button on the Drawing toolbar. If you need just a plain line, the Line button is one button to the left on the Drawing toolbar.

To use an arrow, follow these steps:

1. Click the Arrow button on the Drawing toolbar.

The mouse pointer changes to a small cross.

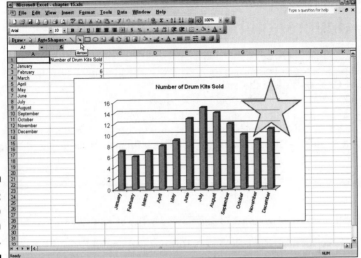

Figure 15-6:
Selecting to
draw an
arrow.

2. **On the chart, click and hold down the mouse button.**

3. **Drag the mouse and the arrow will appear and resize as you draw it.**

   Figure 15-7 shows how I drew an arrow on my chart.

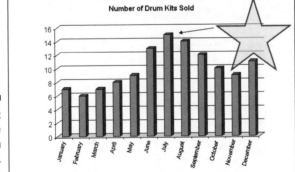

Figure 15-7:
Viewing the
arrow on
the chart.

4. **Release the mouse button.**

Lines, rectangles, and ovals are all inserted into a chart the same way as an arrow. Each has a button on the Drawing toolbar.

Here's how to format the arrow:

1. **Double-click directly on the arrow.**

   The Format AutoShape dialog box appears.

Understanding the order of objects

While working with AutoShapes (and other non-chart items such as clip art) you may notice them disappear! Click outside of the chart to bring them back. There is a depth order to objects. A shape may sit on top of a chart or behind it. One object may be situated between another object and the chart, so it becomes covered up.

Objects are stacked in the order in which they're added to the chart. To efficiently work with shapes and objects, try selecting various shapes and choose Draw⇨Order on the Drawing toolbar. This lets you set the order of shapes with these settings: Bring to Front, Send to Back, Bring Forward, and Send Backward.

---

2. **Click the Colors and Lines tab to bring it to the top.**

3. **Make formatting selections in the Line and Arrow sections.**

   Note that the formatting options in the Area section are disabled, because arrows (lines) have no interior (see Figure 15-8).

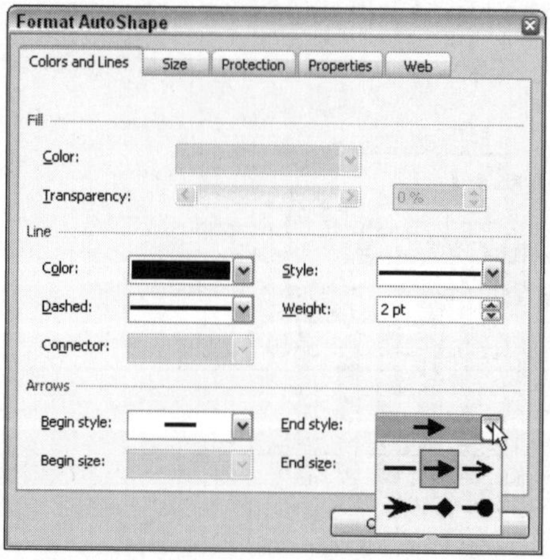

Figure 15-8:
Formatting
the arrow.

Inserting Text

The Text Box button on the Drawing toolbar lets you insert text into the chart. Figure 15-9 shows where the button is on the toolbar.

The method to insert text is about the same as inserting AutoShapes. Here's what you do:

1. Click the Text Box button on the Drawing toolbar.

2. On the chart, click the place where you want to insert text.

3. Enter the text.

Figure 15-10 shows where I decided to enter text.

You can also insert text into a chart by first selecting the chart and then entering text into the Formula Bar. Pressing the Enter key lands the text in the middle of the chart; then you can drag it to where it needs to go.

Figure 15-10 shows that I entered the *Great Work!* text on the left side. I also entered the *WOW!* text inside the star by double-clicking on the star (which lets you enter text inside the shape).

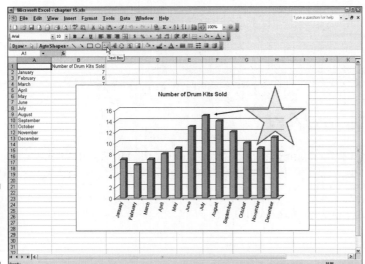

Figure 15-9:
Preparing to
insert text in
the chart.

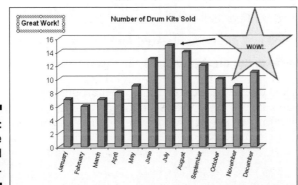

Figure 15-10:
Viewing the
inserted
text.

You can format both the text and the text box. Double-click on the border around the text to open the Format Text Box dialog box, shown in Figure 15-11. Double-click directly on the text to edit it.

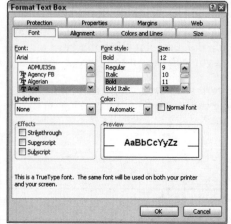

Figure 15-11:
Formatting
text with the
Format Text
Box dialog
box.

Using WordArt

WordArt is a fancy text-generator utility. Clicking on the WordArt button on the Drawing toolbar opens the WordArt Gallery dialog box, shown in Figure 15-12.

Here's how to insert WordArt:

1. **Click the WordArt button.**

   The WordArt Gallery dialog box opens.

2. **Click on the desired format, and click OK.**

   The Edit WordArt Text dialog box opens.

3. **Enter your text and apply the desired font formats (see Figure 15-13).**

4. **Click OK to close the dialog box and see the WordArt on the chart.**

After the WordArt is on the chart, you can move it around, resize it, and change the rotation. Figure 15-14 shows where and how I placed the WordArt. To format or edit WordArt, select it, and then use the WordArt toolbar (which appears when WordArt is selected).

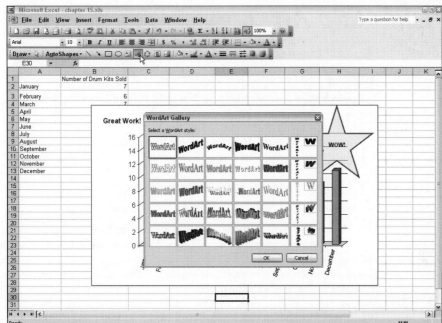

Figure 15-12:
Selecting a
WordArt
format.

Figure 15-13:
Entering
WordArt
text.

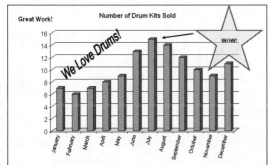

Figure 15-14:
Viewing the
WordArt on
the chart.

Using Clip Art

Microsoft Office comes with a significant amount of clip art. Typically, you search for clips and then insert one or more. Here's how to do this:

1. **Click on the Insert Clip Art button on the Drawing toolbar.**

   The Clip Art Task Pane appears.

2. **Enter a keyword (or keywords) to search on.**

   I entered *Drums*.

3. **Click the Go button to run the search.**

   Figure 15-15 shows the result of my search.

4. **When you find a piece of clip art you want, click the arrow to the right of it and select Insert (see Figure 15-16) or just click on the image.**

Figure 15-17 shows the inserted clip art. I resized it and moved it to have it appear exactly the way I wanted.

When you insert clip art, it probably won't be inserted in the correct place or be the correct size. You can resize and move the clip art as needed.

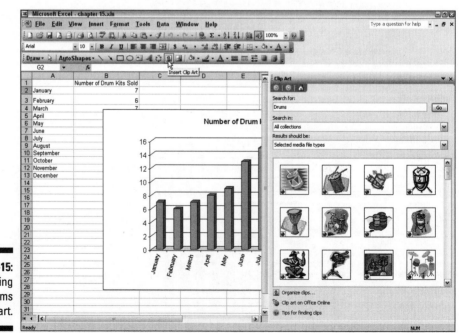

Figure 15-15: Searching for drums clip art.

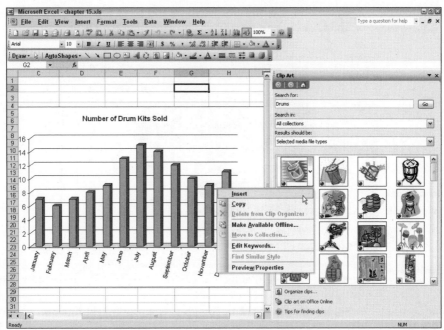

Figure 15-16:
Inserting
the clip art.

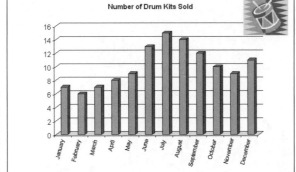

Figure 15-17:
Viewing the
chart with
the clip art.

Inserting a Photograph

Placing a photograph on a chart is another great thing to do to customize a chart — and it's so easy! Here's how:

1. **Click the Insert Picture from File button on the Drawing toolbar.**

   This opens the Insert Picture dialog box.

2. Browse to the directory where you have a photograph file (a `.jpg`, `.gif`, `.bmp`, and so on), as shown in Figure 15-18.

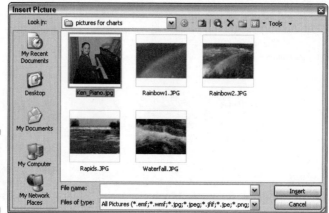

Figure 15-18:
Selecting a picture to insert.

3. Select the photograph file and click the Insert button.

Figure 15-19 shows how the photograph appears in my chart. I had to resize it and move it to where I wanted it to be placed.

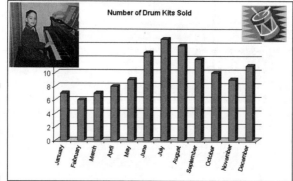

Figure 15-19:
Viewing the photograph with the chart.

Double-clicking on a photograph opens the Format Picture dialog box in which you can make selections to format the photograph.

Part IV
Advanced Chart Techniques

The 5th Wave   By Rich Tennant

In this part . . .

In this part, I cover the advanced features of Excel charts. When you get familiar with everything in this part, you're really a chart star.

Chapter 16 explains how trendlines and error bars work. Chapters 17 and 18 run the gamut of combination charts and user-defined charts. This is really great stuff!

You've heard of word processing templates? In this part, you find out how to make chart templates — and those are real time-savers. Then it's on to pivot charts. Pivot tables are used to summarize complex data, and pivot charts display the summaries. To wind up this part, I show you how to have your charts interact with Word and PowerPoint, and even how to post your charts on Web pages! How's *that* for cool?

Chapter 16

Adding Trendlines to a Chart

● ●

In This Chapter

▶ Finding out about trendlines

▶ Giving a name to a trendline

▶ Extending the trendline to make a forecast

▶ Placing the equation and the coefficient of determination on the chart

▶ Formatting a trendline

● ●

*W*hen analyzing time-based data, the actual data values may be of less interest than whether the values are getting higher or lower over time. Expecting a change in value over time is, after all, the nature of investment. You hope that your value in a stock will increase. If you buy a stock at a value of $25 per share, and three months later it's worth $30 per share, it's not likely that you're concerned what it was worth any particular day during the three-month period. You had expected the value to grow.

This is where trendlines are handy. A trendline smoothes out the up and down bumps in a time-based data series and presents the overall direction of the values over the range of periods. Trendlines are based on mathematical formulas. Don't worry — I don't cover the math here, so you don't have to pull out the old algebra books.

A trendline is based on a data series. When you add a trendline to a chart, you indicate which series the trendline is based on. The trendline appears in a similar fashion to a data series but will appear less chaotic than the source data series line.

Figure 16-1 shows a chart with a trendline. The source data series line is replete with ups and downs. The trendline is the straight line that seems to slice right through the actual series line. The trendline makes clear the overall direction of data values over time.

A trendline can be added to a data series in a Line, Area, Bar, Column, or XY (Scatter) chart.

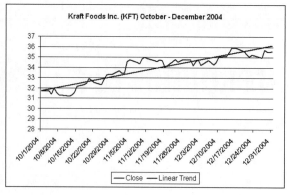

Figure 16-1:
A trendline
shows the
direction of
data values
over time.

Exploring Trendline Types

There are six types of trendlines: Linear, Logarithmic, Polynomial, Power, Exponential, and Moving Average. Each of these trendline types is formulated with a particular mathematical equation. I don't cover the particular math equations here, but you can look them up in the Excel Help system by searching on "trendlines."

To add a trendline to a chart, follow these steps:

1. **Create or open a chart in which the categories are time-scale (dates).**

   Make sure the chart is one of a Line, Area, Bar, Column, or XY (Scatter) chart type.

2. **Select the chart and choose Chart ⇨ Add Trendline, or right-click on the data series and select Add Trendline.**

   The Add Trendline dialog box appears.

3. **Click the Type tab to bring it to the top, if it isn't already on top (see Figure 16-2).**

   The six trendline types are available to select from. A trendline is based on a data series. You must indicate which data series you're adding a trendline to. The data series are listed in the Based On Series list (in my example, there is only one series).

4. **Select a trendline type.**

   If you select Polynomial or Moving Average, you also select the order or number of periods to use, respectively.

5. **Click OK to close the dialog box and see the trendline on the chart.**

   Figure 16-3 shows how my chart came out.

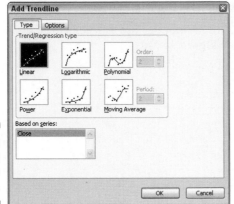

Figure 16-2:
Selecting a
trendline
type.

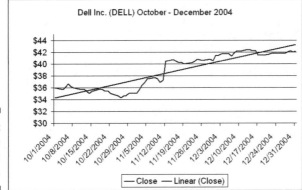

Figure 16-3:
Viewing the
chart with a
trendline.

The trendline helps make clear the overall direction of the data series, which is particularly helpful with erratic data in which seeing any trend by looking at just the data itself is difficult.

Naming the Trendline

Notice in the chart in Figure 16-3 that the legend displays the name for the trendline as Linear (Close). This is simply a combination of the series name (Close) with the trendline type (Linear). Excel provided the default name, but you can change it. Here's how.

1. Double-click on the trendline.

The Format Trendline dialog box appears.

2. **Click on the Options tab to bring it to the top.**

3. **In the Trendline Name section near the top, select the Custom option and enter a name (see Figure 16-4).**

Figure 16-4:
Changing
the trendline
name.

4. **Click OK to close the dialog box and see the change on the chart.**

Figure 16-5 shows the trendline name change on my chart.

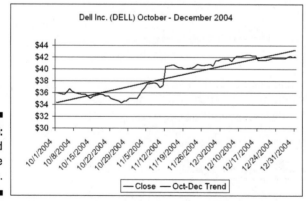

Figure 16-5:
The updated
trendline
name.

The Add Trendline dialog box and the Format Trendline dialog box share two common tabs: Type and Options.

Applying a Forward or Backward Forecast

Seeing the trend of the existing data is interesting enough, but it isn't always what you need. Often, a trend is used to extrapolate and see what values can be expected in the near future. If you have a good reason to believe a stock's value will go higher, you'll invest in it. Forecasting attempts to answer where the value is headed.

You can extend the trendline backward or forward to see where the value might have been and especially where it might go. Here's how to add a forward forecast to your charts:

1. **Double-click on the trendline.**

   The Format Trendline dialog box appears.

2. **Click on the Options tab to bring it to the top.**

3. **In the Forecast section, enter a value for the Forward Periods.**

   The periods match the time-scale of the series data, so if the series data is daily, the entered number is the number of days to extend the trendline. Figure 16-6 shows where I entered 14, to extend the trendline by 14 days.

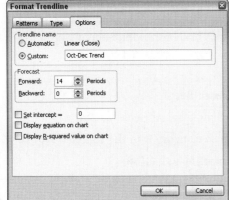

Figure 16-6:
Entering the number of periods for the forecast.

4. **Click OK to close the dialog box and see the change on the chart.**

Figure 16-7 shows that the trendline on the chart now extends past the source data.

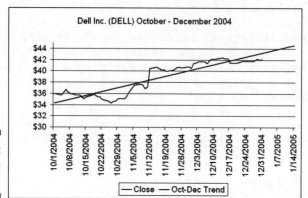

The forecast ability presented here should not be a guarantee of investment performance. If it were, I would be writing *Investing For Dummies!*

Formatting a Trendline

Trendlines can be formatted, which is especially useful on a busy Line chart when differentiating the different series is important. A trendline often is recognizable by its shape, but this is not always true. Therefore, being able to change the style, color, or weight of a trendline may make sense.

To format a trendline:

1. **Double-click on the trendline.**

   The Format Trendline dialog box appears.

2. **Click on the Patterns tab to bring it to the top (see Figure 16-8).**

3. **Make any desired formatting selections.**

4. **Click OK to close the dialog box.**

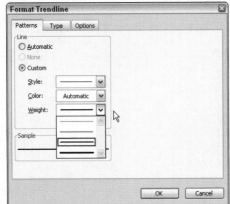

Figure 16-8:
Formatting
the trendline.

Displaying the Equation or the R-Squared Value

On the Options tab of the Format Trendline dialog box are check boxes for displaying the equation and the R-squared value on the chart. Figure 16-9 shows the chart with the equation and R-squared value. Each trendline type is based on a mathematical equation, which is what appears on the chart. The R-squared value is a number between 0 and 1 that signifies how close the trendline values are to the actual data. The higher the number, the closer the values. The R-squared value is also known as the *coefficient of determination*.

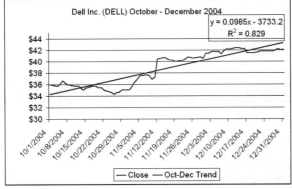

Figure 16-9:
Displaying
the equation
and the
R-squared
value.

On the Options tab is a setting for changing the intercept. This setting interacts with the formula the trendline is based on. Using this setting is a bit involved and requires getting into the nuts and bolts of the underlying equations, which is beyond the scope of this book.

Chapter 17

Using Combination Charts

In This Chapter

- Understanding when different data series should be plotted on different axes
- Plotting data on a secondary value axis
- Setting the secondary axis to plot with a different chart type

At times, you'll need to display multiple series of data in a chart — there's nothing new about that. It could be, though, that one or more series of data does not contain values that are close in range to the other series data. This is a problem because, given that a value axis has a single range, how can you best set the range to accommodate a wide range of values?

Figure 17-1 illustrates the problem. The worksheet shows the closing prices for the Dow Jones Industrial Average (DJIA) and the NASDAQ for December 2004.

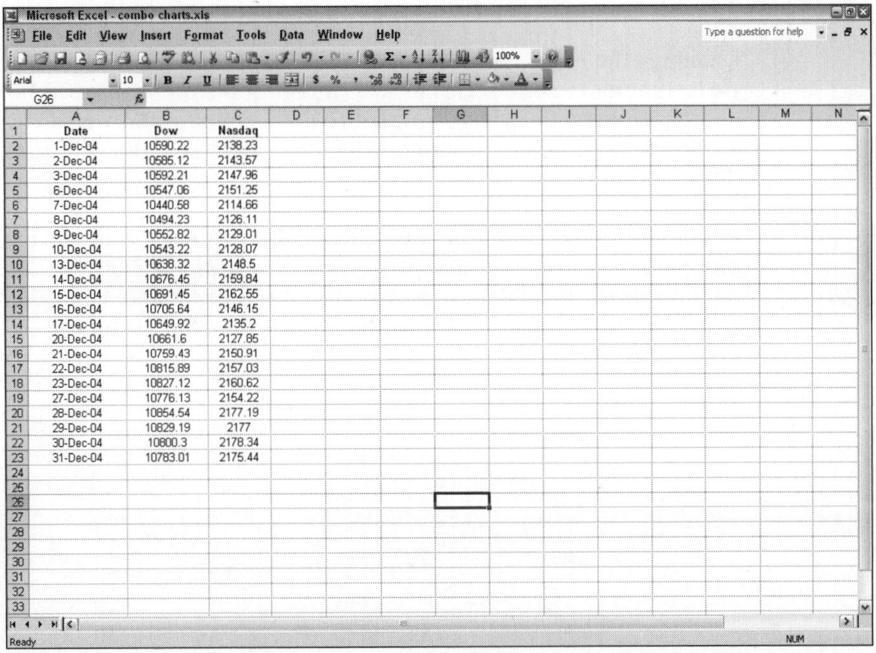

Date	Dow	Nasdaq
1-Dec-04	10590.22	2138.23
2-Dec-04	10585.12	2143.57
3-Dec-04	10592.21	2147.96
6-Dec-04	10547.06	2151.25
7-Dec-04	10440.58	2114.66
8-Dec-04	10494.23	2126.11
9-Dec-04	10552.82	2129.01
10-Dec-04	10543.22	2128.07
13-Dec-04	10638.32	2148.5
14-Dec-04	10676.45	2159.84
15-Dec-04	10691.45	2162.55
16-Dec-04	10705.64	2146.15
17-Dec-04	10649.92	2135.2
20-Dec-04	10661.6	2127.85
21-Dec-04	10759.43	2150.91
22-Dec-04	10815.89	2157.03
23-Dec-04	10827.12	2160.62
27-Dec-04	10776.13	2154.22
28-Dec-04	10854.54	2177.19
29-Dec-04	10829.19	2177
30-Dec-04	10800.3	2178.34
31-Dec-04	10783.01	2175.44

Figure 17-1: Comparing stock indices.

✔ The DJIA values are 10,440.58 through 10,854.54, covering a range of 413.96.

✔ The NASDAQ values are 2,114.66 through 2,178.34, covering a range of 63.68.

Attempting to plot these two series together on a single value axis will lead to a frustrating experience! In Figure 17-2, the two indices are plotted. The range of the value axis is from 0 to 12,000. Both series appear as essentially flat lines. Seeing any ups and downs in the values is impossible.

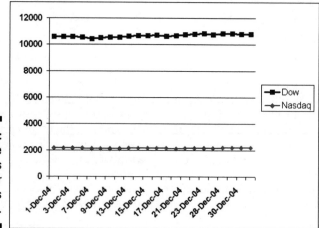

Figure 17-2:
Plotting the two series together produces flat lines.

Changing the *range* (the minimum and maximum) of values of the value axis to accommodate one series makes the other disappear. Figure 17-3 shows the chart with the value range now set to display values between 1,900 and 2,300. The NASDAQ and its ups and downs are easy to see. But the DJIA is off the chart, literally.

In this chapter, I show you how to deal with this nightmare. Imagine trying to plot data only to have it disappear. If this were *Magic For Dummies,* making data disappear would make sense. But this is *Excel Charts For Dummies,* so I show you chart magic, the kind that makes data *not* disappear.

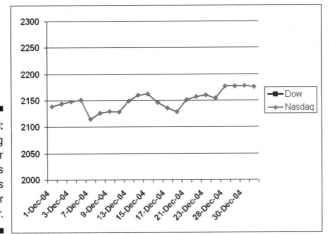

Figure 17-3:
Adjusting
the range for
one series
makes
the other
disappear.

Working With the Secondary Axis

So what exactly is a secondary axis? A *secondary axis* is a second value axis
(not a second category axis) on which you plot one or more series — in the
same way as the first value axis.

The key point is that the secondary axis is set to a different range of values.
Then one or more series can stay plotted to the values on the first value axis,
and one or more other series can be plotted to the second value axis.

A secondary axis typically is a value axis. When two value axes are used,
they're referred to as the *primary axis* and the *secondary axis.*

The best way to see how this works is to try it yourself. The following steps
show how to plot the DJIA and NASDAQ data together. You can use the data
shown in Figure 17-1 or you can use your own data.

1. **Copy the three columns of data shown in Figure 17-1 onto a worksheet.**

   To make it easier, you can copy a few rows — you don't need to copy
   the entire month of data. Or, you can just use some data of your own.
   If you use your own data, structure it like the data in Figure 17-1 — that is,
   the first column has categories (dates in my example), followed by two
   columns of data.

2. **Select the data and choose Insert ⇨ Chart.**

   The Chart Wizard opens.

3. In the Chart Wizard, select the Line chart type, and click Finish.

You can format the chart a bit afterward if you want.

Figure 17-4 shows how my chart turned out. I cleared the gray background from the plot area and applied bold to the fonts in the category and value axis. The two series are plotted on the same value axis, which does neither one justice.

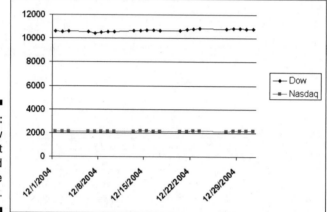

Figure 17-4:
Seeing how the Chart Wizard made the chart.

4. Double-click directly on one of the series lines to open the Format Data Series dialog box.

5. In the Format Data Series dialog box, click on the Axis tab to bring it to the front.

In my example, I double-clicked on the DJIA series line (see Figure 17-5).

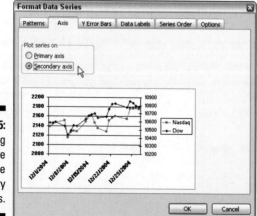

Figure 17-5:
Selecting to plot the series on the secondary axis.

6. **Select the Secondary axis option and click OK.**

Figure 17-6 shows how my chart has turned out. The DJIA is now plotted with values on the secondary value axis — which is to the right of the plot area.

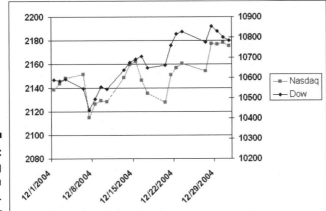

Figure 17-6:
Reviewing
the two data
series.

The chart in Figure 17-6 is exactly what you need. You can now see how both series fared — that is, you can see the ups and downs and, more specifically, you can easily see that the DJIA and the NASDAQ followed similar ups and downs.

You can format a chart like this even more and adjust the range of values on each axis a bit. When you adjust the range on one axis, it will alter the shape of just the lines that are bound to that axis.

The custom chart type Lines on 2 Axes creates a combination chart with two value axes. Select the data, start up the Chart Wizard, select the Lines on 2 Axes chart type on the Custom Types tab, and click Finish.

Mixing Chart Types Together

One of the cooler aspects of combination charts is that you can mix two different chart types together. The data series connected to the first value axis is plotted on one chart type, and the data series connected to the secondary axis is plotted on a different chart type.

Follow these steps to see how this works:

1. **Gather some data onto a worksheet in such a way that the two data series share common categories.**

   The data in one series should not be close in range to the data in the other series (otherwise, there is no need for a combination chart). You can use my data, shown in Figure 17-7.

   My sample data reports the average grade attained for different class sizes — all fictional, of course! I don't want to have any educators calling me up to complain.

2. **Select the data and choose Insert ⇨ Chart.**

   The Chart Wizard opens.

3. **In the Chart Wizard, select the Line chart type, and click Finish.**

   Figure 17-8 shows how my chart came out. I formatted it a bit to make it look presentable. Note, in particular, that I formatted the category axis (at the bottom of the plot area) to have the tick-mark labels not appear — they aren't necessary in this chart.

4. **To set the average grade series to be plotted on the secondary axis, double-click directly on the series line to open the Format Data Series dialog box.**

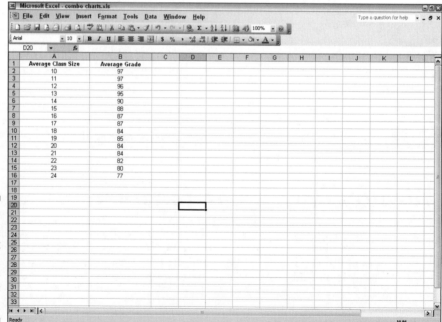

Figure 17-7:
Preparing
to plot
data on a
primary and
secondary
axis.

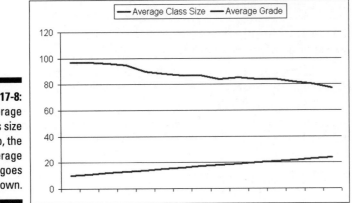

5. Click the Axis tab to bring it to the top.

Figure 17-9 shows how this should look.

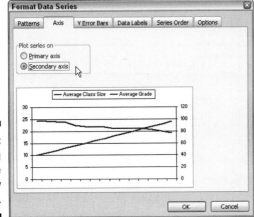

6. Select the Secondary Axis option and click OK.

Figure 17-10 shows how my chart now looks. Notice how the right side of the plot area now has a value axis, and the average class size series line has changed position, because the range of the primary axis (on the left of the plot area) has an updated range of values. The range of the primary axis now better accommodates the average class size series.

7. Right-click directly on the average grade series line.

A pop-up menu appears (see Figure 17-11).

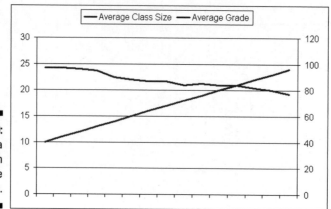

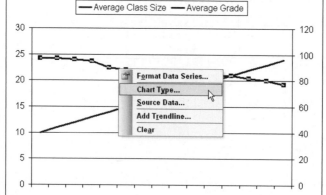

8. **In the pop-up menu, select Chart Type.**

    This opens the Chart Type dialog box.

9. **On the Standard Types tab, under Chart Type, select Column.**

10. **Select the first subtype (see Figure 17-12).**

11. **Click OK.**

    This changes the selected average grade series to be presented as columns instead of a line. Figure 17-13 shows how my chart came out.

    Almost there! You could stop here, but one last good technique is to change the range of the secondary axis to separate out the series a bit.

12. **Double-click on the secondary axis to open up the Format Axis dialog box.**

13. **Click the Scale tab to bring it to the top.**

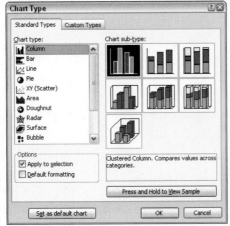

Figure 17-12:
Selecting a
Column
chart type
for the
secondary
axis.

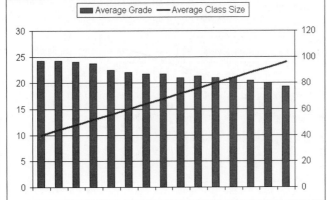

Figure 17-13:
Reviewing
the mixed
chart types.

14. **Change the Maximum value to 200 and make sure to uncheck the Maximum check box (see Figure 17-14).**

15. **Click OK.**

    Figure 17-15 shows how my chart now looks.

Note that, in the chart in Figure 17-15, I added titles for the primary and secondary axes. On a combination chart, the legend is not enough to communicate which series is being plotted to which axis. When you add titles, you avoid confusion.

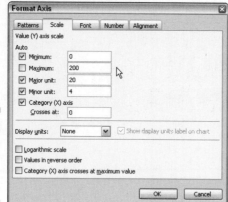

Figure 17-14:
Changing
the range
of the sec-
ondary axis.

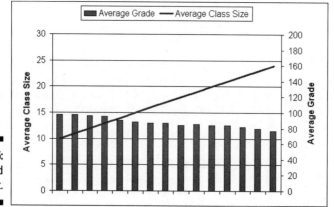

Figure 17-15:
The finished
chart.

Chapter 18

Creating and Saving
User-Defined Charts

*E*xcel provides quite a few predesigned charts. You may not realize it, but when you select a chart type in the Chart Wizard, a definition for the chart type is buried somewhere deep inside Excel. Wouldn't it be nice if you could add your own chart layouts to the list of chart types, so you could reuse your custom layouts over and over?

Well, you can! This feature is really useful, because you may find yourself repeatedly adding elements or using certain formats and styling over and over again. There is no need to go through this drudgery anymore. You create a reusable custom format by creating a chart based on an available chart type, and then adding it to the group of user-defined chart types. In this chapter, I show you just how to perform this brand of chart magic.

Creating a Chart Layout

The first thing to do is to create a chart. Base this chart on a chart type that you want your custom chart to be. For example, create a Bar, Line, Pie, or whichever type of chart your custom chart will be. Even though you'll create a custom chart, it will still be based on an existing chart type.

The difference between a standard or built-in chart type and the user-defined chart you'll create will be formatting and the inclusion of graphics. For example:

✔ Including the company logo

✔ Including names of relevant staff members, phone extensions, and so on

✔ Formatting the chart layout to include a certain color scheme

Figure 18-1 shows a finished chart. It's a bar chart with a variety of formatting, including

✔ A picture of an apple in the background (in the chart area)

✔ A chart title formatted to a bold, italic, 16-point font

✔ Value-axis and category-axis tick-mark labels set to a bold, 12-point font

✔ Data labels set to show values

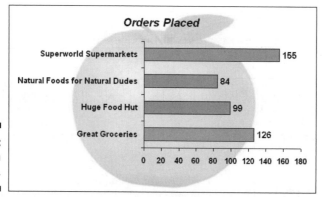

Figure 18-1:
Creating a
chart layout.

In a nutshell, the chart I created has design elements added to it that would be tedious to have to set up each time I created a chart. In the next section, I show you how to save the layout.

Adding a User-Defined Custom Chart to the Collection of Chart Types

Adding a completed chart to the list of chart types is the key to creating a reusable chart layout. First, you need to customize a chart:

1. **Create a new chart, or open an existing one.**

   The data will not be saved with the chart layout, so in that sense, the data is not important. On the other hand, you must use some data to create a chart in the first place.

2. **Insert graphics, change formatting, rearrange the placement of chart objects, and so on.**

   You're creating a new layout, which includes formatting, placement, and inserted items.

3. **With the chart selected, choose Chart ➪ Chart Type, as shown in Figure 18-2.**

   The Chart Type dialog box appears.

4. **In the Chart Type dialog box, click the Custom Types tab, and select User-Defined in the Select From box (see Figure 18-3).**

   Note that an Add button has appeared.

5. **Click the Add button.**

   The Add Custom Chart Type dialog box, shown in Figure 18-4, appears.

6. **Enter a name and description for your chart.**

   Figure 18-5 shows what I entered for my chart.

7. **Click OK.**

   The custom chart has now been added to the list of chart types, as a user-defined chart. Figure 18-6 shows how my chart appears in the list.

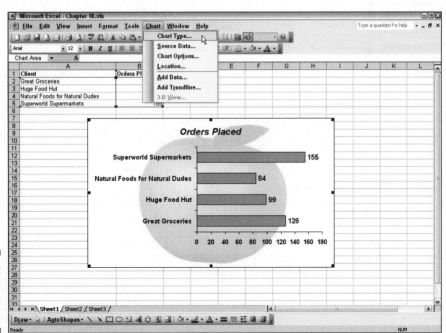

Figure 18-2:
Preparing
to save the
chart layout.

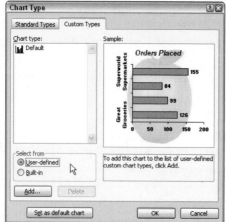

Figure 18-3:
Selecting
user-
defined
chart types.

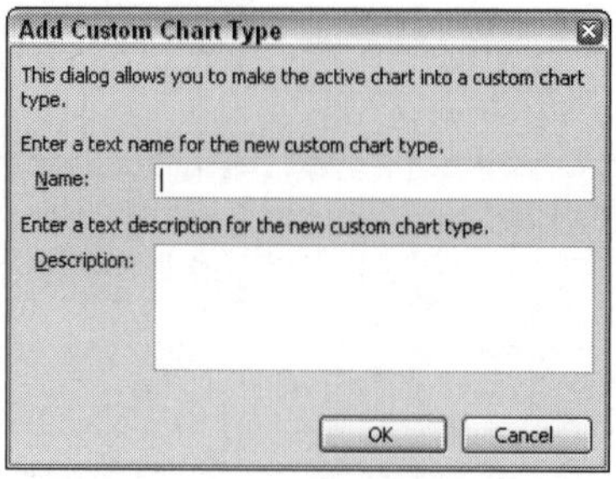

Figure 18-4:
Preparing
to add the
custom
chart type.

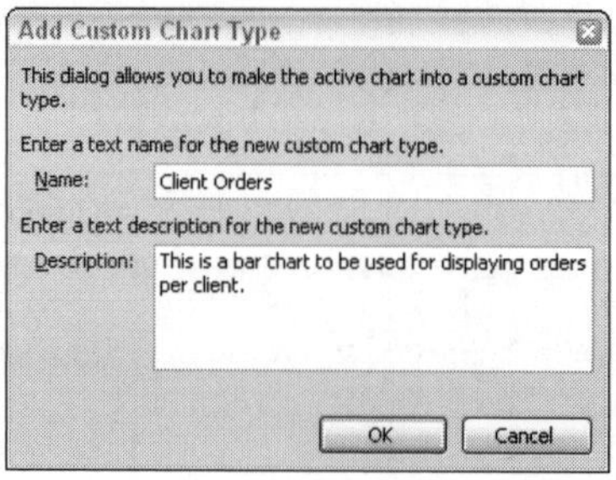

Figure 18-5:
Entering a
name and
description.

The chart layout is now available for use. It will show up in the Chart Wizard or when changing chart types.

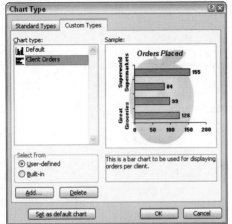

Figure 18-6:
The custom
chart
appears in
the list of
chart types.

Note the Set as Default Chart button on the Custom Types tab in the Chart Type dialog box (refer to Figure 18-6). There is always one chart type that a chart is based on when no other options are selected. For example, when using the Chart Wizard, just clicking Finish will create a chart based on the default type. The default can be one of your custom chart types. You not only can create a reusable chart type; you can have it be the basis for your charts without even needing to select it first!

You can remove a custom chart type by selecting it in the list of chart types and clicking the Delete button.

Using a User-Defined Chart Layout

When it's time to create a new chart, you can use your previously created custom chart layout. Figure 18-7 shows some new data to plot and where in the Chart Wizard the custom chart layout is being selected. Note that the custom chart appears on the Custom Types tab, when the User-Defined option is selected.

Figure 18-8 shows the completed chart. This chart was completed by clicking Finish while still in the first screen of the Chart Wizard. The settings saved with the custom chart type are applied to the new chart.

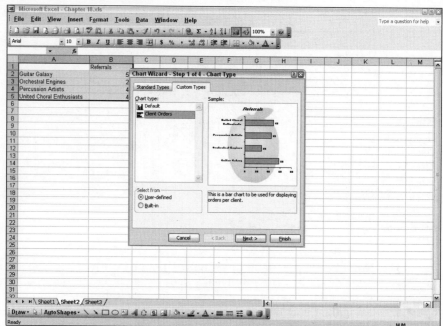

Figure 18-7:
Using the
custom
chart type.

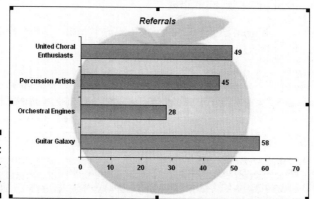

Figure 18-8:
The com-
pleted chart.

Chapter 19

Creating Pivot Tables and Pivot Charts

Data can get complex, and that means utility strength tools are needed to manage it. Lucky for you, Excel puts such a tool at your disposal. Allow me to introduce you to pivot tables and pivot charts.

A *pivot chart* is just a visual representation of the data in a pivot table, so first you need to know what a pivot table is. Figure 19-1 shows a worksheet with data. Each value in column D represents the number of units for each combination of Region, Market, and Product.

Data like this is hierarchal in nature. Cool-sounding technogeek terms like *drill down* and *data warehouse* start to spin around my head when I see data like this. Not to fear: In this chapter, I show you how to work with this stuff.

You can sum up the data in a number of ways. For example:

✔ The total number of units for Product A is 153, without regard to Region or Market.

✔ The total number of units for the East is 80, without regard to Market or Product.

✔ The total number of Wholesale units for Product B is 67, without regard to Region.

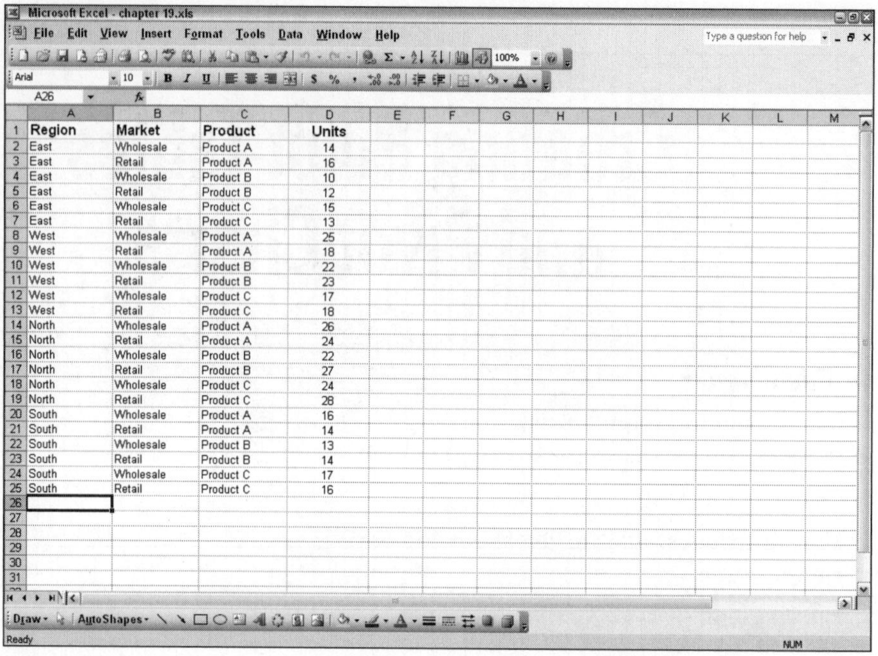

Figure 19-1:
Reviewing
complex
data.

Pivot tables let you see your data in a variety of ways. You can view grand totals, subtotals, and the raw data, too. The layout of a pivot table can be rearranged and, when you do so, you can view different summaries of the data.

Figure 19-2 shows a pivot table built upon the data shown in Figure 19-1. The particular layout of the pivot table is just one way to present the data.

You can easily see certain summaries in the pivot table in Figure 19-2. For example:

✔ There is a total of 148 units for Product C, without regard to Region or Market.

✔ The total number of units for the South is 90, without regard to Market or Product.

✔ There are 18 units for Product A for Retail in the West.

✔ The grand total for all units — without regard to Product, Market, or Region — is 444.

Next, the pivot table layout is altered (I show you how to do this later). The result is a different view of the data, shown in Figure 19-3.

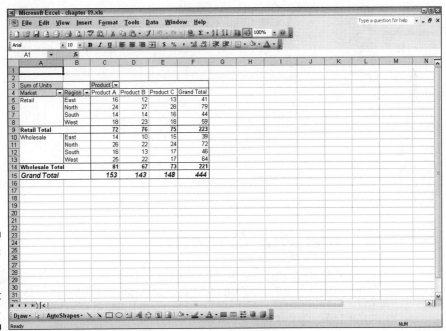

Figure 19-2:
Viewing a
pivot table.

Figure 19-3:
Summariz-
ing the data
in a different
layout.

In the configuration of the pivot table in Figure 19-3, you can easily identify facts such as:

- ✔ The total retail units for Product A is 72.
- ✔ The total wholesale units, without regard to Region or Product, is 221.

Because this is a book about charts, Figure 19-4 shows a chart based on the pivot table in Figure 19-3.

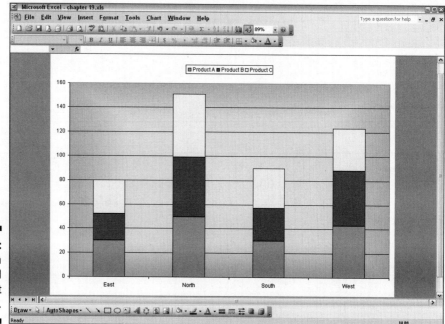

Figure 19-4: Viewing a chart based on the pivot table.

Pivot-table charts are similar to regular charts, but they incorporate methods to filter the pivot-table data — which produces a change in the chart.

Introducing the Wizard

In the following sections of this chapter, I walk you through creating a pivot table and an accompanying pivot chart. The PivotTable and PivotChart Wizard is the Excel utility that helps you get this done. Nothing like a good wizard to help out when you need one!

The wizard has many options and settings, most of which I discuss but some of which you'll need to play around with on your own.

To follow along with the chapter, you need some data, of course! My recommendation: Copy the data I created in Figure 19-1. If you want to use your own data, make sure it has a hierarchal dimension to it (that is, values should exist on combinations of more than one field). For example, in my data, any single value relates to a combination of region, market, and product.

Just a single step is all that's needed to crank up the old wizard and get him going: Choose Data ⇨ PivotTable and PivotChart Report to start up the wizard.

Selecting a Data Source Type and Report Type with Step 1

Figure 19-5 shows the first step of the PivotTable and PivotChart Wizard. In this step, you select the location and type of source data, as well as whether to create just a pivot table, or a pivot table and a pivot chart.

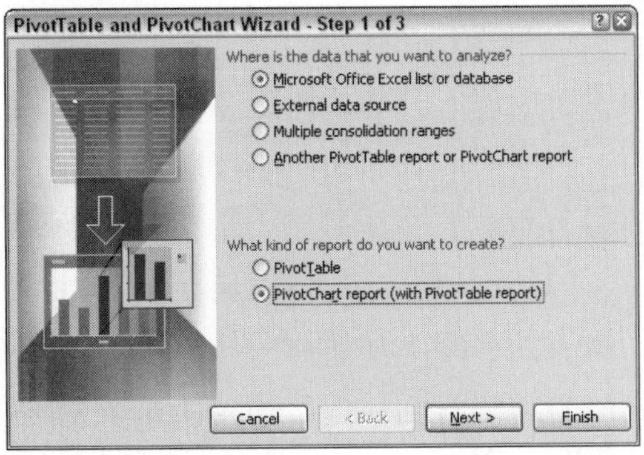

PivotTable and PivotChart Wizard - Step 1 of 3

Where is the data that you want to analyze?
- ● Microsoft Office Excel list or database
- ○ External data source
- ○ Multiple consolidation ranges
- ○ Another PivotTable report or PivotChart report

What kind of report do you want to create?
- ○ PivotTable
- ● PivotChart report (with PivotTable report)

Cancel   < Back   Next >   Finish

Figure 19-5: Making selections in the first step of the wizard.

You have four choices for where the source data is found:

✓ **Microsoft Office Excel List or Database:** The data is sitting on a worksheet. This chapter follows this example.

✓ **External Data Source:** The data is in an external file or database. When you select this option and click the Get Data button, the data source is selected in the Choose Data Source dialog box, shown in Figure 19-6.

 ✔ **Multiple Consolidation Ranges:** Uses data that comes from various worksheet ranges. When you select this option and click Next, the ranges are selected in one of the wizard's subdialog boxes, shown in Figure 19-7.

 ✔ **Another PivotTable Report or PivotChart Report:** Uses data from an existing pivot table in the same workbook.

Figure 19-6: Selecting an external data source.

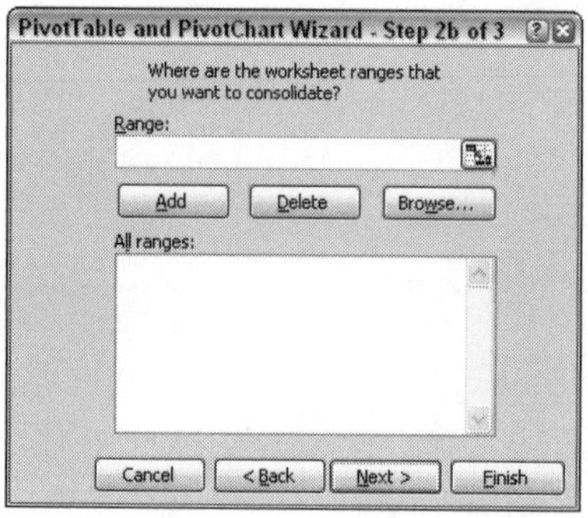

Figure 19-7: Selecting ranges as the data source.

Here's how to select the data on the worksheet:

1. **In the wizard's first step, make sure the Microsoft Office Excel List or Database option is selected.**

2. **Select to create a PivotChart report (refer to Figure 19-5).**

3. **Click Next.**

Selecting the Data with Step 2

In the wizard's second step, you define the range of the data on the worksheet. The second screen, shown in Figure 19-8, may already have the defined range of the data in the Range box. If not, you can select it. Also note that if the data is not selected the wizard will use the contiguous range of data that the active cell is in.

Figure 19-8:
Defining
where the
data is.

If the wizard's second-step screen opens with the data range filled in, you can just click Next and skip to the next section. You may have selected the data before starting up the wizard. In this case, the wizard already knows where your data is.

In Figure 19-8, the mouse pointer is over the control that lets you select data. Here's how to select the data:

1. **Click on the control.**

   The wizard shrinks to just the size of the entry box, as shown in Figure 19-9.

	A	B	C	D
1	Region	Market	Product	Units
2	East	Wholesale	Product A	14
3	East	Retail	Product A	16
4	East	Wholesale	Product B	10
5	East	Retail	Product B	12
6	East	Wholesale	Product C	15
7	East	Retail	Product C	13
8	West	Wholesale	Product A	25
9	West	Retail	Product A	18
10	West	Wholesale	Product B	22
11	West	Retail	Product B	23
12	West	Wholesale	Product C	17
13	West	Retail	Product C	18
14	North	Wholesale	Product A	26
15	North	Retail	Product A	24
16	North	Wholesale	Product B	22
17	North	Retail	Product B	27
18	North	Wholesale	Product C	24
19	North	Retail	Product C	28
20	South	Wholesale	Product A	16
21	South	Retail	Product A	14
22	South	Wholesale	Product B	13
23	South	Retail	Product B	14
24	South	Wholesale	Product C	17
25	South	Retail	Product C	16

Figure 19-9:
Preparing to
define the
data range.

2. **Click on the first cell of the data range, hold down the mouse button, and drag over the full range (see Figure 19-10).**

3. **Release the mouse button.**

   The entry box has filled in with the range of the data.

4. **Click on the small button to the right of the entry to complete the operation (see Figure 19-11).**

   The second-step screen displays the data range in the entry box, as shown in Figure 19-12.

5. **Click Next.**

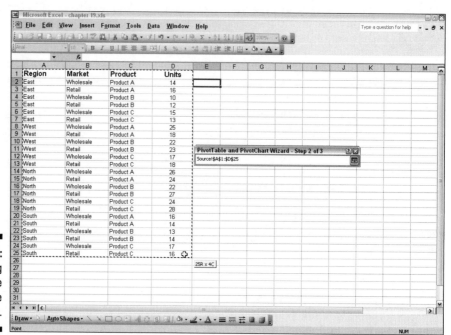

Figure 19-10:
Dragging
the mouse
over the
data.

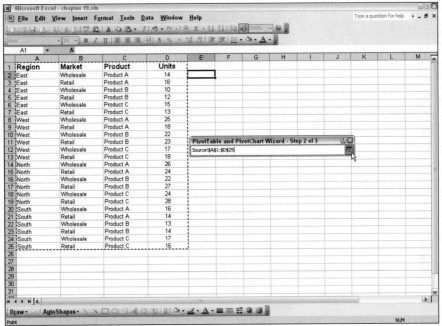

Figure 19-11:
Completing
the entry
of the data
range.

Figure 19-12:
Completing
the wizard's
second step.

Selecting Layout and Options with Step 3

In the third step of the wizard are the Layout and Options buttons. These lead to a number of additional settings.

You can skip creating the layout yourself by just clicking the Finish button in the wizard's third screen. But why miss all the excitement? Creating the layout is where you fine-tune the appearance of the pivot table. Here's what you do:

1. **Click the Layout button to open the PivotTable and PivotChart Wizard – Layout dialog box, shown in Figure 19-13.**

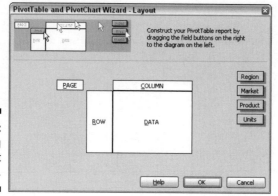

Figure 19-13:
Opening
the Layout
dialog box.

Note that in the dialog box, on the right, are the fields from the source data: Region, Market, Product, and Units. In the middle of the dialog box is an entry grid to which these fields are dragged. This activity creates the layout of the pivot table.

2. Click on the Region field and, while holding down the mouse button, drag the field to the Row box; then release the mouse button.

The Region field is now designated as a row in the pivot table (see Figure 19-14).

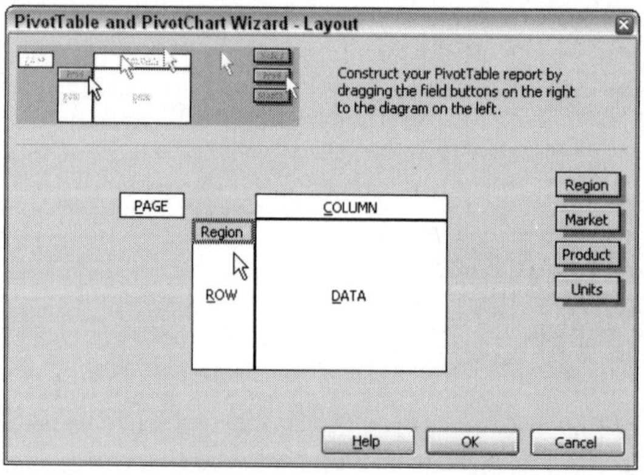

Figure 19-14:
Confirming
that the
Region field
will become
a row.

3. Click on the Market field, hold down the mouse button, drag the field to the Row box, and release the button.

The Market field is also designated to be a row in the pivot table (see Figure 19-15).

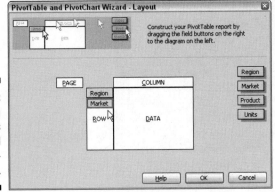

Figure 19-15:
Reviewing
two fields
designated
as pivot-
table rows.

4. **Click on the Product field, hold down the mouse button, drag the field to the Column box, and release the button.**

   The Product field is designated to be a column in the pivot table (see Figure 19-16).

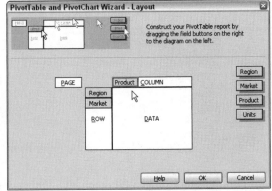

Figure 19-16:
Setting the
Product
field to be a
pivot-table
column.

5. **Click on the Units field, hold down the mouse button, drag the field to the larger Data box, and release the button.**

   The Units field is the field with values that are to be summarized. In the Data box, the name changes to Sum of Units (see Figure 19-17).

   Sum is not the only available aggregation type. See the "Using the PivotTable Toolbar" section, later in this chapter, for further information on how to use other summary options.

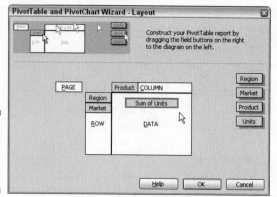

Figure 19-17:
Reviewing the complete layout.

6. **Click OK to close the PivotTable and PivotChart Wizard – Layout dialog box.**

You're now back in the wizard's third-step screen.

7. **Click the Options button.**

The PivotTable Options dialog box, shown in Figure 19-18, appears.

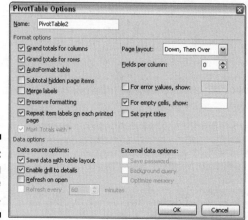

Figure 19-18:
Reviewing pivot-table options.

I don't cover pivot-table options here, but knowing where to find them is a good idea.

8. **Click OK to close the PivotTable Options dialog box.**

You can select to have the pivot table appear on a new worksheet or on the existing worksheet. If you select the existing worksheet option, the pivot table's first cell will be where the active cell is on the worksheet. Or you can enter an address or click on an appropriate cell to contain the upper-left corner of the table. You'll be warned that the table will replace any existing entries in that range.

9. **Click the Finish button in the wizard's third-step screen.**

This creates the pivot table and pivot chart.

Reviewing the Pivot Table and Pivot Chart Report

If you selected to make a pivot chart report in the wizard's first screen, both a pivot table and pivot chart have been created; otherwise, just a pivot table has been created.

Figure 19-19 shows the pivot table, which has been created on a new worksheet. If the chart appears first, click on the new worksheet tab to see the table.

True to the layout, there are two hierarchal rows: Region and Market. The Product field is the column, and Units are found in the middle — both the actual values and sums.

On a separate chart sheet, the accompanying chart has been created, as shown in Figure 19-20.

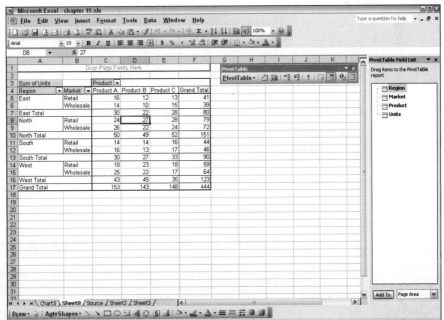

Figure 19-19: Looking at the pivot table.

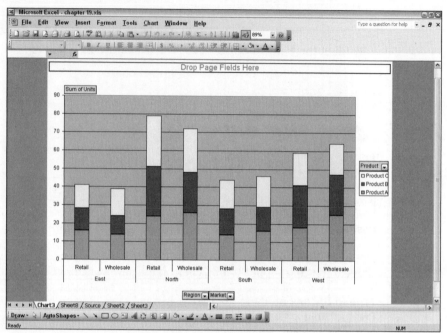

Figure 19-20:
Reviewing
the pivot
chart.

Changing the Layout

The pivot-table layout can be changed by dragging the fields around. Note that in Figure 19-19, the pivot-table rows are Region and then Market. Note, too, that in the chart in Figure 19-20, the category axis has a double set of tick-mark labels. First are the markets, and underneath are the regions. The layout of the chart changes when the pivot-table layout changes. You can do just that by taking the following steps:

1. **On the worksheet with the pivot table, click on the Market field.**

2. **Hold down the mouse button and drag the mouse to the left of the Region field.**

3. **Release the mouse button.**

Figure 19-21 shows how the pivot table now looks.

The pivot chart has also updated, as shown in Figure 19-22. Note that the category labels are now the regions with the markets underneath.

You can move fields around as needed to produce the best results of the data. In Figure 19-23 is one more example — a pivot table in which Region and Product are rows and the Market field is the column.

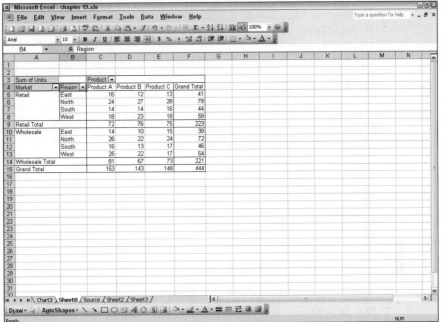

Figure 19-21:
The changed pivot-table layout.

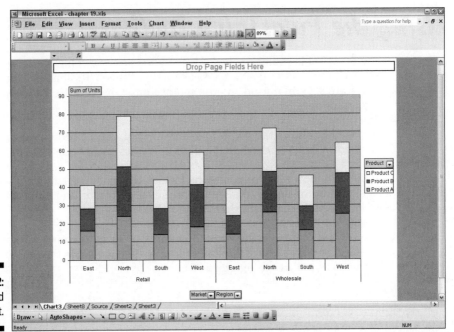

Figure 19-22:
The updated pivot chart.

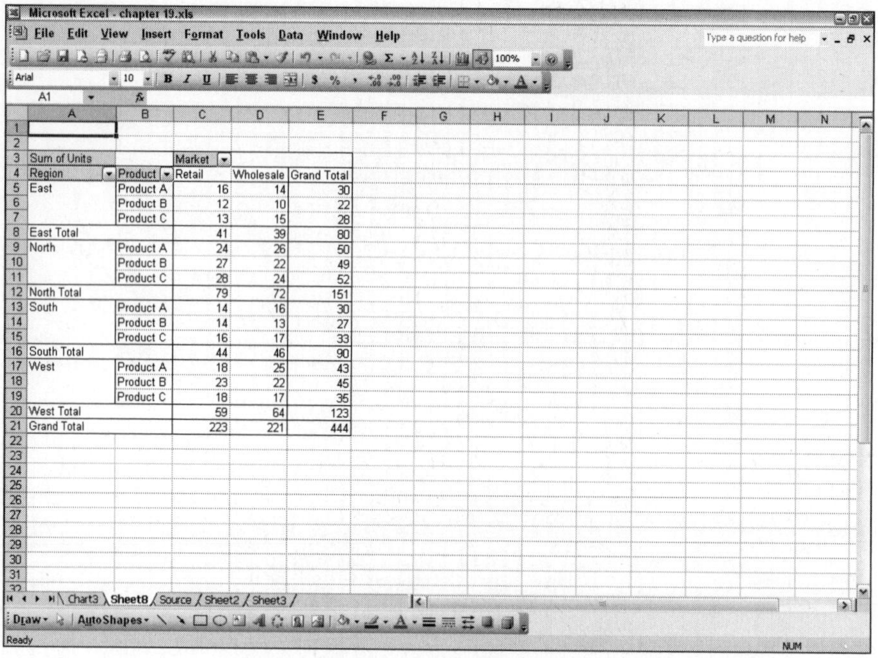

Figure 19-23:
Trying out
different
layouts.

Using the PivotTable Toolbar

The Pivot Table toolbar appears when you click any cell within the pivot table. (If the toolbar doesn't appear, choose View ➪ Toolbars ➪ PivotTable.) There are several buttons on the toolbar, and I discuss a few of the more important ones here.

Figure 19-24 shows the pivot table and toolbar. On the toolbar, the PivotTable drop-down list is opened. In the drop-down list are several options.

In the drop-down list, selecting the Field Settings item opens the PivotTable Field dialog box. In this dialog box are several options on how to summarize and manage the data, shown in Figure 19-25.

The second button on the PivotTable toolbar opens the AutoFormat dialog box. In this dialog box, a number of formats are available that can be applied to the pivot table (see Figure 19-26).

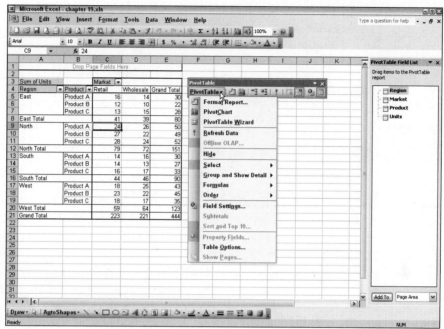

Figure 19-24: Reviewing the toolbar options.

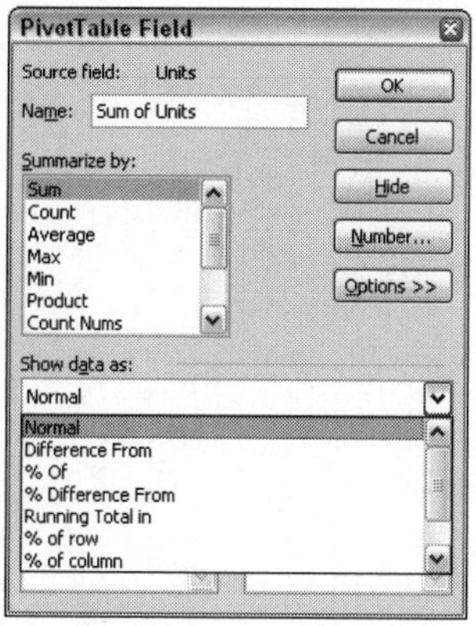

Figure 19-25: Reviewing the aggregation options.

The third button on the PivotTable toolbar opens the Chart Wizard, from which the pivot chart can be changed, as shown in Figure 19-27.

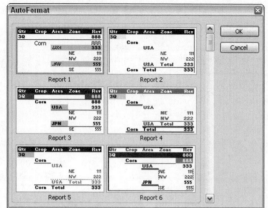

Figure 19-26:
Previewing auto formats.

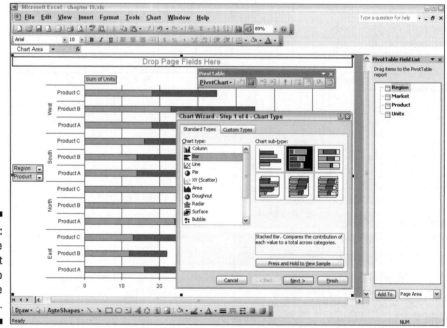

Figure 19-27:
Using the Chart Wizard to change the chart type.

Applying a Filter

In a pivot table, the fields designated as rows and columns appear as drop-down lists. When a drop-down list opens, it lists the values that are in the field. You can then select one or more and filter the pivot table on those values.

Figure 19-28 shows a pivot table in which the Region field's drop-down arrow has been clicked. The values found in the Region field — East, North, South, and West — are available for you to check or uncheck as you want. In Figure 19-28, only the South is being selected — that is, the other regions have been unchecked (they're currently in the pivot table but are about to be hidden).

Figure 19-29 shows how the pivot table looks after clicking the OK button. Only the data for the South is visible.

You can filter on values in all the row and column fields. This lets you fine-tune the pivot table to show just the data you need.

When data is filtered, the associated chart updates as well. Figure 19-30 shows the chart presenting just the data about the South region.

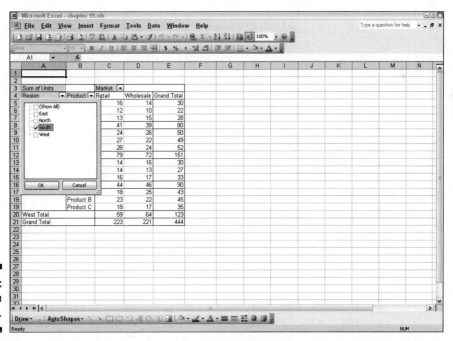

Figure 19-28:
Filtering on
a field value.

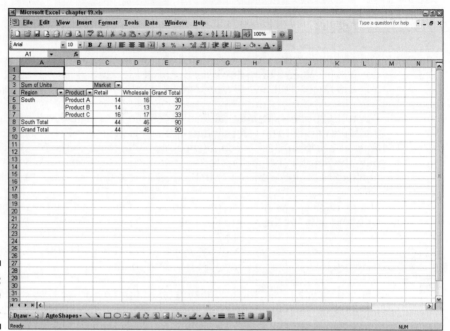

Figure 19-29:
Viewing the
filtered data.

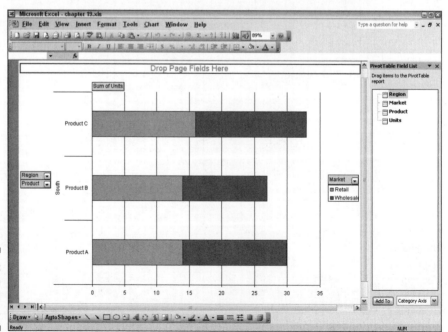

Figure 19-30:
Viewing the
filtered
chart.

Using Page Fields

Fields can be designated as the row or column headings in a pivot table. Fields can also be designated as page fields. When a field is used as a page field, it doesn't appear in the pivot table. Instead, any filtering made to a page field applies to the pivot table as a whole, without the values of the page field appearing in the body of the pivot table.

An example makes this clear. Figure 19-31 shows the wizard screen in which field locations are selected. By the way, I called up this wizard screen by selecting PivotTable Wizard from the drop-down list of the PivotTable button on the PivotTable toolbar (say *that* five times fast!).

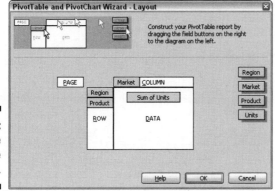

Figure 19-31:
Editing the pivot-table layout.

In the wizard screen, I've dragged the Region field to the Page box. This removes the Region field from being a row field (see Figure 19-32).

More than one field can be designated as a page field.

Figure 19-33 shows how the pivot table now looks. The region is now situated separately above the pivot table.

When the Region field was designated as a row field, it was possible to select multiple field values to filter on. As a page field, only one value can be selected to filter on.

Pivot tables are great for presenting complex data. In this chapter, I show you the basics. My recommendation: Work with them, look up how to use them in the Excel help system, or even research them on the Internet. When you become familiar with pivot tables, you may find yourself using them over and over again.

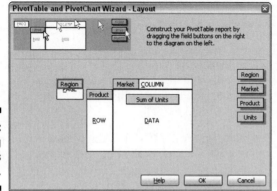

Figure 19-32:
Moving
fields
around.

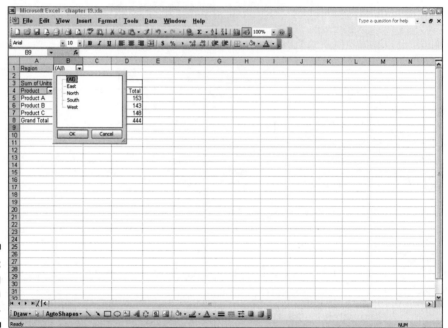

Figure 19-33:
Filtering
with a
page field.

Chapter 20

Interacting with External Programs

*O*ne of the coolest things about working with Excel and other Windows programs is that you can take something created in one program and paste it into another. This is a huge asset when it comes to keeping your creative juices flowing.

PowerPoint presentations routinely have charts in them. Have you ever worked with PowerPoint's native chart utility? It leaves a lot to be desired. Thankfully, you can just as easily drop Excel charts on PowerPoint slides instead. Just work up the charts in Excel and then copy and paste them into PowerPoint. One, two, three, lickety-split, and you're done.

The same goes for other programs such as Word. You can paste an Excel chart into Word and just go about your business. In fact, you have choices when pasting charts into Word or PowerPoint. You can keep a link to the original workbook, you can have the chart be editable with Excel tools but without being linked to the original workbook, or you can just paste the chart as a picture and be done with it.

You can paste Excel charts into many Windows programs, not just PowerPoint and Word.

Even cooler is the ability to put Excel charts on Web pages. Here, too, you have options: You can decide whether to let the chart be editable. And you don't have to be an Internet genius to do this! In this chapter, I show you the nuts and bolts.

Pasting an Excel Chart into a PowerPoint Presentation or a Word Document

Pasting an Excel chart into a PowerPoint slide and pasting an Excel chart into a Word document are nearly identical. The options each programs offers may have slight differences; the available options are likely based on the configuration of the software on your computer.

Getting an Excel chart to appear in PowerPoint or Word really involves just three simple steps:

1. **Copy the chart in Excel.**
2. **Activate the slide or document.**
3. **Select the paste method.**

To see how easy this is, try one yourself. Just follow these steps:

1. **Open an Excel workbook that has a chart in it.**
2. **Start up PowerPoint or Word.**
3. **In Excel, click on the chart once to select it.**
4. **Copy the chart either by choosing Edit ⇨ Copy or by pressing Ctrl+C.**
5. **Go to the other open program (PowerPoint or Word).**
6. **Navigate to the slide or place in the document where you want the chart to be placed.**
7. **Choose Edit ⇨ Paste Special.**

   The Paste Special dialog box, shown in Figure 20-1, appears.

   You may see a slightly different list of items when displaying the Paste Special dialog box on your system.

8. **Select to paste the chart as an Microsoft Office Excel Chart Object.**
9. **Select either the Paste or Paste Link radio button.**

   See "Linking the chart," later in this chapter, for more information on the differences between these two options.

Note: Do not check the Display as Icon check box. See "Selecting to display an icon," later in this chapter, for more information on this check box.

10. Click OK.

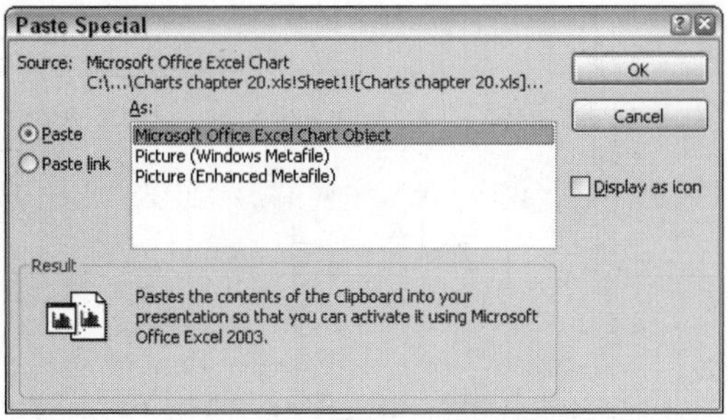

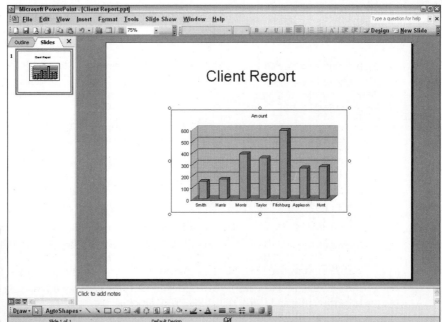

Figure 20-1:
Selecting
how to
paste a
chart.

Figure 20-2 shows how I landed an Excel chart on a PowerPoint slide. Pretty good landing job, don't you think?

In PowerPoint, you can resize and move the chart by clicking on it once (to select it) and using the handles along the border. Figure 20-3 shows how I changed the size of my chart. (I'm proud of my chart and want it to be as big as possible!)

Figure 20-2:
Viewing
the Excel
chart in
PowerPoint.

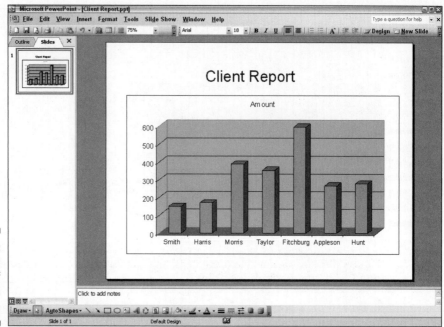

Figure 20-3:
Changing
the size of
the chart in
PowerPoint.

In both PowerPoint and Word, you can resize and move pasted Excel charts.

Editing the chart

If you followed the instructions to paste the chart as a Microsoft Office Excel Chart Object (on your system, the list item may have been named differently, depending on your version of Excel) and not as a graphic, you can edit the chart. Here's how:

1. In PowerPoint or Word, double-click on the chart.

You'll either end up with the chart looking a little bit more like the way it looks in Excel, while still being in PowerPoint or Word, or you'll be in Excel proper. The result of the double-click depends on how the chart was pasted — link or no link.

Figure 20-4 shows what happens when I double-click on my chart in PowerPoint. The tabs from my Excel workbook are now available. I can enter data in the cells, change data, and so on. Note, however, that although in the Excel workbook my chart was on a worksheet, it's now on a chart sheet. I need to activate the Sheet1 tab to get to the actual data. When I'm done editing, I have to activate the chart sheet itself before ending; otherwise, I'll leave the worksheet as the visible object in PowerPoint.

Note that while editing the Excel workbook from PowerPoint, the menu items in PowerPoint have changed to the ones found in Excel.

2. **Whether your chart is still in PowerPoint or Word, or in Excel itself, make a change to the data that feeds the chart by editing the contents of a cell.**

Don't forget to press Enter or Tab to complete the entry.

You can change source data and make formatting changes to the chart. For example, you can change the chart type.

3. **To complete the change, if you're still in PowerPoint or Word, just click somewhere outside of the chart to deselect it. If you're now in Excel, find PowerPoint or Word on the Windows task bar and go back to that program.**

You'll see that the chart has been updated.

You may find that, although your original chart was on a worksheet, it's now also on a dedicated chart sheet. If you're editing the chart while still in PowerPoint or Word, be sure to activate the actual chart sheet before deselecting the chart.

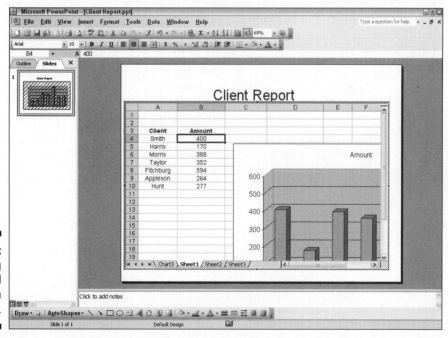

Figure 20-4:
Editing an Excel chart in PowerPoint.

Linking the chart

In the Paste Special dialog box, you have Paste and Paste Link options. The Paste Link option sets up the pasted chart to retain a connection to the original data source back in the Excel workbook. This option is really handy, because the chart in PowerPoint or Word will present the changed state of the data, even though you only made the changes in Excel. Also keep in mind that when there is a link, the file with the source data must be available or the link becomes broken.

But be careful, because this dynamic updating may not be called for at all. For example, if you create a Word document that summarizes business activity for 2005, any chart in the document should not change! What if the chart starts showing data that reflects activity from 2006?

The ability to link a pasted chart back to its original data is not always called for.

Figure 20-1 shows the Paste Special dialog box with the Paste Link option *not* selected. Instead, the plain Paste option is selected. When a plain Paste is selected, there are options for the type of the pasted object. When the Paste Link option is selected, only the Microsoft Office Excel Chart Object remains in the list. Here is a summary of the differences:

Option Setting	What the Options Are
Paste	You can paste the chart as an Excel chart object or as one of the available graphic types in the list. If the chart is pasted as an Excel chart object, then any editing is done within the host program, using Excel features.
Paste Link	You can only paste the chart as an Excel chart object. Any editing is done back in the Excel workbook itself. Double-clicking the pasted chart object starts up the original workbook.

Selecting to display an icon

One of the options in the Paste Special dialog box is Display as Icon. The check box is available only when the chart object type is selected in the list. Selecting a graphic type disables the Display as Icon check box.

When this option is selected, an icon is placed in the slide or document, not the chart itself. Figure 20-5 shows how this appears on a Word document. Double-clicking the icon brings up Excel with the chart displayed.

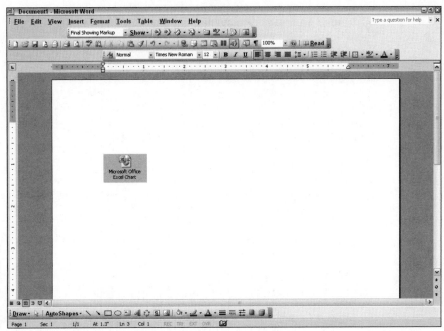

Figure 20-5:
Using icons
instead of
charts.

You may wonder why you'd want to bother with this feature. The advantage is that it saves room in the document. For example, you may have a report that references many charts throughout. By using icons, recipients can just look at the charts they need to see. Assuming a chart can take up a half a page or so, a document with 50 charts has 25 extra pages, unless you use the icons.

Using the icons to make documents shorter sounds like a great idea, but it only works with electronic distribution. If the report is printed, all that will appear are icons.

Converting the chart to a graphic

As you see in the Paste Special dialog box (refer to Figure 20-1), there are options to paste the chart as a graphic. Pasting the chart as a graphic is a good option if you're sure the data will never need to be changed.

A chart pasted as a graphic can be moved and resized. When a chart graphic is double-clicked, the Microsoft Office picture-editing tools and settings become available. This is now a graphic — any connection to Excel is gone.

Figure 20-6 shows a chart that has been pasted as a graphic into a Word document. Clicking on the graphic once selects it and displays the Picture toolbar from which you can do some formatting. Clicking on the graphic twice opens the Format Picture dialog box, which has even more settings. In Figure 20-6, both the Picture toolbar and the Format Picture dialog box are shown.

Using Shift and Copy to create an instant graphic

If you just need a graphic of the chart, you can use a great shortcut. It simply involves holding down the Shift key when you copy the chart. Here's what you do:

1. **In Excel, click once on the chart to select it.**

2. **Hold down the Shift key.**

3. **Choose Edit ⇨ Copy Picture to copy the chart as a picture.**

   Wait a minute! Where did Copy Picture come from!? This is the heart of the technique. When you hold down Shift, Copy becomes Copy Picture under the Edit menu (see Figure 20-7).

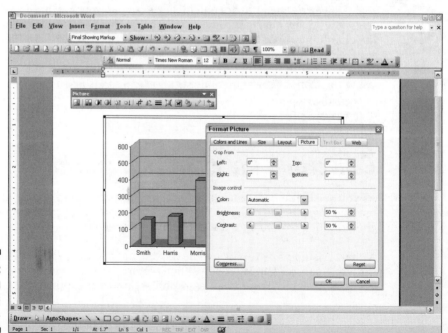

Figure 20-6:
Formatting a graphic of a chart.

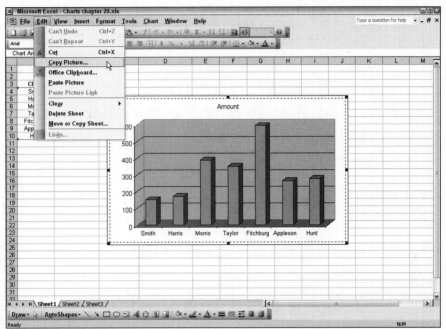

Figure 20-7:
Copying the
chart as a
picture.

When you select Copy Picture from the menu, the Copy Picture dialog
box, shown in Figure 20-8, appears. You can select how the chart should
be copied.

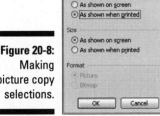

Figure 20-8:
Making
picture copy
selections.

4. Paste into PowerPoint, Word, or any other program.

The only option is to paste the chart as a graphic.

Placing Charts on Web Pages

Back when PCs were in their youth, you had to print an Excel chart if you wanted to show it to someone — that is, unless that person was peering over your shoulder. Then came e-mail: You could send the file to the recipient.

And now there is the Web. You can publish an Excel chart to a Web page and people can view it with their Web browsers. (I wonder what the next technical leap will be? My guess is that the image of a chart will be beamed right into our brains!)

In this section, I show you how to save your chart to a Web page. There are two approaches to this:

✔ Save the chart as a static picture.

✔ Save the chart with the ability to be interactive.

Saving a chart to a Web page

First, you want to get a chart onto a Web page. Here's a walkthrough, with a couple terms explained along the way:

1. **Open an Excel workbook with a chart in it, and select the chart by clicking on it once.**

2. **Choose File ➪ Save as Web Page.**

   The Save As dialog box, shown in Figure 20-9, appears. Although you've used this dialog box more times than you can remember, it now looks different.

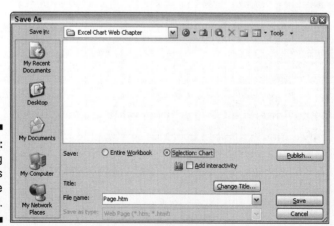

Figure 20-9: Reviewing the Save As Web page options.

3. **In the middle of the dialog box, in the Save section, click the Selection: Chart option.**

   If you don't see the Selection: Chart option, you forgot to select the chart first. If that's the case, close the dialog box and start over with Step 1.

4. **Click the Change Title button.**

   The Set Title dialog box appears.

5. **Enter a title.**

   On the Web page, this title will appear on top of the chart, and on the title bar of the browser. It isn't the standard chart title itself. Figure 20-10 shows how I added a title.

Figure 20-10:
Adding a
title.

6. **Click OK to close the Set Title dialog box.**

7. **Leave the Add Interactivity check box unchecked.**

8. **Because this is a Save As dialog box, use the top part of the dialog box to locate a directory where you want to save the files.**

   Note: A Web page does not have to end up being on the Internet itself. What you're doing here is saving an HTM type of file.

   HTM or HTML file types are the standard for Web pages. HTML is an abbreviation of Hypertext Markup Language.

9. **Enter a name for the file — or keep the default if its generic tone doesn't offend your creative sensibilities.**

10. **Click the Publish button.**

    The Publish as Web Page dialog box, shown in Figure 20-11, appears.

    Publishing offers more options than saving. Saving just saves the file in the manner that all files are saved. Publishing provides options to immediately see the chart on a Web page and to create a link between the workbook and the Web page.

11. **Leave the Add Interactivity check box unchecked.**

12. **Leave the AutoRepublish Every Time This Workbook Is Saved check box unchecked.**

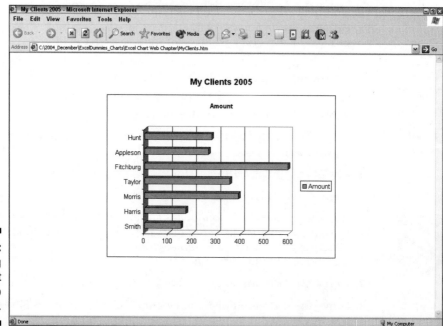

Figure 20-11:
Selecting
publishing
options.

13. **Make sure the Open Published Web Page in Browser check box is checked.**

14. **Click the Publish button.**

    If all went according to plan, you're now looking at your chart on a Web page. Figure 20-12 shows how mine came out.

Figure 20-12:
Viewing
the chart
in a Web
browser.

Because you didn't select to make this interactive, the chart is now a graphic. A couple of files have been created that you should know about. In the directory that you selected in Step 8, there is now a new HTML-based workbook and a new subdirectory. The workbook is not a standard Excel workbook. It's a mix of Excel and Web protocols, and opening it from Excel leads to the display in the browser. If you're curious and brave about files and directories, look inside the new subdirectory. There is the graphic file that is a picture of your chart. Other files may be in there as well — you can ignore those other files, but do leave them there.

Figure 20-13 shows my new file and directory.

Knowing where these new files are may be important to you or someone in your place of work. The Webmaster (if you have one) may want the files so he can put them on the company intranet.

Whenever you want to view your Web-based chart, open Excel and open the file that was created by the publishing process.

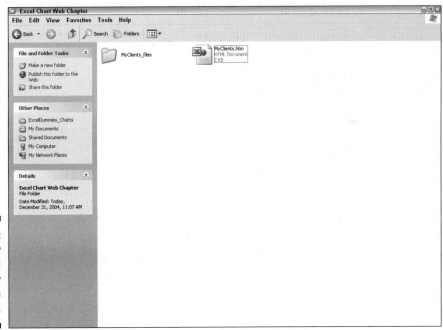

Figure 20-13:
A new file and directory have been created.

Adding interactivity to a Web-page chart

If you followed the steps in the preceding section, you know you skipped the interactivity option. Now I'll show you how to try it out. Some of these steps repeat what you did earlier, but practice makes perfect!

1. **Open an Excel workbook with a chart in it, and select the chart by clicking on it once.**

2. **Choose File ⇨ Save as Web Page.**

   The Save As dialog box appears.

3. **In the middle of the dialog box, in the Save section, click the Selection: Chart option.**

   If you don't see this option, you forgot to select the chart first. If that's the case, close the dialog box and start over with Step 1.

4. **Click the Change Title button.**

   The Set Title dialog box appears.

5. **Enter a title.**

   On the Web page, this title will appear on top of the chart and in the title bar of the browser. It isn't the standard chart title itself.

6. **Click OK to close the Set Title dialog box.**

7. **Check the Add Interactivity check box.**

8. **Use the top part of the dialog box to locate a directory where you want to save the files.**

9. **Enter a name for the file.**

10. **Click the Publish button.**

    The Publish as Web Page dialog box appears.

11. **Check the AutoRepublish Every Time This Workbook Is Saved check box.**

12. **Make sure the Open Published Web Page in Browser check box is checked.**

    Figure 20-14 shows how the various settings in the Publish as Web Page dialog box should look.

13. **Click the Publish button.**

Figure 20-15 show how my chart turned out. Not only is the chart present, but beneath is the worksheet with the data. The data can be changed and the chart will update. In other words — interactive!

One more important thing: During the steps in this section, I had you select to AutoRepublish. This has created a link between the workbook and the Web page. Every time the workbook is saved, the data and chart on the Web page are updated. So you can make changes to the data in the workbook and have the changes appear on the Web page.

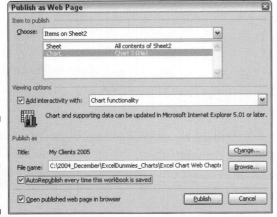

Figure 20-14: Reviewing the Web publishing selections.

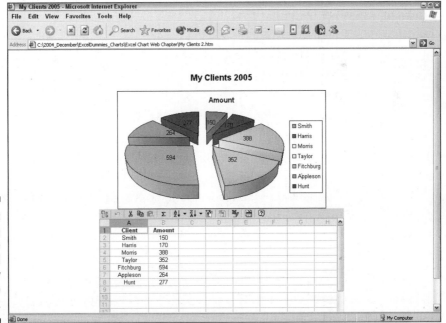

Figure 20-15: Working with the chart and data directly on the Web page.

There is one catch, though: You need to refresh the Web page to see the update. This is easy enough. In Internet Explorer you choose View ➪ Refresh, or just click the Refresh button on the Standard Buttons toolbar or press F5.

By the way, the AutoRepublish link works in one direction only. Changes in the workbook update the Web chart. Changes on the Web chart do not update the workbook.

Refresh the Web page to see updates made to the chart.

Part V
The Part of Tens

The 5th Wave   By Rich Tennant

"Great! It comes with Excel Charts. Now maybe we can factor in where all the money around here is going."

In this part . . .

*J*ust when you think I've shown you all I know, I have another trick or two up my sleeve. In Chapter 21, I show you ten bad charts and what can be done to correct them. Cluttered charts, deceiving charts, bad formatting — they're all here. To balance the bad with the good, Chapter 22 shows some cool charts and diagrams. Here I show you an organizational chart; target, cycle, and radial diagrams; and more. With all these options, you have so many ways to plot. Happy charting!

Chapter 21

Ten Chart Remakes

Some charts are downright ugly. Some charts are cute but hard to figure out. Some charts are too busy. And some charts just don't make any sense.

In this chapter, I show you ten charts that are in need of help. Someone call the chart doctor! Oh, that's me! Never mind. I'll just pack my bag of chart medicines and help these charts get better. Really, all it takes is some common sense.

Removing the Clutter

Having a lot of news to report is exciting — results, statistics, windfalls, short-falls, and so on. What better vehicle is there to showcase all this news than a chart? A chart is a wise choice to be sure, but too much news does not a healthy chart make.

Figure 21-1 shows a chart that reports just a bit too much information. All the information is correct, but good luck figuring out much of it. I always like to use my scientific, instant-chart-impression measuring system. It works like this: Close your eyes, stand in front of your computer, open your eyes, and within 5 seconds say something useful you learned from the chart. I don't think you can do that with the chart in Figure 21-1.

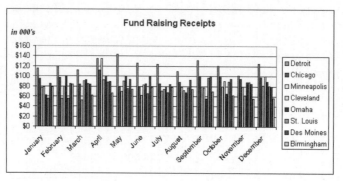

Figure 21-1:
Getting a
headache
looking at
a chart.

The chart in Figure 21-1 is just too busy for its own good. There are too many series to be plotted against the given number of categories. If conveying all this information in one place is really necessary, you need to keep in mind that some things are not meant to be plotted. This type of information would work better on a spreadsheet.

If reading a summary would be faster then figuring out a chart that displays the summary, there is no use for the chart.

The fix, though, is to either remove some of the series, remove some of the categories, or remove some of each. All is not lost — you can deliver more charts, each with less on it. For example, you can create 12 charts — 1 for each month — or just create charts with 2 or 3 cities on each. Figure 21-2 shows such a facelift.

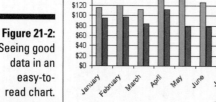

Figure 21-2:
Seeing good
data in an
easy-to-
read chart.

Now when you try the 5-second test, you'll know that Detroit is always higher than Chicago.

Plotting the Unknown

I admit I've been guilty of plotting the unknown. In fact, I hope I haven't done this too much in this book! What I'm talking about is displaying a chart with no clue as to what the chart is showing. Figure 21-3 shows a chart that looks nice, and you can tell a few things about it, but ultimately you realize that you don't know what is being plotted.

Figure 21-3:
Unraveling
the mystery
of what's
being
plotted.

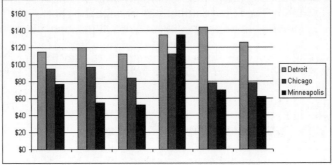

The fix, of course, is to provide a chart title that tells what is being plotted, and categories to illustrate what the dollars are related to. All you can tell about the chart in Figure 21-3 is that the three cities had results at certain dollar values. You can see that there are six categories, but you don't know what they are. Assuming, for argument's sake, that they're time-based categories, such as months, you still wouldn't have the full picture.

Replacing Beauty with Common Sense

The chart in Figure 21-4 is really eye-catching. I've never met anyone who didn't stop and stare at a 3-D Pie chart. It must spark something in the human unconsciousness — like wanting some pie.

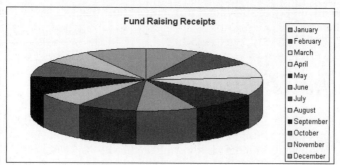

Figure 21-4:
Falling for
looks over
all else.

That just doesn't cut it in chart land. This chart is the wrong type. Seeing much variation among the pie slices is really difficult, because there are just too many of them. The fix, of course, is to change the chart type. This type of data is well served with a Bar or Column chart. It just may not taste as good.

Basic charting protocol dictates that the data is the key to the correct chart type. Select the best type for your data, not the type you think is the coolest.

Looking for Sanity in Chaos

The chart in Figure 21-5 is what happens when an overly excited assistant tells you what a great chart he's going to make for you. Oh, sure, the chart does tell you a lot. It even includes information that has nothing to do with the chart (Max wins the Outreach contest), and even has some bad formatting to boot (the value axis labels should not have decimal points).

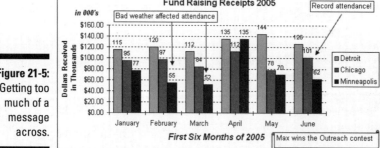

Figure 21-5:
Getting too
much of a
message
across.

The chart in Figure 21-5 suffers from overzealous labeling, to the point of redundancy. For example, the categories are six months, January through June. You can tell that from the names. But the category-axis title tells you that anyway. Likewise, on the value axis, above the labels is a qualifier that tells the amounts are in thousands. But even so, the value-axis title repeats this information.

The way to improve this chart is to remove the extra elements. Doing so may be painful at first, but this sort of cleansing is good for the chart. Remember that, and you'll have an easier time keeping yourself from being too gung-ho the next time you make a chart.

Scaling to the Data

The chart in Figure 21-6 is not that bad. Indeed, worse charts have been tossed around boardrooms and even in some Excel 101 courses. The chart does tell you what it's plotting and it is true to scale — but that scale thing is the problem.

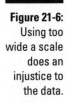

Figure 21-6: Using too wide a scale does an injustice to the data.

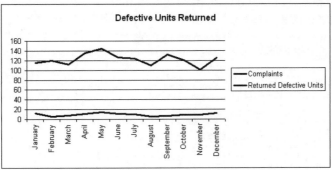

The issue is that the two plotted series are not close in underlying values. This forces one line to plot near the top and the other to plot near the bottom. Actually, this could be a desired effect, perhaps to point out the fact that the two series are not similar. But putting that idea aside, the best thing to do is to plot each series on its own axis.

By converting this simple line chart into a combination chart, each series can be plotted against its own value axis — one on the left and one on the right. Each value axis then covers a range closer to the values being plotted. Figure 21-7 shows how this improvement looks.

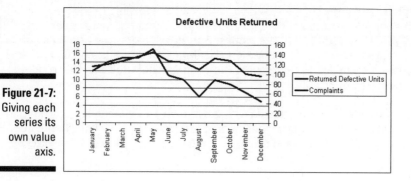

The advantage of plotting each series on its own axis is that each line takes on more of a defined shape. Then you can more easily see how the two series relate. In this example, there clearly is correlation between number of complaints and number of returned defective units.

Easing Off the Categories

Working with the axes scale settings is a key factor in making a readable chart. Figure 21-8 shows how a bad choice in scale settings has produced a chart with too many category labels.

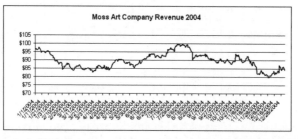

Figure 21-8:
Displaying
too many
category
labels.

Occasionally, so many category labels are necessary — but considering the chart in Figure 21-8, the categories don't add much. This is a view of a year's worth of data. The chart helps to show direction and the ups and downs during the year. Knowing that, on April 21, the value was $85 isn't critical. What is useful to glean from this type of chart is that, in the spring, revenue was depressed compared with the summer and fall. Therefore, using the scale settings to display fewer categories is the fix for this chart, as shown in Figure 21-9.

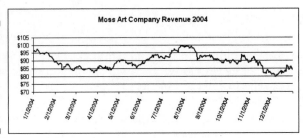

Figure 21-9:
Giving the
categories a
little
breathing
room.

You don't need to display many labels on the axes. A good approach is to consider how little is needed, not how much can be included.

Displaying Nonsense

Sometimes there just isn't any data worth making a chart over. The chart in Figure 21-10 is a case in point. The chart is an XY (Scatter) chart that attempts to point out some relation between the number of customers and the number of deliveries.

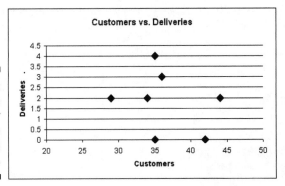

Figure 21-10:
Ignoring the
data just for
the sake
of making
a chart.

The fact is there is no correlation between the number of customers and the number of deliveries. Why would there be? One has nothing to do with the other. It's not like the trucking company called up your customers to arrange a coordinated visit to your place of business. The best thing to do with this chart is to place it in the circular file (a.k.a., the trash can).

Hiding Data

Area charts are prone to hiding plotted data. This occurs when the order of the series forces any series with lower values to fall behind series with higher values. The chart in Figure 21-11 shows the problem.

Figure 21-11: Having a hard time seeing all the data.

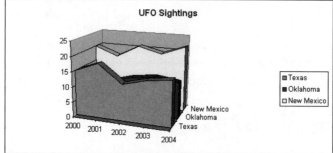

Some of the data values for Oklahoma are hidden behind Texas values. Because Texas has higher values, it should be placed behind Oklahoma, not in front of it. Changing the series order fixes the problem. Figure 21-12 shows the improvement. Now all you have to worry about is the number of UFOs flying over New Mexico.

Figure 21-12: Shuffling the series order brings hidden data into the foreground.

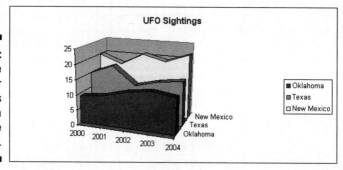

The ability to change series order is a great help when formatting charts, but be sure this makes sense for the data. For example, you wouldn't want to reorder series data if some supporting documentation discusses the series in the original order.

Playing Perspective Tricks

Three-dimensional charts are a blessing and a curse. They certainly spice up the visual, but they can also lead you into trouble. The chart in Figure 21-13 fills the bill. It's simply gorgeous. But should you accept it as is? That is the question.

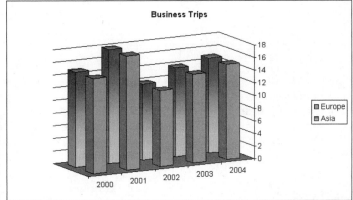

Figure 21-13:
Getting the wrong impression.

The problem with the chart in Figure 21-13 is that it's misleading. Upon viewing it, you would think that Asia has slightly higher values than Europe. Surely anyone can see that! But the fact is that the two series are identical. That's right, if it weren't for the 3-D effect, these two series would appear as perfect twins. Trying different 3-D settings will lead to a better presentation of the data — or a worse one. Trial and error is the way to tell what works. The other option is to change the chart type back to 2-D. You lose the glamour, but you also lose the ambiguity.

Accuracy is always more important than appearance.

Misusing Graphics to Inflate Results

Graphics often make a boring chart more lively. Just leaf through any number of newspapers or magazines, and you'll see what I'm talking about. The issue is that graphics can lead to inflated (or deflated) results. Figure 21-14 shows how this is commonly achieved. The graphic, an airplane in this example, is used twice in the chart. The size of the plane changes, to show a before-and-after comparison.

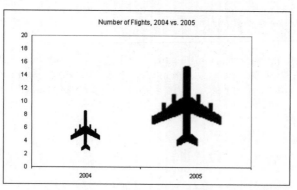

Figure 21-14:
Reporting a
phenomenal
achieve-
ment.

The plane on the right is twice the height and width of the plane on the left, which can only lead you to conclude that the change from before to after resulted in a doubling achievement. But is this the truth? Because graphics can be independently placed in a chart regardless of the data, this opens free license to make results look as good as you want. Surely no one would cheat like that!

The best way to avoid this type of issue is to use graphics with care. Keep an eye open to see if your graphics are misleading. Without underlying data to rely on, the impression drawn from independent graphics in charts really is in the eye of the beholder.

Chapter 22

Ten (or So) Fancy Charts

*L*ine charts, Bar charts — been there, done that. Seen them all and then some. Are you ready for a batch of distinctive charts? You've come to the right place. In this chapter, I show you supply-and-demand curves, a histogram, an organizational chart, an incorporated map, and more.

Getting Supply to Meet Demand

Anyone who has taken Economics 101 (including yours truly) has learned that, above all else, supply and demand meet at some point called the *equilibrium*. The equilibrium is a price point where the price is low enough to keep demand coming, but high enough to keep companies making the product. If the price gets higher, then fewer people will buy, thereby driving the price back down to the equilibrium point. If the price drops, demand becomes greater, and manufacturers raise their price to capitalize on the situation — which lowers demand back to the equilibrium point.

Plotting supply and demand curves is easy. It's really just a Line chart. But unlike most Line charts that seem to plot series moving together, supply and demand curves move in opposite directions, as shown in Figure 22-1. This is just two lines plotted together on the same value axis. The supply series trends up and the demand series trends down, forcing the lines to cross.

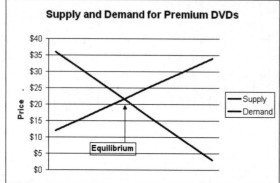

Figure 22-1:
Matching
supply with
demand.

This supply-and-demand chart is very simple. Do not take this as a supply of a real lesson in economics, or my economics degree will no longer be in demand.

Wrapping Up Your Data in Bins

Histograms provide a way to view the occurrence of data points within value ranges that you define. Then the ranges themselves become the categories and the values are the counts of data points within the categories. This provides a view of the frequency distribution. Figure 22-2 shows a histogram.

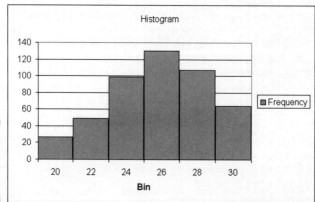

Figure 22-2:
Grouping
data into
bins.

Looks a lot like a Column chart, doesn't it? Well, it is a Column chart, but instead of the columns representing individual data points, the columns represent the groupings.

You plot a histogram the same way you plot a Column chart. The first step is getting the counts of the individual data points into the bins. You can do that manually or through some other means, namely using the Analysis ToolPak add-in. Read the outstanding *Excel Formulas and Functions For Dummies* by yours truly along with Peter Aitken (published by Wiley) for more information on the Analysis ToolPak.

Adding Visual Value with a Map

Charts are often used to plot geographic data. This data could be population counts, temperatures in certain areas, voter turnout, or any number of other things.

Incorporating a map into a chart design provides an extra measure of information. The chart in Figure 22-3 is a perfect example. The data is a set of counts for different locales in Florida. If you know where all the cities are, then the map has dubious value — but if you don't, then the map is a real help. The map is not a graph per se — it's a graphic — but it does help to visualize the data.

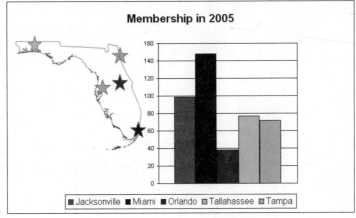

Figure 22-3: Using a map to give the data extra focus.

The map is great for someone who isn't a Florida resident but is curious where the referenced cities are. In this particular example, the tie-in is with the colors. Each referenced city has a star on the map that is of the same color as its counterpart in the legend. (You'll have to trust me on this.)

Maps can be used in a number of ways:

- ✔ As a secondary legend, as shown in this example
- ✔ As a background graphic
- ✔ With data labels placed strategically on the map, instead of being plotted in a chart itself

If you really wanted to go all out, you could research latitude and longitude, elevation, distance between points, weather patterns, and so on, and incorporate these into your design.

Getting Organized

Organizational charts are standard business fare. Strictly speaking, they aren't used to visually display quantitative data. But they sure do look like they belong in a chart book!

Actually, Excel provides six cool-looking diagrams, of which the organizational chart is one. A simple organizational chart is shown in Figure 22-4.

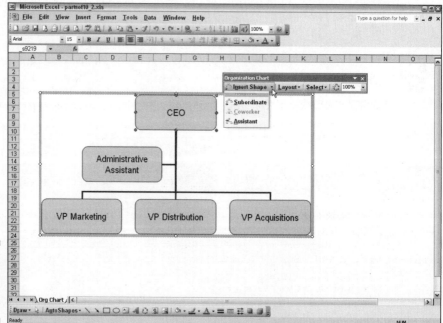

Figure 22-4:
Seeing who
reports
to whom.

To create an organizational chart:

1. **Choose Insert⇨Diagram.**

   The Diagram Gallery dialog box, shown in Figure 22-5, opens.

2. **Select the organizational chart.**

3. **Click OK.**

Figure 22-5:
Selecting
diagrams.

Six diagrams are available in the Diagram Gallery dialog box. After selecting one and clicking OK, the diagram is placed on the worksheet. A Diagram toolbar is visible when a diagram is selected (the name of the toolbar may change to match the type of diagram).

On the toolbar, click the Layout button and then deselect AutoLayout in the menu. This is necessary to really work with the diagrams — otherwise, many of the formatting options remain locked.

In Figure 22-4, the toolbar is being used to add new members to the organizational chart.

Going 'Round and 'Round

The cycle diagram is great for showing a flow that wraps around onto itself. Figure 22-6 shows a cycle of rain, humidity, and evaporation. If you've ever been stuck in the New York City subway in the summer, you know the cycle as heat and humidity, heat and humidity, heat and humidity.

To create a cycle diagram:

1. **Choose Insert⇨Diagram.**

   The Diagram Gallery dialog box appears.

2. **Select the cycle diagram.**

3. **Click OK.**

You can add additional steps by clicking the Insert Shape button on the toolbar.

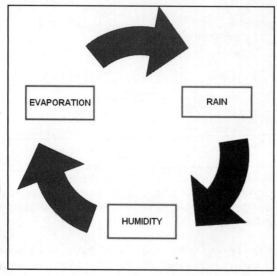

Figure 22-6:
Displaying a
repetitive
process.

Putting the Parts Together

The radial diagram shows individual elements and the combined result. This diagram is useful in many situations, such as showing the individual members who make up a team, the individual processes that produce an output, or the individual ingredients that go into making cookies.

Figure 22-7 gives an example of a radial diagram that lists good habits that help an athlete perform at her best.

To create a radial diagram:

1. **Choose Insert⇨Diagram.**

   The Diagram Gallery dialog box appears.

2. **Select the radial diagram.**

3. **Click OK.**

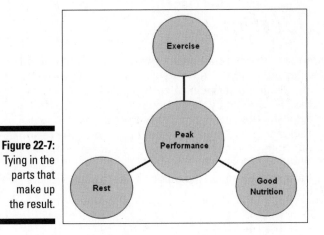

Figure 22-7:
Tying in the
parts that
make up
the result.

Building a Pyramid

If you're like me, you can't help but thinking about food groups when you look at a pyramid diagram. Figure 22-8 shows the pyramid diagram.

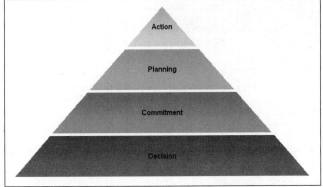

Figure 22-8:
Building
layer upon
layer.

Pyramid diagrams are great for showing how building blocks or sequential steps build up to, or contribute to, a whole.

To create a pyramid diagram:

1. **Choose Insert⇨Diagram.**

   The Diagram Gallery dialog box appears.

2. **Select the pyramid diagram.**

3. **Click OK.**

Looking At the Overlap

The Venn diagram shows where different entities overlap or, to put it another way, enjoy a union. The example shown in Figure 22-9 shows how three different sales departments all end up servicing a certain number of the same accounts. A national chain is handled by the national accounts department, yet the local salesperson visits the chain stores in her area. The national chain maintains a few regional offices, and these are handled by the regional sales manager. Isn't it nice to give a big customer such great service?

Is the overlap good? That's entirely up to the business folks. The overlap by itself is a fact without bias.

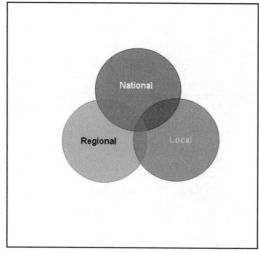

Figure 22-9:
Seeing where efforts are duplicated.

To create a Venn diagram:

1. **Choose Insert⇨Diagram.**

    The Diagram Gallery dialog box appears.

2. **Select the Venn diagram.**

3. **Click OK.**

Going For a Bull's-eye

The target diagram is used to show the steps taken to reach a goal — in other words, the bull's-eye. Figure 22-10 shows a target diagram with four steps. As with all the diagrams, you can add levels to the diagram by using the Insert Shape button on the Diagram toolbar.

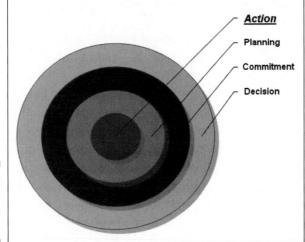

Figure 22-10: Taking steps to reach the target.

To create a target diagram:

1. **Choose Insert⇨Diagram.**

    The Diagram Gallery dialog box appears.

2. **Select the target diagram.**

3. **Click OK.**

Index

• T •

• U •

• V •

Notes

Notes

Notes

Notes

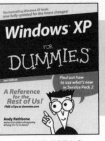

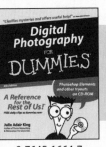 

SPORTS, FITNESS, PARENTING, RELIGION & SPIRITUALITY

0-7645-5146-9

0-7645-5418-2

Also available:
- Adoption For Dummies
  0-7645-5488-3
- Basketball For Dummies
  0-7645-5248-1
- The Bible For Dummies
  0-7645-5296-1
- Buddhism For Dummies
  0-7645-5359-3
- Catholicism For Dummies
  0-7645-5391-7
- Hockey For Dummies
  0-7645-5228-7

- Judaism For Dummies
  0-7645-5299-6
- Martial Arts For Dummies
  0-7645-5358-5
- Pilates For Dummies
  0-7645-5397-6
- Religion For Dummies
  0-7645-5264-3
- Teaching Kids to Read For Dummies
  0-7645-4043-2
- Weight Training For Dummies
  0-7645-5168-X
- Yoga For Dummies
  0-7645-5117-5

TRAVEL

0-7645-5438-7

0-7645-5453-0

Also available:
- Alaska For Dummies
  0-7645-1761-9
- Arizona For Dummies
  0-7645-6938-4
- Cancún and the Yucatán For Dummies
  0-7645-2437-2
- Cruise Vacations For Dummies
  0-7645-6941-4
- Europe For Dummies
  0-7645-5456-5
- Ireland For Dummies
  0-7645-5455-7

- Las Vegas For Dummies
  0-7645-5448-4
- London For Dummies
  0-7645-4277-X
- New York City For Dummies
  0-7645-6945-7
- Paris For Dummies
  0-7645-5494-8
- RV Vacations For Dummies
  0-7645-5443-3
- Walt Disney World & Orlando For Dummies
  0-7645-6943-0

GRAPHICS, DESIGN & WEB DEVELOPMENT

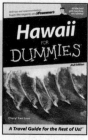

0-7645-4345-8

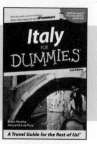

0-7645-5589-8

Also available:
- Adobe Acrobat 6 PDF For Dummies
  0-7645-3760-1
- Building a Web Site For Dummies
  0-7645-7144-3
- Dreamweaver MX 2004 For Dummies
  0-7645-4342-3
- FrontPage 2003 For Dummies
  0-7645-3882-9
- HTML 4 For Dummies
  0-7645-1995-6
- Illustrator CS For Dummies
  0-7645-4084-X

- Macromedia Flash MX 2004 For Dummies
  0-7645-4358-X
- Photoshop 7 All-in-One Desk
  Reference For Dummies
  0-7645-1667-1
- Photoshop CS Timesaving Techniques
  For Dummies
  0-7645-6782-9
- PHP 5 For Dummies
  0-7645-4166-8
- PowerPoint 2003 For Dummies
  0-7645-3908-6
- QuarkXPress 6 For Dummies
  0-7645-2593-X

NETWORKING, SECURITY, PROGRAMMING & DATABASES

0-7645-6852-3

0-7645-5784-X

Also available:
- A+ Certification For Dummies
  0-7645-4187-0
- Access 2003 All-in-One Desk
  Reference For Dummies
  0-7645-3988-4
- Beginning Programming For Dummies
  0-7645-4997-9
- C For Dummies
  0-7645-7068-4
- Firewalls For Dummies
  0-7645-4048-3
- Home Networking For Dummies
  0-7645-42796

- Network Security For Dummies
  0-7645-1679-5
- Networking For Dummies
  0-7645-1677-9
- TCP/IP For Dummies
  0-7645-1760-0
- VBA For Dummies
  0-7645-3989-2
- Wireless All In-One Desk Reference
  For Dummies
  0-7645-7496-5
- Wireless Home Networking For Dummies
  0-7645-3910-8

HEALTH & SELF-HELP

0-7645-6820-5 *†

0-7645-2566-2

Also available:
- Alzheimer's For Dummies
  0-7645-3899-3
- Asthma For Dummies
  0-7645-4233-8
- Controlling Cholesterol For Dummies
  0-7645-5440-9
- Depression For Dummies
  0-7645-3900-0
- Dieting For Dummies
  0-7645-4149-8
- Fertility For Dummies
  0-7645-2549-2

- Fibromyalgia For Dummies
  0-7645-5441-7
- Improving Your Memory For Dummies
  0-7645-5435-2
- Pregnancy For Dummies †
  0-7645-4483-7
- Quitting Smoking For Dummies
  0-7645-2629-4
- Relationships For Dummies
  0-7645-5384-4
- Thyroid For Dummies
  0-7645-5385-2

EDUCATION, HISTORY, REFERENCE & TEST PREPARATION

0-7645-5194-9

0-7645-4186-2

Also available:
- Algebra For Dummies
  0-7645-5325-9
- British History For Dummies
  0-7645-7021-8
- Calculus For Dummies
  0-7645-2498-4
- English Grammar For Dummies
  0-7645-5322-4
- Forensics For Dummies
  0-7645-5580-4
- The GMAT For Dummies
  0-7645-5251-1
- Inglés Para Dummies
  0-7645-5427-1

- Italian For Dummies
  0-7645-5196-5
- Latin For Dummies
  0-7645-5431-X
- Lewis & Clark For Dummies
  0-7645-2545-X
- Research Papers For Dummies
  0-7645-5426-3
- The SAT I For Dummies
  0-7645-7193-1
- Science Fair Projects For Dummies
  0-7645-5460-3
- U.S. History For Dummies
  0-7645-5249-X

Get smart @ dummies.com®

- **Find a full list of Dummies titles**
- **Look into loads of FREE on-site articles**
- **Sign up for FREE eTips e-mailed to you weekly**
- **See what other products carry the Dummies name**
- **Shop directly from the Dummies bookstore**
- **Enter to win new prizes every month!**

* **Separate Canadian edition also available**
† **Separate U.K. edition also available**

Available wherever books are sold. For more information or to order direct: U.S. customers visit www.dummies.com or call 1-877-762-2974.
U.K. customers visit www.wileyeurope.com or call 0800 243407. Canadian customers visit www.wiley.ca or call 1-800-567-4797.

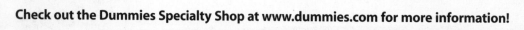